The Impact of
National Health Insurance
on New York

The Impact of
National Health Insurance
on New York

Marvin Lieberman
EDITOR

Published for the
New York Metropolitan Regional Medical Program by
PRODIST   New York   1977

Selected papers commissioned by the
Task Force on the Impact of National Health Insurance of the
New York Metropolitan Regional Medical Program,
July 1, 1974–Septembr 1, 1974

Funded under Division of Regional Medical Programs,
U.S. Department of Health, Education, and Welfare.
This book does not necessarily represent
the views of HEW or the grantee.

Published for the New York Metropolitan Regional Medical Program by
PRODIST, a division of
Neale Watson Academic Publications, Inc.
156 Fifth Avenue
New York, New York 10010

Library of Congress Cataloging in Publication Data

Main entry under title:

The Impact of national health insurance on New
    York.

    Includes bibliographies.
    1. Medical care—New York (City)   2.   Medical
policy—New York (City)   3.   Insurance, Health—
United States.   4.   Medical policy—United States.
I. Lieberman, Marvin.   II.   New York Metropolitan
Regional Medical Program.   Task Force on the Impact
of National Health Insurance.
RA395.A4N743   368.4'2'009747   77-8690
ISBN 0-88202-120-6

Publisher's Note: No effort has been made to superimpose
a rigid uniformity of style or syntax. The authors' wishes
have been followed wherever possible.

Designed and manufactured in the U.S.A.

Contents

Members of the
New York Metropolitan Regional Medical Program
Task Force on the Impact of
National Health Insurance

Chairman
Frederick O'R. Hayes
former Budget Director
 of New York City

Ralph Alvarado
Associate Director
Segundo Ruiz Belvis Family
 Neighborhood Care Center
Bronx, New York

Lowell E. Bellin, M.D.
Commissioner of Health
New York City Health
 Department

William C. Felch, M.D.
practicing physician
Rye, New York

George Himler, M.D.
French Polyclinic Medical
 Center
New York, New York

John L.S. Holloman, Jr., M.D.
President
New York City Health and
 Hospitals Corporation

Robert Merritt
Executive Director
National Association of Health
 Services Executives
New York, New York

William J. Middleton
Board Member
National Association of
 Neighborhood Health Centers
New York, New York

Howard Newman
President
Dartmouth-Hitchcock Medical
 Center
Hanover, New Hampshire

Mrs. Nora Piore
Associate Director
Center for Community Health
 Systems
Columbia University
New York, New York

Mrs. Eva Reese, R.N.
former Executive Director
Visiting Nurse Service of
 New York

Peter Rogatz, M.D.
Senior Vice President
Blue Cross and Blue Shield of
 Greater New York

Jack Sheinkman
General Secretary-Treasurer
Amalgamated Clothing Workers
 of America
New York, New York

Joseph V. Terenzio
President
United Hospital Fund
New York, New York

Lewis Thomas, M.D.
President
Memorial Sloan-Kettering Cancer
 Center
New York, New York

Ray E. Trussell, M.D.
General Director
Beth Israel Medical Center
New York, New York

Marvin Lieberman, Ph.D.
Staff Director, August 1975–
September 1976

Irving J. Lewis
Staff Director, July 1974–
July 1975

Foreword

JESSE B. ARONSON

In 1973, with expressions of interest on the part of President Nixon and of the then Chairman of the House Ways and Means Committee, Wilbur Mills, and again in late 1974, it appeared that prospects for the passage of legislation on national health insurance were better than they had been for some time. Such legislation would have represented a major expansion of federally sponsored medical care programs whose performance was increasingly coming into question. The ten-year experience since the enactment of the Medicare and Medicaid legislation had clearly demonstrated that any major change in one aspect of the health care delivery system impinges on all aspects of the system and gives rise to changes of substantial magnitude throughout the system. At the same time there was concern that in the absence of proper planning any new program of great magnitude might have deleterious as well as beneficial consequences in New York City. Therefore, the board and staff of the New York. Metropolitan Regional Medical Program decided to take preparatory steps to anticipate the impact of national health insurance on New York City and to stimulate discussion of measures that would contribute to an improvement in New York City's health care in the process of implementing national health insurance.

Health care in the United States involves a complex matrix of unwritten, superficially studied, unevenly understood and often unacknowledged relationships. The derangements resulting from federal legislation and other forces affecting the health system have three areas of impact with immeasurable subsidiary ramifications.

First, there are the pressures caused by the increased entitlement to services without the necessary changes in organization of facilities and personnel engaged in providing those services. The more flexible use of personnel in the system is substantially limited by a broad variety of statutes and regulations administered through permits, licenses, and certificates, each catering to a special vested interest; by a reliance on professionals with long educational and experiential prerequisites; by a professional education system patterned to protect the guild-like limited access to the professions. The economic consequences of these pressures could have been foreseen: the rise in the price of specific medical care procedures has greatly exceeded that generated by inflation in other sectors of the economy.

Second, we have the proliferation of new, complex, and expensive diagnostic and treatment procedures. These have been developed through government-funded research, promoted in part by federally-sponsored Regional Medical Program projects and utilized widely as a result of government-sponsored systems of reimbursement. This has increased the capital needs of medical facilities, called for cadres of more and more highly trained professional personnel, and required the employment of a variety of new disciplines of paramedical technicians. At the same time this has stimulated the utilization of new and additional medical procedures heretofore unavailable. It is obvious that the introduction of these factors required major reorganization of services and has resulted in additions to the cost of medical care.

The third major area of impact lies in the fact that large segments of the aged and poor population are now entitled to medical care under auspices of their own choice. Patient care in the charity clinic with its focus on teaching and research is now obsolete. At the same time, the inner city as a site for traditional medical practice has also become a thing of the past. This void has been filled only in part by the few federally-supported neighborhood health centers. This distortion of the previously existing medical care market by the entitlement of these new groups of people has given rise to the "Medicaid mill," the utilization of the emergency room as a facility for primary medical care, over-utilization of some medical service and a significant problem of fraudulent billing for deficient, unneeded, and often unperformed services.

Under the special circumstances existing in New York City, the aforementioned factors have been exaggerated to the nth degree and we can recognize a whole series of sequelae as definitive problems affecting our health care delivery system. New York City has seven medical schools and 20 medical school-affiliated teaching and research hospital centers. Its hospitals offer resident training to thousands of physicians coming from and returning to all the states in the union. In order to provide training, additional examinations and tests are performed, and patients with especially complicated medical conditions are encouraged to come to New York.

When one considers the 60 independent voluntary hospitals, the approximately 25 private for-profit hospitals, and the 15-unit municipal hospital system—not to mention the numerous union health centers, industrial health centers, Health Insurance Plan centers and neighborhood health centers—the complexity of the problem of prognosticating the impact of national health insurance on the delivery of health services is obvious.

This attempt on the part of the New York Metropolitan Regional Medical Program to stimulate leaders in medical care to consider the various facets of this impact must necessarily focus on a few outstanding issues. It is essential that these efforts be continued both before and after national health insurance is under way. In this way, and with the assistance of health planning agencies, major deficiencies in the system can be more easily avoided and positive goals of the system can be identified and implemented.

Introduction

MARVIN LIEBERMAN

The Task Force on National Health Insurance of the New York Metropolitan Regional Program began its work on September 1, 1974, having assembled a group of experts representative of diverse views on the broad range of issues in health care in our region. Persons chosen for the task force were asked to participate on the basis of their background and experience but not necessarily to speak on behalf of the organizations to which they were currently or previously attached. It was not expected that a consensus on the best way to implement a national health insurance program for New York would emerge from discussions on such a controversial subject and one so clouded by uncertainty. But the opening of deliberations was indeed auspicious. The task force was established in response to clear signals from the national administration that passage of legislation on national health insurance was a matter of the highest priority.

With the advent of national health insurance close at hand, the Director of the New York Metropolitan Regional Medical Program, Dr. Jesse B. Aronson, and its regional advisory group sought to assist the New York metropolitan region to ready itself for the proper and effective implementation of the prospective program by an exploration of various options. This effort was not so much an attempt to develop a definitive plan for our local area as much as it was an effort to reduce the confusion and turmoil that would accompany such a major change in policy. Indeed, no definitive plan would be developed since the ultimate shape of the proposal that would be agreed upon by the President and Congress was unknown. The strategy adopted by the staff and the task force was to commission papers on a variety of health care issues of relevance to the problems of New York. These papers would set forth some options that persons with responsibility for implementing the program would do well to consider in the interest of achieving the most beneficial outcome for the health field and for the people it served within our region.

As the task force deliberations concluded in 1976, much had been learned about problems confronting health services in New York, but it had been, at the same time, a chastening experience in that the ultimate shape of the national health insurance program that would emanate from the federal government was no clearer than before. Indeed, prospects for passage of such legislation seemed as remote in 1976 as ever. By the end of 1975 the nation was experiencing its worst post-war recession and an economic downturn that was exacerbated by continuing inflation in the economy at large as well as in the health care field. The President, who had earlier indicated that national health insurance was an important domestic priority, declared a moratorium not only on this but on all other domestic social programs. Simultaneously, a growing awareness of how the cost of one federal program relates to other programs was reflected in the adoption of a new congressional budget process—one which committed Congress to project revenues and expenditures on the basis of an overall plan and which took into consideration the impact on employment and inflation of the policies adopted. Further, during the same period, as the New York City government approached bankruptcy, there was great pressure on local governments in the region to cut back on expenditures for all services including health care. New York's fiscal crisis revealed, for the first time, the limits of its ability to maintain its traditional generous commitment to a wide variety of health and social services.

The inherent instability and volatility of public affairs during the period of task force deliberations may appear to the disinterested observer as a source of great fascination. But to those who seek the formulation and implementation of long term policy, it underscores the fact that choices about policy are made by each of us in great ignorance, and in the face of uncertainty about what will occur in the future. An appreciation of this uncertainty about new policies and their unforeseen consequences may be contributing to the skepticism about government's capacity to embark successfully on major new initiatives in health and other services. Still, serious disillusionment with efforts to achieve national health insurance is unwarranted. We cannot say that the ambitious social programs of the past, such as those of the Great Society, failed because of their inherent design, or whether, instead, the combination of inadequate administration and decreased funding were the underlying causes for our present skepticism and disillusionment. Even if the inherent design of specific parts of the program was faulty, it did not argue for a total dismantling of the programs without an examination of alternatives that might prove more effective. Indeed, despite the frustrations of the past, we must, if we are serious about the problems, continue to explore solutions to the questions of access to and delivery of health services. We must try to deal as effectively as we can, not just with the design phase of policy, but with the consequences of intervention. The understanding that government action leads to consequences that are unpredictable should teach us to approach major interventions with a more experimental attitude, with a more thorough review of policy options and with a readiness to substitute and change as conditions require. In this respect, the deliberations of the task force and the papers presented would make a contribution.

If the note of skepticism and the perception of more limited horizons is unwarranted from a national point of view, the local perspective is different. New York City and New York State have, traditionally, seen themselves as innovators in social policy that ranges from education to welfare and health, yet we have, at the same time, demonstrated a remarkable capacity to sweep aside problems of administration and accountability. The diminished fiscal capacity of the city and state demands a relatively more limited role for city and state initiatives. But if we are to maintain any sort of commitment at all to social services, a much more effective and consistent administration and monitoring of programs will have to be achieved. It is in this respect that federal action applied equally on behalf of all citizens, as well as federal leadership in administration and planning are required if state and local governments—and the private sector—are to successfully adapt social policy to local circumstances. Many of the failures on the local scene derive from a perception that state and local governments, as well as the private sector, are all in an opposition role vis-à-vis the federal government. The absence of strong federal leadership is behind the failures and extravagances in local areas. This, if anything, is one of the major lessons of Medicaid. A lack of understanding in Washington of the impact of federal decisions and non-decisions on the local area has contributed to the alarming disarray in local affairs. Federal initiatives in health not only are compatible with local initiatives but are required if the necessary local adaptations of national policy are to prove successful. Similarly, if local health planning efforts are to succeed, policy formulation and planning at the federal level must be improved; as it is, local efforts take place in a power vacuum where conflicting demands result in a too great response to parochial interests.

Two errors need to be avoided as we consider national health insurance. The first exaggerates our ability to achieve policy consensus by bringing people together in meetings for the purpose of exchanging information and ideas or for sharpening the issues. The second error ignores the role of the executive branch in policy leadership both in early and in implementation phases. Congress alone cannot be expected to overcome the difficulties in formulating a coherent policy. This is so because of the inherent complexity of the problem and because of the difficulties stemming from jurisdictional disputes among congressional committees and conflicts between congressional leaders. Even if Congress were to pass a thoughtful and well designed program, unless both it and the executive branch pay close attention to the problems of implementation and phasing-in, the program will fail to meet our expectations. Here the distinction between what is necessary and what is sufficient must always be kept in mind. Passage alone of implementing legislation is

3

necessary, but it is not sufficient to achieve any set of coherent goals. We often lose what we have gained by lack of attention to the implementation process.

There is a danger that the expression of skepticism about the effectiveness of public policy interventions by government will paralyze efforts to correct our early mistakes and to build on our successes, however modest these may seem to be. To emphasize problems of increasing costs, inefficiencies, fraud, maladministration and unsatisfied aspirations is not to say that these are the only aspects of health policy and administration that deserve attention. To stress these things does not mean that we lose sight of the unmet needs for health services or of the need for relief from the economic burden of health care costs. Nor is it to ignore the accomplishments in health services—the great extent to which we have already developed magnificently trained personnel and superbly equipped health facilities; the great strides we have made in fulfilling the aspirations of people for better health care.

At the conclusion of the task force deliberations Congress was no closer to a resolution of the fundamental direction of a national health insurance program than it was at the beginning. The alternative possibilities presented with varying chances of realization were: (1) continuation of the present mix of public and private programs such as Medicare for the elderly and disabled, Medicaid for public assistance and the medically indigent, and private health insurance as an incident of employment; (2) establishment of a government-financed, full-time, salaried health service to be either centrally managed or managed on a decentralized basis; (3) establishment of a public mandate that all employers take out private health insurance programs for their employees at some minimum level of benefits with catastrophic insurance protection [perhaps funded by the government], continued operation of Medicare for the aged and with movement toward a federalized Medicaid program; (4) a federally administered program financed through both payroll taxes and general revenues with universal eligibility, comprehensive benefits and national rules. While the Nixon-Ford administration had supported proposal (3), later proposals by the Ford administration indicated a scaling down toward a more voluntary approach, with catastrophic benefits the only provision that would either be mandated or publicly supported. Proposal (4) was most significantly featured in the Kennedy-Corman Bill and was endorsed by various labor and consumer groups.

Very early in our deliberations the staff identified the pervasive issues—the themes and problems for task force discussion, and it was around these themes and issues that papers were commissioned for discussion at task force meetings. In addition, seminars and meetings were convened at which a variety of matters relating to national health

4

insurance was discussed. At these seminars decision-makers in health who were not members of the task force had an opportunity to participate in our deliberations. These themes are well set forth in the staff prospectus and interim report of the first staff director of the task force, Professor Irving Lewis. The issues include primary and ambulatory care, cost controls, the relation between public and voluntary hospitals in New York City, planning and resource allocation, governance and accountability of the health sector, as well as a review of special programs. Also included are the lessons of Medicare and Medicaid, the organization of maternal and child health services, issues in long-term care for the chronically ill and the impact of national health insurance on labor and collective bargaining. What follows in this introductory report are the comments of the staff director on the discussions of the task force and the papers presented.

Primary Care

According to Karen Davis of the Brookings Institution, among the goals of a national health insurance program are better access to high-quality care, improved efficiency and effectiveness of health services and better control of costs. In this context primary and ambulatory care are of outstanding significance. When they are properly organized as a substitute for, rather than an addition to, more expensive inpatient care, these expanded services are among the most important steps that can be taken to achieve the goals of access, improved efficiency and lower costs. Here the question of timing or phasing becomes critical. We must have some capability to provide expanded primary care in place either before the advent of national health insurance or during its early stages of implementation. Further, the national health insurance program that is ultimately adopted should encourage the expansion of primary care and at the same time reduce our commitments to inpatient services by cutting down on the number of hospital beds in proportion to our population.

As news of the fiscal crisis in the city and of changed expectations on the federal level were considered, the theme that pervaded the task force discussion was the recognition that resources for health care were much more limited than we had realized. Thus the simultaneous expansion of primary care with the contraction of the most expensive but often least efficient components of our health care system was seen as the single most promising step that could be taken in the New York region. A major shortcoming in health services is the lack of good primary care including first contact and continuous care, coordination of specialized care and preventive health maintenance. While there was agreement on the need for more primary care, there was disagreement on how it was to be achieved. The hospital's role in primary care and the extent to which local public health agencies can take the lead in expanding their primary care programs were sources of full discussion by the task force.

The possible alternative roles of the hospitals in health care was of prime interest and was reflected in commissioned papers which described far-reaching alternatives. The papers were meant to stimulate discussion and to provide an atmosphere for thinking out a particular approach to an issue; they were not meant to attempt a definitive solution of the problem. Certainly, however, the authors of specific papers believed that their proposals were serious and merited diligent attention.

George A. Silver, M.D., Professor of Public Health at Yale University School of Medicine, urged that New York City undertake to provide primary care in free-standing units in clinics now operated by the New York City Health Department. These clinics would be responsible for contracting with groups of physicians and would supervise records, operations and generally monitor the quality of care rendered. Voluntary hospitals could participate in the plan but the major thrust of the paper was on separating ambulatory care from hospitals and on "decoupling" the hospital from primary care. According to Dr. Silver not only are these services poorly managed by hospitals, but outpatient services—when financed as hospital operations—are required to support an unduly massive overhead imposed by the hospital's pattern of staffing and services. An annual fee per client would be established based on the projected cost of services. The Silver proposal would require a reduction in the bed capacity of the hospital system, utilization of the remainder of health institutions for long-term care, refurbishing and equipping health department clinics and salary or capitation arrangements for physicians who work in these clinics. New York City, which now spends Medicaid funds on unlimited fee-for-service reimbursement for primary care to clinics and physicians could expand services while not increasing expenditures. Several alternatives are described to achieve this goal. Dr. Silver takes on two important and powerful segments of the health care system in New York: the hospitals which would lose control over their ambulatory care "teaching material," and the physicians who would no longer be able to carry on independent entrepreneurial activity, at least with public funds.

Members of the task force raised a series of serious objections to Dr. Silver's approach, although a few endorsed his approach as cost-effective. Those taking issue with Dr. Silver suggested that many things are not clear about how it would work: Would the program be only for poor or lower income patients? Would it not continue separate systems for rich and poor? How would the groups recruit physicians who might not want to work in isolation from the hospitals? Would the interim arrangements that would have to be made until the system was operative increase tremendously the cost of outpatient care? Was the scheme, with its provisions for federations and for city health department supervision, entirely too complex, and would it not develop the same excessive overhead that presently characterizes hospitals?

Some members of the task force suggested that the proposal should be modified sharply. There was agreement that it is imperative to reallocate funds from very costly inpatient care to ambulatory care, but that at the same time there has to be a close relationship between the physician and the hospital necessary to insure proper follow-up. Primary care units should be associated with hospitals; perhaps not physically detached from institutions but organized instead as a separate or discrete department with status equal to other major operations.

Experimentation with the use of small teams of practitioners working in centers and paid on a capitation fee was suggested as a basis deserving of careful examination. Dean Wilbur Cohen of the University of Michigan School of Education, former Secretary of Health, Education, and Welfare and a special consultant to the task force, suggested that, under national health insurance, regions throughout the country should be provided with funds on a per capita basis to permit experimentation with new forms of primary care.

Another option which might foster improved access to primary care on the part of families might be the formal enrollment of the family with a specific source of medical care, whether individual physician, small team, organized group, neighborhood health center or hospital clinic. Except on an emergency basis, or if there were a referral by the primary care provider, care obtained outside this source would not be reimbursed. This approach, together with new methods of compensating providers, might encourage the proper management of care through all elements of the system. Using this system, care could then be evaluated according to the type of provider. By establishing clear responsibility for care to the specific providers selected by patients, processes of accountability could also be implemented. The health department would have a role to play in epidemiological studies and quality of care monitoring and, working together with the Professional Standards Review Organization, would assure that a high quality of health care at reasonable levels of effectiveness and efficiency would be attained.

In parallel with Dr. Silver's proposal, Dr. Betty J. Bernstein, Associate Director, Citizens' Committee for Children, prepared a paper on maternal and child health services which projects a program of primary care centers for prenatal and early childhood care from birth to six years of age. Under her proposal the New York City Health Department surveys the needs in the city and determines the number of facilities that would be necessary. The health department, together with the new Health Systems Agency and its sub-area councils, would be responsible for quality of care and for controlling costs. The health department would also set standards which cover physician extenders, certified midwives and pediatric nurse practitioners. Patient ombudsmen would also be included as part of the team. The primary care centers would have an affiliation with back-up hospitals, and referrals could be made only to approved specialists.

Dr. Catherine DeAngelis, Director of Pediatric and Ambulatory Care, University of Wisconsin Hospital, and a specially invited guest at a task force meeting, had some interesting comments on Dr. Bernstein's paper. She stressed that the element of a "single provider" at any given time is essential to the plan. Consumers may change providers, but prior registration would be required. The importance of health education was emphasized. Persons must become responsible for their own health and the health care of their children to a greater extent than is the case today. This emphasis includes the maintenance of a health record, but Dr. DeAngelis was more skeptical about the use of computers than was Dr. Bernstein. The problems that have emerged in the use of computerized systems lead one to conclude that the adoption of such mechanisms is not realistic, both because of the very great expense and because the quality of the system is so dependent on the ability of the persons who design and maintain it.

Dr. DeAngelis described how Dr. Bernstein's recommendation for primary care for children could be linked to secondary and tertiary health care. The primary care component which, according to Dr. DeAngelis, forms the basis for most of Dr. Bernstein's paper, might function through nursing schools, public schools, health stations or even neighborhood apartments converted into clinics. These clinics could be staffed completely by nurse practitioners, nurse midwives and special education people in the schools. Health care provided in these primary clinics would include routine physical examinations, immunizations, screening, health education, pre-school for handicapped children, minor illness care and pre- and post-natal care. Dr. DeAngelis suggests that the secondary component, to which the primary care providers could direct patients with problems, could be conducted in small hospitals or multi-disciplinary practice clinics. Secondary units would be staffed by nurse practitioners, nurse midwives, general practitioners, family practitioners, pediatricians and obstetric/gynecologists. These would be the sites also of sub-specialty clinics. The care provided in these secondary areas would involve diagnosis and treatment for illness requiring hospitalization but not requiring extensive resources (such as pneumonia, hernia repairs, long-term illnesses, routine deliveries and most emergency care).

8

Finally, Dr. DeAngelis recommended that all tertiary care be conducted in a medical center. These centers would be staffed by subspecialists including neonatologists, pediatric cardiologists, pediatric hematologists, pediatric nephrologists, etc., and high-risk obstetricians. The kind of care managed in the medical center would involve major illnesses and complex surgical cases. Emergency care for severe burns and major neurological trauma would be found in selected medical centers.

In the medical school centers, physicians concerned especially with primary care will be integral parts of the medical school faculty, with full hospital admitting privileges. Their coordination of care for their patients would not only prevent fragmentation, but would serve also as an excellent model for medical students and residents to follow.

The other discussant of Dr. Bernstein's paper, Dr. Alfred Yankauer, Professor of Maternal and Child Health, University of Massachusetts Medical School, pointed out that the assumptions of her paper went beyond that of national health insurance and looked rather towards a national health service. Not only must this issue be faced, according to Dr. Yankauer, but before we plunge into a radical restructuring of services, we should undertake pilot projects to determine the impact on child and maternal health.

Like the response to Dr. Silver's paper, reaction from the task force to Dr. Bernstein's paper was mixed. There were doubts that such a proposal, requiring as it would substantial funds, could be implemented in the face of diminished resources for all kinds of services, even if it were considered desirable in the first place. During the discussion comments were made on the present federal strategies of providing project and formula grants to reshape the delivery system and to bring services to under-served groups of people. The plethora of fragmented health projects for family planning, Title XX under the Social Security Act and maternal and infant care are difficult to track or to evaluate. What is required is the support in resource development for health services which would help to implement successful experiments and to phase out those demonstration projects where the results are poor.

Cost of Health Care

In addition to the current economic problems of unemployment and inflation confronting the economy, a major obstacle to the passage of national health insurance is the fear that any national health insurance package will contribute to the growing inflation of health care costs. In the seminar sessions and in the task force discussions there were some useful preliminary observations about questions of costs which should

9

help to clear up some of the confusion which has emerged and which threatens to prevent progress in resolving this important problem.

To deal adequately with the problem of rising costs of health care, we should differentiate between total expenditures for health care and the costs for each unit of service. Further, the costs per unit of service, say, per inpatient hospital day, must be distinguished from costs per case or disease episode. If only the most complicated cases are admitted to hospitals and many under-utilized health facilities are closed, costs per inpatient day might increase while total expenditures for health care decreased.

Control over utilization is often perceived to be a device for reducing total expenditures in a particular program. But so long as the health care system has excess capacity these costs will be met from other programs. Controls over availability of facilities must go hand in hand with controls over utilization of services if real savings are to be achieved.

As the fiscal crisis of the city came into proper perspective, members of the task force were struck with the fact that in the past there was little recognition that resources for health care are finite. We had passed through a period in which a remarkable increase in public and private expenditures on the federal, state and local levels for health care had taken place, and it was plain that, in the face of drastic cutbacks in reimbursement and in layoffs of employees in health and other services, this was not going to continue. It was in this context that the question of imposing a cap on expenditures for health care was raised in task force meetings.

The notion of a cap, or ceiling, on expenditures for health is somewhat ambiguous. A commitment from Congress that expenditures or budget estimates should not exceed a certain amount does not bind other levels of government or the private sector. Similarly, one must distinguish between a cap on expenditures for a specific component of health services and a cap on total health expenditures. Issues of equity are also raised by ceilings on expenditures. Is it fair to impose a cap on a program which deals with a specific set of beneficiaries, especially those dependent on government programs? If freezes on costs in the health field are seen to be temporary, they will lead to increases either in anticipation of the freeze or, after the freeze is lifted, as a justified catch-up measure. It is clear, however, that, as Dr. Leveson points out in his paper, the health field does not react as do other markets which are more subject to competitive forces. Some sort of control through ceilings—especially on reimbursement—seems to have become a permanent feature of the health care scene. But the method of implementing the ceilings leaves much to be desired. It is difficult to manage institutions or to respond to special problems that occur in the face of the uncertainty created by the failure to promulgate new reimbursement rates at the intervals promised.

10

Perhaps a more constructive notion of a cap on health expenditures is the proposal to allocate a specific fund to each geographic area in the country and then to permit the reallocation of this fund among alternative uses within the region. But the crucial questions here include the level of funding and the criteria put forth by the central government by which regions would govern or at least influence the allocation. In the absence of a proper balance between local initiative and central direction implementation of this type of scheme would be very different.

There are other reasons for skepticism on the question of controls on health services. Our attempts to achieve greater refinement in administering controls often flounder in the face of inadequately trained and poorly compensated personnel. There is increasing skepticism about just what difference an additional sum for a new outlay for health services might make to a particular health problem. Yet proper though it may be this skepticism does not support the contention that health services have only to do with "curing" or preventing illness and not with "caring" as a contribution to the quality of life. With all its inefficiencies, health services are often held to higher standards for their contribution to human well-being than are other services in our society for which billions of dollars are spent by consumers. As Professor Uwe Reinhardt pointed out in the National Reporter Conference on Health Policy last April, health care is a source of gainful income for a large sector of our population; indeed cuts in health services do not necessarily lead to expenditures for alternative employment in other sectors in the economy.

In this connection, in our concern for controlling the cost of health care in the New York area, we should not lose sight of the unique and irreplaceable contributions of the great teaching hospitals not only to the health of the people of the city of New York but also of the vital role they play as a national health resource. These institutions attract patients, students, and researchers throughout the world. Any National Health Insurance Program will have to make provision for the special place of these organizations.

During the course of task force discussions, references were made also to the problems of enforcement of standards of care, and to the cases of fraud and abuse of services that appeared in the press and on radio and television. A more effective enforcement of regulations already on the books was seen as one way of eliminating the wanton abuses. For example, additional resources for auditors and prosecutors might have a salutary effect. However, in any review of abuse the task force was sensitive to the distinction between systematic failure and mere lapses in administrative control. For example, for private practitioners, it is the differential in payments between Medicare and Medicaid (where there is little financial incentive to participate) that accounts, at least in part, for the problem which has created Medicaid mills.

11

Several methods have been developed for the more effective utilization of resources allocated for health care and for controlling costs. Among these are utilization review programs under Medicare and Medicaid, state certificate-of-need legislation and hospital rate-setting. Under utilization review programs, committees of physicians and other health professionals are charged with responsibility for preventing unnecessary hospital admissions and excessive lengths of stay in hospitals. Certificate-of-need legislation has, with varying degrees of success, been used to deny hospitals the permission to build new and unnecessary beds and to establish duplicating services.

In deliberations, in seminars, and in briefing sessions the task force has spent a good deal of time discussing the issue of prospective reimbursement of hospital costs. Prospective rate reimbursement has been fostered by the amendments to the Social Security Act as well as through Public Law 93-641, the National Health Planning and Development Act of 1974. It appears that while many interesting experiments in prospective reimbursement are underway, the techniques are considered by most serious students of the subject to be at a relatively primitive stage.

There is general awareness that current methods of reimbursing hospitals on a retrospective cost reimbursement basis have not worked and must be abandoned. Work still remains to be done on developing prospective payment mechanisms that set maximum levels of reimbursement in advance, that are based on analyses and review of budgets and with incentives for efficient performance. Indeed, it must be noted that prospective rate regulation does not deal with inadequacies in the systems which provide health care. Nor has adequate linkage been developed between rate setting, utilization review and quality-of-care review activities such as authorized by the Professional Standards Review Organizations established by the Social Security Amendments of 1972.

Among the most interesting experiments taking place is that in Rhode Island where, under an arrangement among the Social Security Administration, Blue Cross and the Rhode Island Health Department, the Social Security Administration has a contract with Blue Cross. A state-wide limitation on total allowable operating expenses is established through negotiation. For example, in fiscal year 1975 what is described as a "maxicap" (a limit on the rate of increase in costs) of 13.85 percent was established. In 1976 a "maxicap" of 11.5 percent was agreed to. An analysis of each hospital's entire budget takes place and, prior to review and analysis by the state health department and Blue Cross, there is peer review through the hospital association. Individual operating expense budgets are then negotiated and the final hospital budget is subject to cost finding based upon the past principles of reimbursement of each third party. The prospective rates for reimbursement are then established. In any one hospital, a lesser or greater amount may be supplied so long as the entire hospital system does not exceed the percentage increase in the "maxicap." In addition, it is possible under this kind of system for the state to introduce the Health Systems Agencies and the Health Planning Agencies into the process of cost determination. Any savings that the hospital receives could be allocated according to plans by the Health Systems Agencies.

Rhode Island's experience must be viewed with caution since transferring the experience from one state to another must take into account the difference in the relative size and complexity of the hospital systems in New York State and Rhode Island. In order to adapt the Rhode Island system to New York, the review of hospital budgets would have to be decentralized due to the great number of hospitals in the state. There would, perhaps, have to be some assurance that the responsible planning agencies were competent, efficient and fair in their analysis of budgets.

In the upstate New York area, there will be a significant attempt to carry forward the experiment begun in Rhode Island. A recently announced contract between the Office of Research and Statistics, Social Security Administration and Blue Cross Association, working with the Hospital Association of New York State, two upstate Blue Cross Plans and 23 hospitals in the Rochester area is in effect for a two-year period ending December 1978. A "maxicap" program linking prospective reimbursement with a health service plan in some form and an overall community budget for health care will be developed. The experience obtained in tying together planning and prospective reimbursement will be closely watched by those who are interested in better ways of allocating resources for health care facilities and services.

At the writing of this report the evaluation studies that the Social Security Administration contracted for have not been published. There are indications that the administrators closest to the problem of reimbursement are sharply divided about the effectiveness of such programs. At a seminar on cost control sponsored by the Task Force in February 1975, a spokesman for the Bureau of Health Insurance in the Social Security Administration expressed great skepticism about the possibility of using prospective reimbursement to effectively control costs. On the other hand, at another meeting, the research personnel responsible for reimbursement projects and demonstrations in the Social Security Administration were guardedly optimistic in their statements.

Senator Talmadge, chairman of the Subcommittee on Health of the Senate Finance Committee, has made some proposals for changes in Medicare and Medicaid reimbursement which may foreshadow the shape of things to come in any national health insurance program. There is recognition that reasonable cost reimbursement is inflationary because of the absence of limits on what should be considered "unreasonable." Furthermore, there are neither incentives for efficient performance nor sanctions for poor performance. The emphasis in the Talmadge amendments is to establish "performance-based" reimbursement systems which would provide hospitals with incentive payments to "reward" and "stimulate" efficiency. Great efforts will be made to develop standards for classifying and comparing hospitals.

Another area of concern is the very controversial issue of the method of payment for physicians which is usually summarized in the phrase "fee-for-service vs. capitation payments." In the present method of reimbursement under Part B, Title XVIII of Medicare, customary and prevailing fees are reimbursed and physicians are permitted to charge patients the difference between the government's payment (including the co-insurance feature) and the charge to the patient. Only if the physician accepts an assignment of the claim by the Medicare beneficiary and thus obtains immediate payment is the physician limited to the customary and prevailing fee. Yet, if the schedule of fees were to be reduced, the physician would be discouraged from accepting assignments. With the reduction in the profiles of prevailing fees under Medicare which have taken place, fewer physicians today accept assignments than previously. Indeed, the percentage of physicians participating in assignments has declined.

In order that the patient might have a greater portion of his bills covered, among the measures under consideration in national health insurance legislation are incentives other than speedy payment to encourage physicians to accept assignments.

Payment of physicians at customary and prevailing fees subject to a cutoff limit has received a good deal of criticism. Opponents of this approach suggest that it subjects patients to additional costs and may be inflationary. The failure to mandate assignment of claims also has received opposition on the grounds that it encourages uneven standards of care. If fee-for-service is to be a viable method of compensation of physicians there must be negotiation of rates of payment that are equitable to physicians while protecting patients against additional charges.

The pattern of low unit payments under Medicaid has led to a relatively low level of participation under Medicaid and to the proliferation of Medicaid mills or shared health facilities. Under Medicaid there is a so-called "vendor payments" program by which providers including physicians are paid directly by the welfare agency or other fiscal intermediaries, and are not permitted to bill patients themselves.

It has been alleged that in many shared-health facilities, a profit can be made even with low unit payments for services by means of providing extremely brief visits, excessive delays on treatment regimens and drugs and by permitting a wide variety of specialists to see the patients, albeit very briefly. (In California, in those situations where Medicaid has been furnished under capitation payment arrangements with various groups of practitioners, other abuses have emerged. Under this type of program, since compensation is received regardless of whether or not services are performed, the tendency has been to discourage the patient from obtaining services.)

Abuses under fee-for-service and capitation arrangements often lead critics to suggest that the problem is inherent in the method of delivery of service. Yet in neither case of payment has adequate regulation and monitoring been given a chance to eliminate shortcomings in the program, nor have fair levels of reimbursement for physicians' services been developed. Despite the lack of assurance that any one method of physician compensation is free from difficulties, greater experimentation with methods of compensation, in addition to fee-for-service arrangements, is widely supported by administrators and students of health services. Although only a minority of physicians might prefer salary or capitation arrangements, it is important to stress that a substantial number of physicians are presently working under other than fee-for-service. The number of physicians who will participate in other than fee-for-service arrangements depends upon the level of compensation and upon the type of physician recruited. For example, it is believed by some that pediatricians, as a group, would be more willing to accept different compensation arrangements than would other physicians. It is for this reason that Theodore R. Marmor of the University of Chicago argues for a universal pediatric service provided by pediatricians and other physicians on a capitation basis, although he would not alter the method of payment for other specialists.

Governance and Accountability

In the New York City area many questions are being raised by the spokesmen for both voluntary and public hospital facilities about the propriety of the arrangements whereby the other hospital system is organized, financed and managed. To a large extent the debate is academic since, on the one hand, in the absence of universal financial entitlement to health care, the voluntary hospitals would be unable to care for the medically indigent patients who have no other source of care than that provided in public institutions. On the other hand, there seem to be no serious proposals that the New York City Health and Hospitals Corporation should take over the operation of voluntary hospitals. Staff

15

of the task force have identified problems arising out of the increasing proportion of public funds paying for care of all, which are linked to concerns about efficiency, effectiveness and responsiveness.

By governance we refer to the structure which sets the goals and makes the decisions about allocation of resources within the institutions to achieve its goals of health care. Complicating the issue of goal-setting are the numerous constituencies and external agencies that tend to influence the goals of a health care institution. There are a variety of governance mechanisms in health, each one having its special supporters such as individual proprietorships, corporate profit-making, not-for-profit corporations, public corporations and public operation by departments of government. Furthermore, in some parts of the country, hospital districts exist as a level of government themselves, with a power to tax analogous to local school districts.

With the proliferation of advisory boards and planning and regulatory bodies, the issues of governance need to be clarified. We tend to emphasize nominal structures instead of real differences. For example, the public and not-for-profit governance arrangements permit a greater variety of decision-making arrangements than is normally realized. A public health agency can be autonomous or can be tied down to a variety of overhead agency constraints, just as a not-for-profit corporation may be run by a small group or may have a variety of rules for the selection of its management and boards of directors.

Accountability refers to that process whereby persons or units in some position of authority render an accounting to an external, superior agency or to the public at large for their efforts to achieve asserted goals— including efficiency, quality, responsiveness and propriety of performance. The major problem in discussions of accountability is the lack of precision about the agency *to whom* one is accountable and *for what* one is accountable. Charges of lack of accountability unaccompanied by specifications of the process and subject of accountability should not be accepted at face value.

The issue of municipal versus voluntary hospitals is tied into the question of the proper arrangements for governance and accountability. It is now the case that a very large percentage of the total resources of voluntary institutions derive from public funds, but public funds have always played a significant place in the operation of charitable service institutions in the United States. With greater demands for participation in the society from persons who hitherto have been either excluded from such participation, or who have not sought participation, one issue is the way in which voluntary institutions will broaden their constituency and how the new constituency will be brought into the structure of governance.

On the other hand, if we ever reach the point at which all persons are entitled to comprehensive health benefits, then the special role of municipal hospitals for the poor will have to be reconsidered. When this occurs, the demand for a single standard of care will no longer be academic but a challenge that can no longer be ignored. The question will not be easily resolved however, because there are conflicts between the desires for full access to services, for control of the best institutions and for the desire of groups to control their own institutions.

The great strength of voluntary hospitals lies in their relative freedom from budgetary control from the city and in their ability to tap support from a variety of constituencies, as well as the prominence of their leaders in social, business, financial and religious circles. Yet as the growth of public expenditures has led to an increase in regulation, the autonomy of the voluntary hospital has gradually diminished. The new factor in voluntary hospitals, and to a lesser extent in the public hospitals, has been the rise of the professional manager. Management in voluntary hospitals has fewer external constraints than does management in public sector hospitals, but is nevertheless subject to a multiplicity of regulations imposed upon them by governmental agencies at all levels, such as the requirements for onerous and sometimes conflicting reporting.

Hospitals in the voluntary sector derive their greatest strength from the loyalty of the particular constituency which they represent. Indeed, as resources of support diminish, strains among voluntary hospitals are bound to increase. At the same time a major weakness is their inability to work with each other in a coordinated way that would ensure services and management. Dogmatic attacks by one sector on the other shed little light on the fundamental question of whether a particular hospital is needed and who can pay for its support. In the present period, the ultimate battle will be within each sector to see which hospital rather than which system survives. For the present, as attempts are made to limit the number of hospitals, attention is focused primarily on the trials and tribulations of the public hospitals; too many of the hospital plants in the municipal system are obsolete; there are too many hospital beds; many hospitals will have to be shut down.

The ultimate question of governance will have to be postponed until the issue of entitlement is settled. Once the matter of entitlement is settled the conflict will not be over nominal control of the institution but over such issues as how the medical staff relates to the hospital, the role of education, the relation of the medical schools to the local practitioners and the question of academic physicians. These disputes will become extremely important and will complicate the ultimate solutions.

A serious question that is raised periodically is whether the public hospital system can establish a viable management capability. Indeed, one of the reasons for the creation of the Health and Hospitals Corporation was the desire to free the hospitals from direct control by the city overhead agencies in their budget and purchase functions and the establishment of a quasi-independent public corporation that would permit the improvement of management. At the time of the creation of the hospitals corporation, supporters argued that the municipal hospitals could be reorganized to be run more like voluntary hospitals. Complicating this was the presence of a strong central staff operation both within the hospital department and the corporation. Opponents argued that the creation of the corporation would remove the hospitals from the supervision of the mayor, thus leaving him free to ignore the needs of the corporation and to no longer be held accountable for poor performance by corporation hospitals.

Another premise underlying the shift to a corporation was that the public hospitals were fundamentally a business-like operation. It was argued that with the passage of Medicaid and Medicare, municipal hospitals would no longer be dependent on city funding for their continued satisfactory operation. There were at least two fallacies in this approach. The first was the view that adequate funding from third-party sources was indeed available, when, in fact, the hospitals continued to be dependent on support from the city. The working poor and other persons not covered by public assistance or Medicaid would continue to require support by the city for their medical care in municipal institutions. The second error was to assume that the solution to systematic mismanagement and extremely rigid governmental controls would be achieved by separating one sector of government and making it independent. Management confusion and the lack of adequate financial reporting systems in city government would not be solved by this device. The current fiscal crisis in city government demonstrates the need to review and overhaul the management and the accounting systems and policies that caused the havoc. The tendency at present is to bring the municipal hospitals back under public financial control for, in one way or another, public funds are decisive elements in the costs of their operation.

Another complicating factor in the public hospital system is the development of two powerful constituencies—the leaders of ethnic groups served by the hospital who now play a major role in its management, and the unions of public employees who work in these institutions.

Since the beginning of the corporation there has been relatively little public exploration of the long-term role of public hospitals in New York City. Such a discussion is beginning now on the matters of how physicians should relate to hospitals in terms of the future of affiliation contracts. In informal discussion there is advocacy for further closing of the least utilized or most poorly equipped facility. Other alternatives include the sale of municipal hospitals to voluntary institutions or the conversion of a municipal hospital to a voluntary hospital with a community board. There is an important distinction between converting a municipal hospital into a voluntary hospital by sale of one institution to the other and its resulting incorporation into the existing voluntary hospital and the conversion of the municipal hospital into a public hospital in which the board is representative of elements of the local community.

While these matters cannot be resolved today, now is the time to begin to clarify some of the confusion surrounding the debate. This can be done by separating the issues from the buzzing mass of slogans. These issues include, but are not limited to, the following: (1) elimination of underutilized elements and of inefficient operations in both systems; (2) the sharing of services and facilities among voluntary and municipal hospital systems; (3) broadening the base of governance of voluntary hospitals to include an examination of how trustees are selected, what their qualifications are and what roles they perform; (4) modern accounting and management procedures for municipal hospitals; (5) balancing of patient service, health research and teaching functions in all hospitals, whether public or private; (6) developing improved relations between hospitals and their local communities; (7) developing networks within and among the voluntary and public hospital systems.

Study Prospectus

IRVING J. LEWIS

This paper was prepared by the staff of the task force as a primary agenda item for the first meeting of the task force on October 11, 1974. It was presented as both a substantive and procedural outline of an admittedly experimental, but in our judgment essential, planning activity.

Legislative Outlook

Congress has many different bills on national health insurance before it, and legislative predictions are always risky. Nevertheless, there is growing consensus that a compromise bill should and will be enacted before too long. President Ford has urged enactment of a bill, and Congressman Wilbur Mills, Chairman of the House Ways and Means Committee, has actively tried to secure agreement in his committee. In recent discussions, we have heard that the administration has agreed that, regardless of source of financing, coverage for each person should be mandatory, as Wilbur Mills believes. The present long-range planning of HEW assumes that NHI will be fully operational by 1980.

On many points the policy-makers are in agreement. These are:

1. Use of federal appropriations, subsidy and taxing powers;
2. Coverage of low-income persons by use of general revenues in a national plan, thus phasing out Medicaid;
3. Strengthening state and local, or area, planning and development agencies;
4. Encouragement of Health Maintenance Organizations (HMOs) and use of other incentives to improve quality and lower or control costs;
5. Benefits to include coverage of outpatient services, and
6. Phasing in benefits over several years.

The largest areas of disagreement are those that deal with whether the administration of NHI should rest with the Social Security system and be funded through a payroll tax, or with the private insurance companies and the payment of private premiums. At this time there seems to be some willingness to settle this issue on the basis of the fiscal intermediary concept followed in Medicare. We must point out that the debate stresses financing and only pays lip service to the problems of organizing and delivering health services. Even at that, it is an advance over the debate surrounding Medicare in 1965.

Overall cost, the impact of NHI on the federal budget and its relation to the present inflationary situation, together with the questions of (a) deductibles and co-insurance and (b) sources of financing are obvious political questions that are still very troublesome to resolve. Although one view is that the outcome could be no more than a "catastrophic" insurance bill, the very fact of the worsening economy may actually lend urgency to the need for tight cost controls coupled with more extensive insurance.

The federal government, then, will establish a new framework for financing the purchase of health care; within it will be predetermined (a) eligibility, (b) benefit coverage, (c) sources of financing and (d) some broad parameters on administration, regulation and control, especially costs. At the same time, the delivery of health care will be viewed as a responsibility of the communities—private and public; state and local. We can be sure, however, that basic changes in the financing of health care will have enormous impact upon the health-care delivery system. These changes will not outlaw but will, undoubtedly, modify what has been the basic force shaping our present structure of medical care—the fee-for-service system—and the roles played both by professionals and by institutions, especially hospitals.

The Task Force Job

The objective of this RMP task force is to uncover the changes that the new financing system and concepts are likely to engender, and to inquire whether we can mold these changes and the delivery system's response to them so as to benefit the entire community, consumers and providers alike, in both private and public sectors. The political decisions or compromises that will be made on the sources of funding a system for universal entitlement to a basic set of personal health services may lead to waste, to administrative inefficiencies and to the perpetuation of certain inequities, but so long as a mandate emerges from Congress for universal entitlement, the issue of financing may well turn out to be secondary to the community's problem of organizing the delivery system.

The community's problem becomes clearer as we realize that we are probably approaching a situation in which, for a variety of political reasons, there will be an effective ceiling on the financial resources for health care. This prognosis derives initially from two well-known factors: (1) the rapid rise in health care costs, unit and total, and (2) the increasing federal budgetary stake in payment for health. The probability of facing eventual closed-end funding becomes more certain in the face of a worsening economy and the competition for funds for other more compelling societal demands—e.g., housing—upon both the GNP and the federal budget. The relatively lower priority given to health in comparison

21

with food and shelter; the increased cost pressures of medical technology; the stagnating economy; the enormous rises in health expenditures since 1965—all these are likely to combine and to highlight for many analysts of health care the impossibility of continuing unchanged the present methods of fee-for-service payment and cost-pass-through reimbursement. In their place, in some form in NHI, we will have controls over charges and fees, prospective reimbursement, fixed budgets or capitation systems for defined populations.

In the long run these changes in financing and the need for cost controls may have to find expression in some form of local organization or structure able to oversee the allocation of resources of men, money and materials. Inevitably, a public stake in setting priorities opens up issues of public accountability and governance and consumer involvement.

The predictions are coming true that the concern of third party payers—both public and private—with the cost impact of how health services are delivered will be reflected in provisions for cost control and incentives. But we can be sure that the approach of these payers will remain, as always, essentially financial. The Ways and Means Committee, conservatively oriented as it is, will not address itself to the impact of these provisions or of new benefit coverages upon health care programs. The task force will have to identify for New York City—each community being different—the major components of that impact (whether intentional or unintentional) and to assess the available options for advance planning so that both the outcome of NHI may be favorable and its limitations well identified.

It is useful to keep in mind the systematic interaction among considerations of (1) financing (costs), (2) utilization (efficiency), (3) quality (content) and (4) availability (access) of health care services. The eventual outcome of responsiveness to community demands—or needs— for health care will depend upon how these considerations are put together in a balanced relationship. Since legislative mandates and guidelines from many sources will come into play, it is only at the community level of delivery that the proper balance can be achieved.

Work Plan

Task Force Membership Members have been asked to serve as *individuals*, rather than to *represent* their interests. The deeply fragmented or pluralistic character of the health system tends to keep most decision-makers in their present groove. While the members clearly bring different points of view to bear upon our effort to define the public interest, the task force is not expected to be representative of all the special interests in health care.

Task Force Panels We are recommending that the task force function as a committee of the whole so that the full range of points of view can always be covered on all issues. On occasion, however, the task force may feel that a small panel should attack a specific subject with the aid of one or more consultants on an ad hoc basis.

Position Papers Subject to task force discussion and agreement, the staff has put together a broad work plan set forth below. To illuminate and focus the meeting agenda, we will depend upon the commissioning of position papers or studies by other persons familiar with the New York scene. Papers will especially address options for action and the identification of responsibilities, but will not necessarily make specific recommendations for action. We think it is important that the task force members enhance the process of dialogue by bringing their own points of view and knowledge to bear upon each issue.

Seminars As a further input of information to task force deliberations, and in support of the overall project objective of attracting the attention of a wide variety of New York decision-makers, we plan to hold three to five seminars. These will be chaired by Mr. Lewis and will be attended by 25–30 invited local participants. The seminars should help us to develop ideas and sharpen key issues. Brief oral presentations will be made by several invited consultants as a basis for leading off the discussions, and while participants will be drawn principally from the New York area, consultants will be drawn from other areas as well. Task force members, of course, will be welcome to attend. Seminar topics can be infinite in number. The staff think that the priority topics are (1) primary care, (2) changing public/private responsibilities, including governance and accountability, (3) cost controls and quality of care and (4) special groups of problems such as the elderly, mothers and children, the mentally ill and long-term care.

Issues

The impact of NHI on New York City health programs raises an almost limitless number of issues. The staff have identified a group of study areas which we believe are inevitably raised by NHI and which are of top priority for New York City. Commissioned papers and other reports on the following subjects will develop the essential data and will contain options for possible action, as well as indications of pitfalls to be avoided by decision-makers.

1. Primary Care How can the expected substantial extension of benefits for ambulatory services be translated into the organized provision of

23

better primary care? National health insurance does not directly address the major health systems problem of primary care; rather it stresses payment for outpatient services. The field of primary care is fraught with questions of definition, but the key concepts are first contact, continuous care and preventive care, all largely ambulatory. What are the new regulatory, planning and developmental strategies that are needed in primary care; where are the most critical substantive needs; what utilization can be expected? Further, what new investment resources will be required to meet the new, forecasted demands for primary care so that access to financing care runs parallel to the availability of services?

The impact of NHI on various forms of providers needs examination in its own right, but the examination tends to come together under the rubric of primary care. The basic organizational issue will probably relate to reorganizing OPD clinics and emergency rooms, both in voluntary and municipal hospitals, but we also need to know what the outlook is for private practice—in terms of availability, style of practice and increased productivity. Health department facilities, HMOs and existing prepaid groups such as HIP are part of the review. Finally, health centers supported by federal grants, such as family and neighborhood health centers, various maternal and child health centers and mental health centers need a special review to examine their continued financial availability under NHI.

2. Impact on Health Care for the Poor   What will be the impact of national health insurance on the delivery system of health care to the poor and what is the forecast for continuing state and local responsibility for such care? The uncertain funding that prevails under Medicaid and Medicare should yield lessons to be applied here. Judgments will be needed on the short and long-term role of the local and state governments both in providing and in paying for health care for the poor. Since deductibles and co-insurance will undoubtedly be part of any NHI package, we have to have some sense of the composition of the groups who are likely to fall "between the cracks," and make plans for the arrangements—whether financial or provider-oriented—that will be needed for these "working poor" who will still be without access to financing. Obviously, then, we need to know what the budgetary impact of NHI will be on the New York City and other local budgets. We need a sober appraisal of this major municipal responsibility.

3. Resource Allocation, Planning, Regulation and Control   What new or redesigned local structures, and what adjustments in state and local relations should we develop in order to provide for resource allocation, planning, regulation and control? It is not yet clear how tightly the new

24

federal health planning legislation will be linked to national health insurance, or how NHI will provide for planning. Yet there is bound to emerge, both from the federal planning bill and from the NHI arena, a new, broad range of planning, regulatory and developmental responsibilities which should stimulate the improved organization of care, as well as aid in the movement toward rational allocation of health care resources of men, money and facilities. This "managerial" function will be largely decentralized from Washington and poses at least these areas of concern: (a) overall organization in New York State and New York City for health planning and development, and changes in existing CHP/RMP/Hill-Burton structures; (b) relations between state and local government in the regulation and control of health services, facilities and manpower, and (c) organization of the functions of overall data collection and analysis relating to utilization, efficiency, costs and finances, geographic settings, forms of care, etc., which are essential for rational allocation of resources and planning.

4. Quality of Care Assessment   How will we assure quality-of-care assessment under NHI? Although the impetus for PSROs (Professional Standards Review Organizations) was cost and utilization control, and its present jurisdiction is Medicaid/Medicare, the likelihood is that the PSRO will be carried over into NHI as a main tool for the assessment of quality. There will no doubt be problems of integrating the local PRSO mechanisms with the newly emerging local planning, regulatory and developmental functions, as well as with city and state health department functions of monitoring and auditing health care. We will have to assess the present status of the PSRO program and grapple with the basic question of how to define and assure quality of care. This is especially critical in respect to differences between the voluntary and public sector. Current assessments of quality stress techniques of credentialling and of process review. Can and should we seriously consider moving to assessment of quality in terms of criteria of outcome, excessive utilization, availability and accessibility, and other measures of performance?

5. Accountability and Governance   What adjustments in the existing public/private, i.e., pluralistic, system of governance and public accountability will be required or desirable, given publicly-ordered changes in financing? Apart from the broader questions of structures for resource allocation, planning and control, we will have to face numerous questions of new forms of governance and accountability. With a more extensive insurance coverage for ambulatory care, and with new forms of organization by voluntary and public hospitals to render such care, will some form

25

of districting of services be needed as a rationing device? What are the implications for (a) board of trustee membership, (b) community and consumer advisory boards and (c) consumer involvement in setting priorities? What restrictions on its freedom can the voluntary hospital anticipate?

Assuming the continuance of the municipal hospitals' affiliation contracts with the medical schools, how does NHI affect the relationships between the municipal and voluntary systems? Universal entitlement may accelerate the movement to create a unified or coordinated hospital system which can provide a single standard of care and use its resources efficiently. What, then, are the *structural* implications, and what further structural, jurisdictional and governance changes would occur in the New York City Health and Hospitals Corporation?

6. Cost Containment and Efficiency   What will be the applicability and likely effect of the various techniques of cost control and financial incentives for New York City, and to what extent will they come under local control and direction? With the basic push for cost controls—and indeed its acceleration in today's weakening economy—we can expect that all possible methods of cost controls and incentives will be permitted or ordered under NHI initially. The federal government will look to the states to assume a major role in containing costs. The problem is that costs are only part of the concern for the mix up of cost-quality-utilization-availability which has to be handled in a balanced way at the local level. The data system mentioned in the earlier section will be essential to deal with this concern.

There are many ways to get at the issue of costs. At the *community* level there are: (a) capital expenditure control, (b) PSRO review, (c) Health Maintenance Organization (HMO) development, and (d) investment in new lower-cost services. *Provider*-oriented measures include: (a) utilization review, (b) prospective rates and lump sum budgets, (c) incentive reimbursement, (d) fee schedules and (e) prior authorization of services. A special feature of cost containment which will receive increased attention under NHI is regionalization of high-cost specialty services. In this connection, there is at present a tendency to move from a geographic or functional concept to a network concept, thus avoiding problems of districts, defined populations and major alterations of hospital programs.

These controls and incentives represent a hodge-podge of techniques and do not all appear in one NHI bill. The big problem, since cost containment is a clear NHI objective, is, first, to assess the utility of these techniques in New York, and second, to establish the extent to which they will fall under local control or direction. Thus, hidden in the cost question

26

is the major question of state and local relationships in the organization and delivery of health care programs.

7. Manpower and Education   What are the manpower requirements and what are the implications for educational programs for differing types of manpower? Internship and residency programs, including specialist training, are increasingly the subject of national studies ordered by the fiscal committees of the Congress. In addition, despite recent negative Senate action, we are probably moving toward systems of control over the geographic and specialty distribution of physicians through the medium of approval of internship and residency programs. Such manpower controls over New York City hospitals, both municipal and voluntary, would have an enormous and direct impact on health care programs and on the capacity of the system to meet the demands generated by NHI. Of special interest would be the extent to which manpower controls would be exercised in order to move physicians into primary care, and the nature of the medical school/voluntary hospital response to such controls.

The health industry is not only a major employer in New York City at present but, with the decline in manufacturing jobs, it represents an important potential source for new jobs. We need to examine state, local and private job training programs in terms both of quantitative and qualitative impact so that job expectations can reasonably match job reality under NHI, and so that the "required" manpower will, in turn, be available to meet demand.

8. Changing Role of Industry and Labor in Employee Health Benefits   What will be the continued responsibilities of labor and management in collective bargaining for health benefits, and how can these groups be involved more effectively in cost and quality control efforts? National health insurance, as well as the general efforts to improve the delivery system for primary care, will have both an organizational and a budgetary impact on labor-management relations and on union health and welfare plans. This will be of especial significance in New York City. Issues to be studied include the future need for labor health centers, the continuing role of collective bargaining for uncovered services, labor-management sponsorship of HMOs and other major organizational efforts and their involvement in cost and quality-control efforts.

*9. Unique or Uncovered Areas   As a result of NHI and the response to it by the health care system, certain groups or problem areas will still be in a unique situation. If we are to avoid the errors of optimism under Medicare/Medicaid and plan for continued responsibilities at the local level, we shall have to be prepared to see how national health insurance takes care of such problems as:

1. long term care, including care of the chronically ill and elderly;
2. mental health, drug addiction and alcoholism;
3. maternal and child health.

We can, at this time, assume only limited help for the above from national health insurance. We will probably find a need for continued municipal and state activity, including substantial funding, especially if some of the present federal funding is reduced.

Interim Report and Reflections, July 16, 1975

IRVING J. LEWIS

While we continue to develop additional papers on significant issues and plan for the resumption of task force meetings and seminars or conferences after the summer recess, it is timely that the task force take stock of its work to date, assess what it has learned thus far and determine what would be the most fruitful future course of inquiry.

Legislative Outlook

The prospect for enactment of federal legislation appears much less favorable than when the task force was organized. The general slide in the economy, the tight federal budgetary policy, the reorganization of the committee and leadership structure of the House of Representatives, the loss of Wilbur Mills—all have led to a major change in the mood of Congress. Undoubtedly, the mood has been conditioned by the unwillingness of the administration to submit its own proposal, although President Ford has, in general terms, endorsed the eventual enactment of national health insurance.

Thus the major legislative configurations remain substantially what they have been. The Health Security Bill of Senator Kennedy, the old Nixon Comprehensive Health Insurance Program (CHIP), the National Health Care Services Reorganization and Financing Act, the state health commission bill of Chairman Ullman and the Long-Ribicoff catastrophic health insurance bill (the Catastrophic Health Insurance and Medical Assistance Reform Act) are the principal contenders. The AMA has now moved to its own version of the Nixon CHIP Bill. The flurry over extension of health insurance for the unemployed has now subsided in the jurisdictional controversy between the Rogers health subcommittee (Interstate Commerce) and the Rostenkowski health subcommittee (Ways and Means). Both groups are scheduling hearings and building up written records.

The major issue, which is clearly ideological and will be settled only in a political context, is whether we use the Social Security system as the mechanism both for financing and policy control, or whether we use a mandated system within the framework of private health insurance. The weakening of the economy has probably made both the opponents and proponents of the Social Security plan agreeable to waiting until the 1976 election. Thus, it is becoming very probable that there will be no enactment until 1977 and no implementation until 1979 or 1980. This is the heart of the public/private sector ideological debate, and it is not likely to be decided merely by a marshalling of facts. Rather, like the decisions in 1965 on Medicare, it will reflect fundamental attitudes towards the role of government and will be settled in a political context. Indeed, it may well be a critical election issue in 1976.

Once the basic financing framework is established, most of the other issues seem to be negotiable, but progress toward agreed-upon goals will be made step by step. Among these issues are the scope of benefits or services, the use and size of deductibles and co-payments, the federalization of Medicaid and the abandonment of the traditional grant-in-aid financing and administration of programs for the poor, the coverage of dental care and long-term care and the application of HMO and PSRO legislation. Finally, the whole area of so-called cost constraints is susceptible of significant compromise. In fact, after one has reviewed in depth the many proposals flying under the label of cost constraints, it is not at all clear how significantly they do constrain costs. But legislation will undoubtedly include one or more cost constraining elements like prospective reimbursement, differential fee schedules, capitation, certificate-of-need, public utility regulation, etc. While these different policy and technical approaches may influence the *price* of medical care to individuals, there is no legislative proposal sufficiently comprehensive yet to control the overall cost, i.e., the size of the health dollar. In the last analysis this may come down to the budgeting technique.

This all seems to point to the view that the bill around which compromise will be sought has probably not yet been introduced. We could still see some version that extends insurance only to mothers and children, or we could see compromise on the "catastrophic" approach.

A Theme of Skepticism

The task force proceedings have encompassed seven task force meetings; four invitational seminars on issues of primary care, cost controls, governance and accountability and long-term care, and the production of a series of commissioned and staff papers. The theme which runs increasingly through these proceedings can be summed up in the one word "skepticism." Following hard upon the deep skepticism that national health insurance will be passed at all is the skepticism that, if passed, it will bring any substantial benefits to individuals or to health programs, or that it will yield any substantial budget savings to the City of New York. Moreover, while we have been able to delineate a number of points of interaction between health planning and national health insurance, there is a parallel skepticism that the federal legislative and executive structure is sufficiently well put together to provide realistic policy leadership in planning. Finally, there is a healthy skepticism that the health planners themselves have firm enough ideas about what health planning is and is intended to accomplish.

Apart from the obvious malaise in the American society which seems to be paralyzing democratic action, this skepticism appears to me to drive from the realization, *fortified by these task force proceedings*, that major changes in the organization and delivery of health care in New York are not merely necessary but inevitable if national health insurance is to make any difference, at least to New York City. But we all know how difficult it is to accomplish even slight changes. There is considerable agreement that the existing institutional structures, i.e., the providers, are firmly entrenched in what we venerate as the pluralistic health-care system. Public or private, these providers have tremendous influence over the way in which the present system operates, and it is not clear that any of the pending proposals for national health insurance will have sufficient leverage to be effective in changing structures or in changing the way in which care is provided.

Because of the strategic role of providers, new legislation and the consequent administration of it must alter the degree of freedom that providers now possess if any real change is to occur. Unfortunately, political realism also teaches that, without substantial additional funding, new legislation may have little leverage for change. Yet, the consensus grows that it is cost control and not additional funding, that the health system must anticipate. As a consequence, the future may well see the continued operation of an imperfect medical market, where the flow of money and the lure of dollars, even at a low unit-cost level, will attract new entrepreneurs, e.g., an expansion of the Medicaid mill to the NHI bill.

The skeptical view is not a very attractive outlook for reformers of the health care system, and suggests to the task force that our biggest contribution may be a negative one—to face up to what is do-able and what is not do-able under NHI, and to identify the great difficulties in meeting the excessively high expectation that advocates of NHI may build into the legislation. It especially counsels us to guard against over-promising the under-served populations in terms of what the health care system can do for them. It may mean that we will have to accept a certain amount of indifferent, or even poor, medical care in order to avoid undermining the entire system by over-promising. Finally, it directs our attention to the municipal hospitals as the inadequately funded part of the system and that which most needs improvement if lives are not to be endangered.

While the skeptical view has much to commend it, it does not help to resolve the dilemma which faces us. For some years the idea has gained currency that society's problems in health care do not derive from lack of funds in the health system. (Adjusting for higher than national average per capita costs, I would estimate that New York City's health industry amounts to $4.5 billion to $5 billion. Our Medicaid per capita costs alone are close to $1,500—staggering amounts for products of unknown value and quality.) The problem is seen, rather, as one of reallocating resources between services, e.g., from inpatient to outpatient care, or among groups, e.g., from well-served populations to the under-served "working poor." Further, it is maintained that the resource problem will lead, in time, to a realization that resources for health are finite, and we may therefore expect the imposition of budget ceilings. Under such circumstances, the income of providers will presumably be limited, thus compelling more efficient and productive behavior on their part.

The forecast of more limited resources and budget ceilings for health does not square, however, with the skeptical outlook that says that only new financial incentives which bring pressure to bear on the entrenched provider interests will produce any change at all. If the anomaly is there then the outlook can only be for continuation of the present chaotic and inflation-prone financing system with its consequent escalation of utilization, unit prices and total costs. We thus come full circle.

At this point in our deliberations and with no specific legislative formulation before us, it is difficult to propose a resolution of the dilemma; yet it must be recognized. It means that, in New York City, unless there is a major change in the organization of the health care system, the impact of national health insurance is not likely to result in achieving NHI objectives of improved access to care, greater equity and cost control.

Unless we assume the paralysis of the democratic process, resolution of the dilemma would seem to require (1) creating a local organizational framework for allocation of resources, and (2) the enactment of some form of budget ceilings. If the Social Security system is to be used for financing, the framework will be a federal framework. If there is to be mixed financing, then the evolving Health Systems Agency is the most logical instrument for that framework. It would have the capability, in its planning—both long and short-range—and in its powers over federal funds, capital construction and new service developments, to exercise a consistent pattern of thoughtful choice among alternative uses of financial resources for health care.

Among the many issues that the task force has reviewed there are three that stand out both for their significance and for the opportunity for further discussion. They are (1) primary care, (2) bed supply, and (3) the role and functioning of municipal hospitals.

32

Primary Care

Through our studies and deliberations we have been able to arrive at a consensus that it is at the level of primary care, especially ambulatory, that the impact of NHI will be most likely felt. The users most especially affected will be the "working poor," for whom some kind of sliding financial liability will probably be enacted under national health insurance. To the extent that this group now receives care, it is more dependent upon the municipal hospital OPD and the emergency room system than are either the poor or the well-to-do. But the ability of the system to meet the anticipated new demand by the "traditional" practice of medicine is limited, not necessarily by overall manpower constraints, but by the movement of physicians away from the poorer areas of the city (except insofar as 300–400 Medicaid mills have brought them back to deliver a health care of questionable quality). While the increased demand of 10 percent or so resulting from national health insurance (perhaps 2 to 3 million visits) seems to be within the capacity of the system at large, the potential inflation of physician fees through a "usual and customary" approach may simply turn the Medicaid mill into an attractive NHI mill at a higher unit price.

The hospital, both voluntary and municipal, is, of course, a natural option as a major locus of delivery of primary ambulatory care. In fact, the present shortfall of private primary care has already made the hospital a major provider. But enhancement of its role is seriously debated on both cost and suitability grounds. In respect to costs, hospital-based ambulatory care is the highest. Certainly the present reimbursement structure reflects this, with Medicaid rates running well over $50 and $60 per billable visit. In fact, all rates for institutions like neighborhood health centers carry very high rates. How much of the outpatient cost structure is an accounting artifact, and how much the cost reflects a truly higher-cost way of delivering ambulatory care is difficult to know. Both factors are present, and hospitals attribute the major portion of their operating deficits to the care of indigent ambulatory patients who lack third-party coverage for such care. Since reimbursement is on full average cost and not marginal cost, it is probably given that hospital OPDs will be "losers" and run deficits.

Apart from cost questions, the suitability of the hospital in its present form as a deliverer of primary care under NHI has been seriously questioned. With its excessive reliance on the physician to determine access to care and priorities of service, the hospital, especially the voluntary hospital, has a self-image as a provider of partial rather than full services. The public hospital, with its teaching hospital or medical school affiliation, bears the same characteristic. In either case, ambulatory care takes second place to inpatient care. The accountability of hospitals, both municipal and voluntary, for the full care of the community or of any well-defined population, is very vague, and yet such accountability would seem to be critical if and when we face finite resources and the need to choose among priorities.

Against this negative picture is the task force study of "Ghetto Medicine," ("Organized Ambulatory Services and the Enforcement of Health Care Quality Standards in New York State" by Steven Jonas) which—apart from costs—makes valid a positive hospital role in the delivery of primary care. It has become clear, at any rate, that if NHI will substantially improve the financial picture for hospitals, hospitals will have to assume an accountable care-giving function. The hospital may not wish to do so, or be really capable of doing so. Therefore, we have had developed an alternative proposal for "decoupling" the hospital from primary care. The proposal sees the hospital as "the unchangeable cutting edge of the research and laboratory-oriented medical teaching system," and constrains it to playing an increasingly limited role in the medical care system. The proposal would, starting with the municipal system, separate ambulatory care from inpatient care in both financial and program terms, and would rely on free-standing primary units with which patients would identify consistently. Teams, not individual physicians, would constitute the basic care-giving units, and groups of such team units would be associated with specialized hospital clinics. Such an alternative may well be too radical but it is, in the staff's judgment, a carefully thought through program which differs substantially in its direct address to the question of how to achieve efficient use of finite resources.

Bed Needs

If national health insurance adds substantial outpatient entitlement, the hope is that total care will shift to a "more normal" or "rational" pattern of distribution between inpatient and outpatient service than is presently obtainable. No one knows what this pattern should be, but it is certain that the shift will not occur unless new beds and beds now in use are controlled. If budgetary resources are to be a critical constraint, the cost of new benefits will become an unnecessary high-expense add-on unless beds are controlled.

The technique for determining "need" for beds continues to escape us, but it is crystal clear that not every hospital that exists today must exist in terms of meeting society's needs most effectively. While the technique for the closing of hospitals has eluded society, making the most of our resources requires that we not commit ourselves to precisely the same set and number of resources that exist today.

Beyond that, nationally, we face a bed supply for acute and general-care needs of from 25,000 to 60,000 in excess of need, depending upon the analysis reported. New York City is clearly a part of that phenomenon. Despite a constant and, in fact, declining population, the number of general-care beds in New York City rose from 37,515 to 37,743 from 1966 to 1974, at the same time that beds in New York State were falling from 87,926 to 84,388. Moreover, approvals for additional beds in New York City exceeded 4,000 in 1972, and many of these are now being built.

Against these facts are further considerations: (1) length of stay in New York City far exceeds the national average; (2) occupancy rates of many voluntary hospitals are too low, and those of municipal hospitals are falling precipitiously. The literature and our experience both demonstrate that where third-party coverage is available, bed availability is the most important determinant of bed occupancy. Since keeping bed supply very tight is an essential strategy for creating a rational system under NHI and for reallocating resources, we should seriously consider adopting a moratorium on all hospital construction not yet underway, and on all new proposals for the replacement of existing facilities. Further, the city should hold the line on voluntary beds when municipal beds decrease and should deliberately use the leverage of decreasing the number of municipal beds to bring about a reduction in the number of general-care hospital beds in the whole system.

The Role of the Municipal Hospitals

The task force is only now beginning to address the question of the role of the municipal hospitals under national health insurance. The role will be determined in the light of (1) NHI coverage, (2) city budgetary resources, (3) needs of special populations, (4) patient preferences and (5) overall health service system requirements. It is timely to assess that role, for the capability of the hospitals is being seriously eroded under the hammer of the city's fiscal crisis. The decline of the hospitals run by the United States Public Health Service gives New York City ample warning of how hospitals can be "nibbled to death."

The enactment of Medicare/Medicaid seems to have been accompanied by a shift of both inpatient and outpatient care to the voluntary hospital and private-physician sector. While Medicaid cutbacks in eligibility and benefits reversed the trend somewhat, the shift may recur under an expanded NHI. We see nationally, as well as in New York City, substantial declines in the occupancy of large public hospitals, so that 70 and 75 percent rates of occupancy are frequent. At the same time, the voluntary hospital has developed a total dependency upon the public-funded third-party payment systems. If NHI is to be accompanied by an expanded ambulatory role for the voluntary hospitals (and NHI mills) we will no doubt witness a further decline in the use of municipal hospitals, including those of New York City.

The justification for re-examining the role of the municipal hospital system may seem theoretical, but it is effectively buttressed by consideration of the city's fiscal situation and of the assessment of future municipal priorities should national health insurance be enacted. New York City now spends more than twice as much per capita on health programs as any other major city. About 25 percent of the city budget is for health programs, and about 15 percent of the total tax levy is for health. Within a year or two the tax levy for health programs will be well over $1.6 billion.

In light of the long-term fiscal outlook for New York City and of the option of transferring costs to national health insurance, the magnitude of the municipal effort is bound to be reviewed most critically by the mayor and his staff. Under the most generous NHI plan our best estimate of city tax levy savings is around $900 million. These are fairly crude figures, and better estimates will be insisted upon as the fiscal crisis lengthens. Instead of allowing the estimates to reflect fiscal considerations alone, we ought to ensure that they are derived from a careful assessment of the logical role of the municipal hospitals and that patient preference and the capacity and willingness of the voluntary system are also taken into account.

Meanwhile, we should examine with some seriousness the possibility of a hospital consortium, such as is developing in Hartford, and which can lead, if successful, to more integrated, corporation hospital structures. The consortium is an arrangement for dividing among member hospitals the responsibility for the health care of a total population, thus minimizing the duplication of services and unnecessary costs. The total hospital system in New York City is too vast to take on, but a major demonstration could be mounted in one area, e.g., the Bronx. The task force should consider this possibility for a new public/private entity and, perhaps, build on the opportunity inherent in the opening of North Central Bronx and the new Lincoln Hospitals.

Ambulatory Care in Voluntary Hospitals

HERBERT LUKASHOK and ERIC PLOEN

This paper is a preliminary effort to analyze: (1) the cause and dimensions of voluntary hospital deficits in present operations of ambulatory services; and (2) the impact that national health insurance is likely to have on ambulatory services in the voluntary hospitals, focusing particularly on ways to encourage the development of primary care services as a program commitment of the hospitals.

Cause and Dimensions of Voluntary Hospital Deficits in Ambulatory Services

With the advent of Medicare and Medicaid in 1966, institutionalized ambulatory care entered an era of great expectations from the point of view of both consumer and provider. Utilization of both emergency rooms and clinics rose, particularly during the 1966–1973 period. For example, total visits in 1968 were 7 percent above the 1964 levels; for the period 1968–1973 however, utilization rose by approximately 500,000 visits—about 10 percent—with 24 percent overall during the 1966–1973 period.

Table 1
Ambulatory Visits—New York City Voluntary Hospitals[a] —1966–1973

Year	Emergency Room	Outpatient Clinic	Total	% of City Total
	(Millions of Visits)			
1966	1.22	2.82	4.04	45.0
1967	1.31	2.90	4.21	47.5
1968	1.41	3.13	4.54	51.3
1969	1.44	3.12	4.56	51.2
1972	1.54	3.35	4.89	49.0
1973	1.58	3.41	4.99	49.3

[a]Voluntary hospitals provide about one-half of all hospital ambulatory care in the city.

Pressures on hospitals for the delivery of ambulatory services continued during this entire period as the working poor continued to seek primary care services in a hospital setting despite the Medicaid cutbacks of 1968 and 1969. In addition, as practicing primary care physicians left the economically depressed areas, the delivery of primary care services fell largely on hospital outpatient and emergency departments, both voluntary and municipal.

37

Although the levels of utilization increased, the outpatient departments and emergency rooms of New York City voluntary hospitals were not structured or staffed to meet this demand for primary care. The result was fragmented care, with specialty rather than primary orientation, overcrowded facilities, long waits, no doctor-patient relationships and a consequent high degree of patient dissatisfaction.

The Medicaid cuts of 1968 and 1969 resulted in 750,000 persons being dropped from the program. Whatever progress was being made by hospitals to develop comprehensive family-oriented ambulatory care was slowed because of the fiscal pressures resulting from these cuts. Although the New York City "Ghetto Medicine" program of December 1969 (initially designed to finance deficits) sought to impose certain quality and organizational standards to achieve comprehensive family-oriented ambulatory care, it did not possess sufficient financial leverage to meet both the deficits already being incurred and the new cost increases caused by the required reform and expansion of the program. When the City of New York failed either to match or to allocate approximately $8.5 million of state monies that were made available for the 1973–74 fiscal year, the program suffered a further loss of $17 million.

In 1974 alone, the net revenue shortfall for ambulatory service to New York City voluntary hospitals was in excess of $50 million, an amount not sustainable either by the City of New York, the State of New York, private philanthropy, or the hospitals. The following tabulation traces the revenue shortfall for ambulatory services incurred by twenty representative New York City voluntary hospitals which collectively provide about 62 percent of clinic and emergency services. Fully 73 percent of the cumulative loss of $165,847,763 incurred in rendering ambulatory service care during the years 1970–1974 is attributable to clinic losses, the remaining 27 percent is accounted for by emergency services.

Table 2
Clinic and Emergency Service Loss

		(Net of Governmental Subsidies)
1970		$ 24,539,012
1971		27,817,772
1972		34,565,243
1973		36,931,962
1974		41,993,774
	Total	$165,847,763

The main factors contributing to these large deficits in ambulatory care operations are:

38

1. Most important: 45 percent of clinic patients are not covered by Medicare or Medicaid or by any other form of third-party reimbursement, even though they are charged on a sliding-fee scale for out-of-pocket payments. On this basis, hospital income is far below cost.

2. A revenue control program which became effective January 1, 1970 gave the New York State Commissioner of Health the power to control the rates paid to hospitals for inpatient services. Thus the marginal surpluses from these rates which hospitals had previously used to finance ambulatory care disappeared.

3. In 1971 the Associated Hospital Service of New York eliminated a community service factor which was related solely to losses incurred by voluntary hospitals in the rendering of ambulatory and emergency services. (By state law this factor will be reinstated in 1975.)

4. The Federal Economic Stabilization Program also affected the hospitals. Beginning with the price freeze in August, 1971 and continuing with Phase II and III through March, 1974, hospitals in New York State came under both federal and state control. The third-party payors which were under state control only (Blue Cross and Medicaid) applied the lowest rate increase permissible either by state or federal computation.

5. The enactment of Medicare and Medicaid imposed certain criteria for locating both direct and indirect costs so that the federal programs would be free of those costs connected with persons not covered by the programs. As a result, functional costs were determined; i.e., the total of direct and apportioned indirect costs were applied to each hospital cost center, including the ambulatory service departments. The consequence was that per visit costs for clinic and emergency services appeared to increase markedly, since the apportionment process viewed the ambulatory service departments as separate, distinct units, and not just incremental add-ons to basic hospital services. Medicare was also particularly interested in separating hospital from physician costs since the physician component was reimbursable under Part "B," even for hospital-based physicians.

We close this section of the paper with a summary of a case study that demonstrates the fiscal implications for a hospital if it were to close its clinics.

Because of the extraordinary losses being incurred in the provision of clinic services, St. Luke's Hospital Center in New York recently engaged Touche Ross and Company, CPAs, to study and report to the St. Luke's Board of Directors on the financial options available to reduce operating losses. One option was to drop outpatient services. This option was presented in order to estimate the financial impact of eliminating this major service which was the single largest contributor to the operating loss. (It was determined that the center could not discontinue the emergency room due to its being central to the center's operations and its goal of community service.)

The following points present the rationale, assumptions and concerns associated with this option:

(a) All direct costs and one-half of indirect costs would be eliminated.

(b) Indirect costs not eliminated would be redistributed to other inpatient and outpatient categories.

(c) No estimate is made of potential impact on the emergency room which would be bound to incur some unquantifiable increase in demand.

(d) The impact of the elimination of clinics on hospital programs is not clear. With no clinics it would become necessary to contract with other hospitals in order to provide outpatient experience for resident physicians so as to maintain the residency programs. Inpatient admissions may decline.

The financial analysis of the option was as follows:

Table 3

Clinic[s]	1973 Direct Cost	1973 Allocated Indirect Costs	1973 Total
Elimination:	$1,655,337	$2,427,816	$4,083,153
Non Elimination:	$1,655,337	$5,024,000	$6,679,337
	0	$2,596,184	$2,596,184

Remainder as percent of total prior to elimination............................ 40%
Savings as percent of total prior to elimination 60%

Impact of National Health Insurance

For the purpose of this analysis, it is reasonable to assume that with the advent of national health insurance there will be universal entitlement for ambulatory care in physicians' offices, health centers, group practice units and hospitals. Since the present critical deficits in the operation of outpatient departments are a direct consequence of no third-party coverage for roughly 45 percent of the patient load, and since these patients would be covered for ambulatory services under national health insurance, hospitals would thus be reimbursed for care which has until now incurred substantial loss.

It seems highly unlikely, however, that reimbursement to hospitals through national health insurance will be open-ended, following the precedents set in the original Medicare and Medicaid legislation. There seems to be universal agreement that tight reimbursement controls will be employed. Such controls might take the form of prospective reimbursement on the basis of approved budgetary needs, or of strict use of peer grouping to limit costs, or of direct limitations on revenue through price controls.

Even with these constraints hospitals will realize markedly increased income for ambulatory care. The question then becomes one of determining how to use the leverage of increased dollars to encourage hospitals to incorporate viable primary care programs as intrinsic parts of their outpatient services. The very formulation of this question assumes that the hospital will continue to function as the central resource for the delivery of medical care to the community. This means that it will provide primary care presumably to patients of all income levels. It suggests two possible alternative approaches to supply: restructuring outpatient departments as group-practice primary-care units, or providing the hospital with the capacity to develop outreach services that would function as satellite clinics or neighborhood health centers.

The trend towards the institutionalization of primary care services in large urban areas will continue even when consumers have the financial resources through NHI to choose a solo, fee-for-service practitioner. The assumption, therefore, is that utilization of the hospital's ambulatory services for primary care will continue to increase, and that the increase will be accelerated if hospitals have the resources and the commitment to respond by improving and reshaping their OPDs. Increasingly, as physicians affiliate with such hospital staff, programs on a part- or full-time basis will witness a slow decline of solo private practice.

Programs Presently Available

Pressure on hospitals for the restructuring of ambulatory services will probably not come specifically from national health insurance legislation or from subsequent regulations. Rather, governmental stimulus and influence on a federal level will be likely to be forthcoming from those programs designed to provide underpinning to the health-care system in preparation for national health insurance. Two such broad programs are already here—the PSROs and the HMOs. Most important in this connection will be legislation creating the nationwide network of organizations to be known as Health Systems Agencies. Still moving through the Congress, these regional agencies will probably be given, in addition to their widespread planning authority, the responsibility to approve the expenditure of federal funds for health care activities and programs. It is probably within this framework that the federal govern-

41

ment will have the mechanisms, fiscal and otherwise, to stimulate hospitals to develop comprehensive programs for the delivery of primary care services.

In New York, however, at both state and local levels, there is additional machinery already available that could be useful in accomplishing this objective. The same article 28 of the New York State Public Health Law that requires the approval (as to public need) of the state health commissioner for the construction of new or additional hospital beds, authorizes him to "inquire into the operations of hospitals and to conduct periodic inspections of facilities with respect to the fitness and adequacy of the premises. . . . and *standards of medical care.*"

Further, the law also states that "the State Hospital Review and Planning Council shall adopt rules and regulations . . . to effectuate the purposes of this article including—(a) the establishment of requirements for a uniform statewide system of reports and audits relating to *quality of medical and physical care provided.*"

Within the state hospital code mandated by article 28, there already exists a provision relating to the quality of care in ambulatory services. Section 703.3 provides that facilities must submit to the department a plan providing for "comprehensive medical evaluation for such patient visits on a periodic basis" and for "continuity of care when such patients require hospitalization, home care or emergency care. . . ." This section also provides that outpatient facilities should schedule "not more than 5 patients per hour with an allowance of at least 30 minutes for the first complete patient workup."

On a city level, the standards for ambulatory services developed by the Department of Health of the City of New York to enable hospitals to receive "Ghetto Medicine" subsidies represent a most creative attempt to tie money to program development and improvement. The general and specific conditions required of the voluntary hospitals provide a solid foundation for the delivery of comprehensive family-centered primary care by their outpatient departments. There are obviously serious difficulties in the supervision and enforcement of these codes and standards. The point to be emphasized, however, is that the precedents as well as a framework already exist in New York to encourage hospitals to adopt those programs deemed desirable, necessary and in the public interest.

42

The Implications of National Health Insurance for Ambulatory Care Services in New York City

CHARLES BRECHER, KAREN BRUDNEY, and
MIRIAM OSTOW

The long years of debate in the United States concerning society's responsibility for the health care of the citizenry are culminating in the probable enactment of some form of national health insurance (NHI). This suggests that nationally we perceive financing as a primary constraint on the efficacious and equitable application of our great medical capacity for enhancement of the health of the people. Alternatively, it suggests that at least on this one aspect of health care we have been able to achieve consensus as to policy. However, a decade of experience with financial entitlement to health care for selected portions of the population has indicated that such programs evoke unanticipated consequences, not only for their beneficiaries but for the system as a whole. Accordingly, much thought now is being directed toward the implications of pending legislation.

Ambulatory care, while it accounts for a minor portion of all medical expenditure, is the component of medical care which is universally utilized, which has been affected least by voluntary insurance, and which has priority in the concerns of the individual citizen regarding our system of medical care. Medical planners, too, have been increasingly critical of the failures of the medical system in meeting ambulatory care needs; accessibility, costs, and quality have all been judged unsatisfactory.

This paper focuses on New York City where, despite an agglomeration of institutional and manpower resources unmatched in the nation and perhaps in the world, a large sector of the population is insufficiently served. Our purpose is to provide both background information and suggestive ideas for an analysis of the implications of NHI for ambulatory care services in New York City. We undertake three specific asks: (1) to make explicit some assumptions about the NHI program whose implications are to be discussed, (2) to describe the present patterns of utilization of ambulatory care in New York City, and (3) to offer suggestions about the probable outcomes and possible alternatives for ambulatory care after enactment of an NHI program.

Assumptions About a Probable NHI Program

Predicting the content of any piece of legislation, much less one which is surrounded by controversy, is risky. What follows merely represents the combined views of the authors on what is probable with respect to three issues—coverage, benefits, and mechanisms of payment. Other important issues such as methods of financing and the role of the private insurance industry are not considered, since these will not affect patterns of ambulatory care directly. These assumptions are presented chiefly as a basis for further discussion.

Coverage

Almost by definition, an NHI program must provide universal coverage. That is, all persons, regardless of age, income, or employment status, will be afforded similar benefits. Although there have been discussions of alternatives, such as a comprehensive health program for children (dubbed "kiddie care") or health insurance benefits for recipients of unemployment insurance, this paper will consider only the implications of a universal program.

Benefits

Almost all of the contending NHI proposals include payments for a wide range of hospital and physician's services. The more significant differences among the present bills relate to the use of coinsurance and deductibles, which together are referred to as out-of-pocket liability. The variation in out-of-pocket liability among these proposals is extensive. The Kennedy-Corman (formerly Kennedy-Griffiths) proposal provides "first dollar" coverage, that is, there is no out-of-pocket expense for the services of the physician. In contrast, the Long-Ribicoff proposal is referred to as a "catastrophic" bill because for most families it would provide no medical benefits until a deductible of $2,000 had been met.

Some indication of how this important issue may be resolved can be drawn from compromise bills submitted by the Nixon administration and by Senator Edward Kennedy in the second session of the 93rd Congress. Both bills incorporate income-conditioned deductibles and coinsurance. The reasoning behind the use of these copayment mechanisms is three-fold:

(1) Copayments limit the total tax dollar cost of an NHI program.

(2) Copayments limit excessive utilization of services.

(3) Income-conditioned copayments reduce the inequity associated with imposing out-of-pocket requirements on poor families.

The way in which income-conditioned copayments may be designed is illustrated in both the Kennedy-Mills and Nixon administration bills. Although specific provisions differ somewhat, both bills create three

44

groups, each with a different level of out-of-pocket liability. The first group consists of low-income individuals and families who face no out-of-pocket expense for medical care. The second group consists of those with incomes slightly above poverty levels. The out-of-pocket amount they are required to pay is a percentage of their incomes; the maximum is set at a maximum-income level. For example, in the Kennedy-Mills bill a family of four is required to pay up to 25 percent of the portion of its income falling between $4,800 and $8,800 annually. The third group consists of all families whose incomes are above the maximum level set for the sliding-liability group. This group is required to pay deductibles and coinsurance up to a fixed maximum out-of-pocket liability of $1,000 per year under the Kennedy-Mills bill.

In order to consider the effect of such a program on New York City it is necessary to fill in some of the details of the benefit provisions. Table 1 shows the size of each group if the general income criteria used to establish the three groups in the Kennedy-Mills bill were applied to the present population of New York City. (See Appendix A for an explanation of the method used to estimate the population groups.)

The no-liability group is similar in number and income levels to the population now receiving Medicaid in New York City. With some possible exceptions to be noted later, the nature of assumed NHI coverage for this group is similar to the present entitlement under Medicaid. The sliding-liability group consists of families that are close to the poverty line (the "near poor"). In the above estimates a family of four with an income between $4,800 and $8,800 is placed in this group. (Higher or lower figures are used for larger or smaller families, respectively.) This group represents approximately one-quarter of the population. Finally, there is the majority of the population, those whose incomes are considered high enough to permit payment of a substantial deductible ($150 per person in the Kennedy-Mills bill) as well as an additional coinsurance charge (25 percent), up to some maximum figure ($1,000 per family in the Kennedy-Mills bill). It is largely in terms of these three groups that we shall describe the present patterns of ambulatory care and the implica-

Table 1

Distribution of the Population of New York City in 1973 Using the Income Criteria Specified under the Kennedy-Mills Bill

	Number of persons	%
No liability	1,437,000	19
Sliding liability	2,010,000	26
Maximum liability	4,278,000	55
Total	7,725,000	100

tions of an NHI with income-conditioned deductible and coinsurance features.

Data relating to characteristics other than income and family size are unavailable. Demographic factors such as age and sex which are related to the demand for different types of care are required to make accurate projections of the impact of expanded entitlement. In addition, such data would permit a more detailed delineation of current patterns of care.

Mechanisms of payment

A third critical characteristic of any NHI plan is the way in which those who provide care are paid. Two aspects are important: the principle of payment and the procedures for collection.

With respect to the principle of payment, our assumptions relate more to what will *not* be included than to the exact nature of the program. Specifically, exclusive reliance on institutional budgeting, capitation payments, or both is improbable. However, voluntary enrollment in an organization financed by capitation payments, e.g., Health Maintenance Organizations (HMO), is likely to be permitted, provision being made for applying NHI benefits to the annual premium.

For those who do not enroll in an HMO, free choice of physicians and clinics is likely to be retained. Both the Kennedy-Mills and the Nixon administration proposals provide payment for institutional ambulatory care (hospital clinics and emergency rooms) on a cost-related basis, although the utilization of prospective rather than retrospective formulas is specified. Physicians in private practice will continue to be paid on a fee-for-service basis, but the precise nature of the fee system is an open issue. Options include fixed fees which are determined unilaterally by the government (as it determines fees for Medicaid in New York State), fixed fees which are formally negotiated between representatives of physicians and government (as in Canada), and the "customary and reasonable" principle (as used for Medicare). An additional complication is the possibility of different arrangements for each population group. For example, the payment of fixed fees for services to those in the no-liability group and of unregulated fees for services to those in the maximum-liability group would be permissible under the Nixon administration bill.

Procedures for collection are another important issue about which no precise assumptions can be made. Either the government or the providers of care will have to assume responsibility for collecting out-of-pocket liabilities. Providers are given responsibility either when benefits are paid to the consumer after he has paid the provider or when NHI benefits are paid to the provider, less any deductible or coinsurance charge. The government assumes responsibility for collection when NHI payments are made in full to providers, and the coinsurance or deductible charges are collected from the consumer by the government.

Various combinations of principles of payment and procedures for collection are possible for each of the population groups. The Nixon administration bill, for example, proposes that full reimbursement, including copayments to the provider, come from the program itself (or the insurance carrier) rather than directly from the consumer. However, for the maximum liability group, physicians could charge fees above the insurable amount and collect these additional sums directly from the patient. The Kennedy-Mills plan is slightly more complicated. Institutional providers would receive all payments from the program and the government would be responsible for collecting copayments and deductibles. Physicians, however, have the choice of receiving "customary and reasonable" fees as full payment directly from the government or, if charging more than the customary and reasonable fee, of billing the patient for the entire amount—leaving collection of the reimbursible portion to the patient. While it is impossible to predict the nature of any future bill, some of the implications of alternative arrangements will be discussed later in this paper.

Summary of assumptions

The remainder of this paper is based on the assumption that any probable NHI program will (1) cover virtually the entire population, (2) contain income-conditioned copayments, and (3) continue the principles of free choice and fee-for-service in the selection and payment of physicians. NHI will, as its name implies, be an *insurance* program providing financial protection only. Changes in the organization of services will not be mandated; in fact, the task of this paper is to identify the implications of such a program for the nature of ambulatory care in New York City.

Present Patterns of Ambulatory Care

Present patterns of care can be described in terms of two important features—the volume of care received by the population (i.e., rates of utilization) and the types of providers from which the care is received. For New York City we have identified seven general categories of providers: physicians in private practice, outpatient departments of voluntary hospitals (both clinics and emergency rooms), outpatient departments of municipal hospitals (both clinics and emergency rooms), the various programs sponsored by the Department of Health of the City of New York, the group practices operating within the city under the Health

47

Insurance Plan of Greater New York (HIP), health centers which are operated or sponsored by labor unions, and a miscellaneous category incorporating various other types of free-standing clinics. Each of the three population groups identified earlier may be described in terms of the volume of care its members receive and the locus of that care (see Table 2).

Medicaid

As noted earlier, the approximately 1.4 million New Yorkers who would have no out-of-pocket liability are virtually the same group as those now covered by Medicaid. Of the present Medicaid population, almost 59,000 are enrolled in HIP, but the vast majority are not a part of any capitation system and depend upon a variety of providers for their care. In 1973 this Medicaid group visited physicians in all settings approximately 10,814,000 times, for an estimated average utilization rate of 7.5 visits per person per year. This figure is significantly higher than the national average both for all persons (5.0) and for those in the lowest income range (5.6).[1]

More than 45 percent of the Medicaid visits are provided in an institutional setting, that is, in a location other than a private physician's office. The largest source of institutional care for this group is hospital outpatient departments (OPD) and emergency rooms (ER), which together account for more than 3.6 million visits. The voluntary sector provides a larger share (56.6 percent) of OPD visits while the municipal hospitals account for the larger share (52.5 percent) of ER visits. Clients of Medicaid also account for a large number of visits (604,000 or 33 percent of all visits) to various programs of the Department of Health, and account for a substantial share of visits to free-standing clinics.

While much of the discussion of ambulatory care for the poor focuses on institutions, it is important to note that the majority of the ambulatory Medicaid visits (almost 55 percent) are to private practitioners. This figure would be higher if private psychiatric and methadone-maintenance treatments were included. Much of this private practice is concentrated among a small number of practitioners. Although available data do not permit a description of the concentration of services, it is possible to document the concentration of Medicaid payments among providers of care. Table 3 presents the total payments, total number of participating physicians, and the share of payments accounted for by the 10 percent of physicians with the highest payments. Among general practitioners, more than 65 percent of the payments are made to 10 percent of the physicians, among all specialists approximately 64 percent of the payments went to the top 10 percent, and in selected specialties the figure reaches as high as 79 percent. Thus, while Medicaid has provided access for the poor to private practitioners, much of this care is pro-

Table 2
Estimated Ambulatory Services in New York City in 1973 by Population Group
(Number of Visits)

	Persons in group (No.)	Voluntary OPD	Municipal OPD	Voluntary and proprietary ER	Municipal ER	Health department programs			Free-standing facilities			Private practice	Total visits
						Child health	School health	All others	HIP	Union centers	Others		
Maximum liability—													
Total	4,278,000	986,000	750,000	239,000					2,157,000	666,000		NA	NA
Enrolled in GHI	1,052,000											2,760,000	
Enrolled in HIP	584,000								2,157,000				
Union centers										666,000			
Patients	108,000												
All others	3,534,000												
Sliding liability—													
Total	2,010,000	1,016,000	2,175,000	369,000	851,000	360,000	413,000	406,000				NA	NA
No liability—total	1,437,000	1,410,000	1,079,000	561,000	619,000	177,000	248,000	219,000	216,000		495,000	5,789,000	10,814,000
Enrolled in HIP	59,000								216,000				
All others	1,378,000										495,000		
Totals	7,725,000	3,411,000	3,254,000	1,680,000	1,708,000	538,000	662,000	625,000	2,373,000	666,000	990,000	NA	NA

*Totals may disagree slightly due to rounding.

OPD = hospital outpatient department. ER = hospital emergency rooms. NA = data not available. HIP = Health Insurance Plan of Greater New York. GHI = Group Health Incorporated

Source: See Appendix B

49

Table 3
Medicaid Payments to Physicians, Fourth Quarter 1973

Category of physicians	Total payments	Total participating physicians (No.)	% of total payments to top 10% of physicians
All physicians	24,221,430	7,747	64.6
General practitioners	5,900,847	2,662	65.1
All specialists	18,320,583	5,085	63.7
Selected specialties			
All internal medicine	4,858,310	1,305	62.8
(cardiovascular disease)	(481,767)	(144)	(74.4)
All psychiatry and neurology	3,015,511	699	62.3
Pediatrics	2,821,609	532	57.1
All surgery	1,721,066	911	63.0
(orthopedic surgery)	(179,904)	(164)	(64.1)
Radiology	1,545,658	178	65.0
Obstetrics and gynecology	1,443,698	429	56.0
Pathology	193,711	83	68.3
Physical medicine	118,679	70	78.8

Source: The Department of Health of the City of New York

vided by physicians seeing almost exclusively a population eligible for Medicaid.

The cost of providing ambulatory care to the Medicaid population is great (see Table 4). The Department of Health of the City of New York reports that in 1973 about $365.6 million, or about $254 per client, was spent on ambulatory care services under Medicaid. The total consists of $175.2 million for institutional facilities, $126.2 million for private practitioners, and $64.2 million for other providers. The discrepancy between the institutional share of total visits, 45 percent, and of total expenditure for physician care, 66 percent (of the combined total of clinic and private physician payments), underscores the high unit cost of ambulatory care under present institutional arrangements. The Medicaid expenditures are financed as follows: approximately 25 percent comes from city tax funds, 25 percent from state funds, and 50 percent from federal funds.

In the pattern of utilization by the Medicaid population, three features are conspicuous. First, the absence of any out-of-pocket liability produces high rates of utilization. At a rate of 7.5 visits per person per year, New York's Medicaid population sees physicians more often than most other segments of the population.

Second, one may infer from the Medicaid experience that mechanisms of payment may exert an important influence on the locus of care. New York's Medicaid program reimburses institutional providers on a cost basis, while private practitioners are paid according to a fee schedule set by the state government. Fees have been set low ($7.80 for a visit to a general practitioner), while few limits have been imposed on the payments to institutions. Thus, as of 1975, Long Island Jewish Hospital was receiving $73.50 for a visit to its OPD. Consequently, clients of Medicaid have encountered little difficulty in receiving care from voluntary as well as from municipal hospitals. In contrast, many physicians have been reluctant to serve Medicaid patients; those who do so often must alter their style of practice. They may promote shorter, more frequent visits in order to raise their incomes and may "specialize" in Medicaid clients in order to achieve economies of scale in the clerical work associated with Medicaid billings. A striking illustration has been the proliferation of "Medicaid mills," groups of private practitioners located in or near low-income areas which provide high-volume care of questionable quality to clients of Medicaid. Conversely, Medicaid failed to realize the objective that its early proponents had envisioned, i.e., to enlarge the number of private practitioners in the central city and to provide access to a broad range of private providers through the availability of payment.

Third, the experience of Medicaid suggests that consumers prefer voluntary to municipal hospital care and prefer private physicians to either. Immediately after the implementation of Medicaid, the total number of clinic visits, which had been increasing, leveled off (1967). However, diametrically opposing trends in utilization appeared within the

Table 4

Medicaid Expenditures for Ambulatory Care, 1973

	Millions of dollars
Institutional facilities	175.2
Municipal hospitals/clinics	59.2
Voluntary hospitals/clinics	101.0
HIP premiums	6.7
Methadone maintenance clinics	8.3
Private practitioners	126.2
Physicians	81.4
Podiatrists	8.0
Optometrists	6.0
Ophthalmic dispensers	.9
Therapists	.3
Chiropracters	1.6
Other vendors	64.2
Pharmacies	43.9
Laboratories	8.7
Appliance vendors	5.4
Transportation	6.2
Total	365.6

Source: Department of Health of the City of New York

institutional sector—an increase of 11.8 percent in the voluntary hospitals paralleled a decrease of 9.4 percent in the municipal hospitals (see Table 5). For the following two years total visits continued to decline while the shift to the voluntary hospitals persisted. With the subsequent reduction of eligibility for Medicaid (1968–1969) and the decrease in fees allowed private physicians (1969), total clinic visits again began to climb and municipal visits again increased.

The near poor

No data are available concerning the use of private practitioners by the more than two million New Yorkers who would face a sliding liability under the assumed NHI program. Thus, it is not possible even to estimate an overall rate of utilization for this group. However, since incomes are low and private insurance, if any, is likely to provide only limited ambulatory care benefits, it may be assumed that the use of private practitioners is lowest in this group.

Table 5
Trends in Utilization of Outpatient Departments, 1963–1973

	Number of visits		
	Total	*Voluntary hospitals*	*Municipal hospitals*
1963	5,588,026	2,675,485	2,912,541
1964	5,790,968	2,682,990	3,107,978
1965	6,236,261	2,941,313	3,294,948
1966	6,194,939	2,767,596	3,427,343
1967	6,201,519	3,095,561	3,105,958
1968	5,973,357	3,127,326	2,846,031
1969	5,901,810	3,118,627	2,783,183
1970	6,072,856	3,117,193	2,955,663
1971	6,330,705	3,199,395	3,131,310
1972	6,651,913	3,356,503	3,295,410
1973	6,665,481	3,411,329	3,254,152

	Percentage change from previous year		
	Total	*Voluntary hospitals*	*Municipal hospitals*
1964	+3.6	+ .3	+6.7
1965	+7.7	+9.6	+6.0
1966	−0.7	−5.9	+4.0
1967	+0.1	+11.8	−9.4
1968	−3.7	+1.0	−8.4
1969	−1.2	−0.3	−2.2
1970	+2.9	0.0	+6.2
1971	+4.2	+2.6	+5.9
1972	+5.1	+4.9	+5.2
1973	+0.2	+1.6	−1.2

Source: Health and Hospital Planning Council of Southern New York

The financial barrier which limits access to private practitioners for the near poor is less significant as a barrier to institutional services (Table 2 and Appendix). Over all, we estimate that six million visits, or approximately three per capita, provide care to this group in organized settings. This compares to an estimated 3.5 institutional visits per capita for the Medicaid population, indicating only slightly less access for the near poor. However, the near poor depend far more heavily on municipal facilities than does the population which is eligible for Medicaid. Municipal hospitals and Department of Health clinics account for 69 percent of the institutional visits among the near poor, compared to 47 percent for Medicaid clients. The frequent inability of families that are near poverty to pay for care—either through Medicaid or out-of-pocket—evidently has limited the willingness of voluntary hospitals to provide them with outpatient services, although a significant number of visits are provided in the voluntary sector.

This group now appears to have the lowest overall utilization rate and the most restricted choice for the locus of care. An inability to meet the full cost or prevailing charges for ambulatory care limits access to private practitioners and, to a lesser extent, to voluntary hospital clinics. Consequently, the major source of care for members of this group is municipally financed services provided by the Health and Hospitals Corporation (HHC) and the Department of Health.

There are considerable costs to the city government for providing care to the near poor. In the 1975 fiscal year New York City provided HHC with a subsidy of approximately $270 million for the costs of care to patients not covered by some third party, including Medicaid. Since an estimated 85 percent of all HHC inpatient care is covered by some third party, a substantial portion of the subsidy is required to cover the costs of ambulatory care. All of this subsidy is funded from local tax revenues without any state or federal assistance. In addition, the budget for the Department of Health of the City of New York, 45 percent of which is supported by state and federal aid, is now $116 million. We estimate that the share of the HHC subsidy attributable to outpatient services and the portion of the Department of Health budget devoted to direct personal health services together total roughly $230 million. This indicates an expenditure by municipal government of approximately $115 per person in the near-poor category. An estimate of the total cost of care for this group would have to add to this amount the sums paid directly by consumers and the deficits incurred by voluntary hospitals in providing ambulatory care to this group.

The maximum liability population

The majority (55 percent) of New Yorkers have family incomes sufficient either to pay directly for their ambulatory care or to purchase

53

insurance which, at least partially, covers the costs of ambulatory services. The current patterns of care for this large group can best be described in terms of four subgroups: those enrolled in HIP, those utilizing health facilities sponsored by their labor unions, those enrolled in a Group Health Incorporated (GHI) plan, and all others.

As a whole, this population makes relatively little use of hospital-based ambulatory care. The 4.3 million persons in this group account for an estimated two million hospital clinic and ER visits or about 0.5 visits per person. This compares with 2.2 hospital outpatient visits per person for the near poor and 2.5 visits per person for Medicaid clients. Moreover, as much as 50 percent of their hospital visits are for ER rather than OPD care, in contrast to the Medicaid population and the near poor, among whom only 32 percent and 28 percent, respectively, of the hospital visits are for ER care. Thus, the majority of the population with maximum liability makes relatively little use of hospital-based ambulatory services other than ER care.

Approximately 584,000 persons who were not Medicaid clients were enrolled in one of the 29 HIP groups in New York City. This population visited the HIP facilities an estimated 2,157,000 times for an average of 3.7 visits per person. This rate is lower than the national average, suggesting that the prepaid group-delivery structure provides satisfactory care with a lower volume of visits or that HIP enrollees also make use of other providers, even though this requires some out-of-pocket expenditure.

There are 22 union-sponsored health clinics in New York City. Of these, however, only nine provide comprehensive services in a variety of medical specialties. Six additional clinics provide general medical services only, three exist merely for diagnostic and screening purposes, one contains only dental and podiatric facilities, and one contains only dental facilities. The two remaining union health centers, those of the National Maritime Union and the Seafarers Union, function as check-out points for departing seamen; their clientele consists primarily of transients.

Figures for the nine comprehensive-care clinics indicate that a total of 638,000 union members and their families are eligible to receive care. Only 17 percent, or 107,500, actually use the facilities. For many, the health clinic is located inconveniently; others may simply prefer alternative sources of care for personal reasons. For those relying on the comprehensive centers, we estimate the average number of visits per year to be 6.2. (See Appendix B for the source of this estimate.) Since this figure includes only those persons who made at least one visit, it naturally is higher than the average for other groups or for the national population. Further, a disproportionate share of utilizers are retired union members who also are eligible for Medicare.

GHI covers an estimated 1,052,000 New Yorkers, making it the largest source of private ambulatory-care insurance. It has no facilities for the provision of medical services, and serves exclusively as a mechanism for financing the care purchased by enrollees from a panel of physicians (among whom they have free choice). Originally, participating physicians all agreed to accept GHI fees as payment in full; now, the enrollee has the option of accepting reimbursement of a fixed amount per service and paying out-of-pocket the excess charged by some providers. No precise utilization figures are available for New York City enrollees alone, but among the entire GHI population the estimated number of physician visits per person is 2.6. This low figure requires explanation. Most obvious are a number of factors suggesting favorable selection: enrollments are drawn from the regularly employed population with presumably good levels of health, and few, if any, enrollees are more than 65 years of age, the group which manifests the highest rates of utilization. Employed enrollees also are less likely to spend the time required to seek medical care for trivial complaints than the unemployed, who may disregard the time-cost. It may be hypothesized further that, given the choice offered by New York City to its civil servants (who constitute the largest fraction of enrollees), high utilizers of medical services might elect to join HIP rather than GHI in order to realize the economies of a completely prepaid plan. Finally, actual utilization may be understated due to the failure of some enrollees to file small claims.

The costs of care vary among the four subgroups. The 1975 HIP premium for a single adult was $112.08, for a two-person family $224.40, and for a family of three or more persons $336.60; similar figures for GHI are $75.48, $148.56, and $224.28. (HIP premium rates were supplied by the Research and Statistics Office of HIP. GHI rates are those in effect for municipal employees in fiscal 1975 and were supplied by the Office of Labor Relations, City of New York.) Comprehensive data are not available on the costs of operating union health centers, but figures from one plan, the Union Family Medical Fund of the Hotel Industry of New York City, indicate an annual per patient cost of approximately $158.[2] For the remaining segment of the maximum liability population, there is no way to estimae current expenditures for ambulatory care.

Implications of NHI

How would the present patterns of ambulatory care be affected by NHI? For purposes of discussion, the following propositions are set forth as possible consequences.

(1) The extended entitlement to health-care financing provided by NHI will effect little initial change in the volume of care sought by persons in both the maximum-liability and the no-liability groups.

To the extent that out-of-pocket expense determines demand for ambulatory care, NHI should not alter patterns of utilization at either the upper or lower ends of the income-distribution spectrum. Medicaid now provides the indigent with the same entitlement available under any likely form of NHI. Therefore, the rate of utilization should remain unchanged. Those at or above the median income level have been able to afford to purchase out-of-pocket the major portion of their ambulatory care. Analysis of out-of-pocket expenditures from a national survey in 1970 reveals that approximately half of the utilization by the maximum-liability population would not exceed a $150 deductible (see Table 6). Beyond this, expenditures would be subject to coinsurance; hence, few families are likely to have sufficient medical expenditures to entitle them to care at no further cost to themselves. For this reason, utilization should remain at or near present levels.

The restraining effects of copayment provisions may conceivably be counteracted by the development of special coverage by private insurance companies to supplement NHI. Such supplementary coverage should protect the individual against all or most out-of-pocket liability and could significantly increase utilization. In 1973 such private programs were utilized by 57 percent of all Medicare clients to supplement or complement Medicare coverage.[3]

(2) There will be a significant increase in the volume of care sought by those in the near-poor or sliding-liability group.

The approximately two million New Yorkers who have incomes slightly above Medicaid eligibility levels will benefit most from NHI. They will be able to purchase physicians' services for a limited out-of-pocket

Table 6
Annual Out-of-Pocket Health Expense Among Upper-Income Groups,
1970 (% Distribution)

	Income	
Expenditure	$10,000-$14,999	$15,000 or more
None	5.9%	3.3%
Under $50	18.5	9.8
$50-$99	21.1	21.4
$100-249	33.8	35.1
$250-499	13.8	19.0
$500-999	5.3	8.2
$1,000 or more	1.7	3.4
Total	100.0	100.0

These figures include insurance premiums; however, subsequent medical increases in cost probably offset this factor. Because of the difficulties of adjusting these figures, we have simply used them as a reasonable approximation.
Source: National Center for Health Statistics: Personal out-of-pocket medical expenditures, 1970, *Monthly Vital Stat Rep.* (Suppl.) *22:* April 1973.

expense, whereas now they must bear the full cost or rely upon municipally subsidized services. It is impossible to predict accurately the magnitude of this new effective demand for physician services. However, if we assume that the present low utilization by this group, estimated at 3.5 visits per person (excluding any utilization of private care), will rise to the national average of 5.0 per person, an increase of between two and three million visits annually seems likely. This is probably a conservative estimate, and a closer approximation of the Medicaid population's rate of utilization due to the modest copayment requirements obviously would expand the volume of care which would be demanded even further.

(3) Much of the new demand will be directed toward private practitioners.

Much of the new demand among the near poor will be directed to private physicians' offices rather than to institutional sources of care. We base this prediction on the assumption that the preferences of this group are similar to those of their fellow citizens with both lower and higher incomes. The preference for private practitioners is evident in the present patterns of utilization by both upper-income families and Medicaid clients. The near poor now rely on municipal hospitals for much of their care. Once their out-of-pocket expense for ambulatory care remains constant regardless of the locus of care, these people will attempt to exercise their preference for private providers, who will be confronted with newly generated demand as well as with a shift of existing demand from the hospital sector.

Additional pressure on private practitioners is likely to come from the indigent, who may seek a larger share of their ambulatory care from this source. The Medicaid population is currently restricted in its access to private physicians because of the low fee structure, but if a more favorable fee structure is adopted under NHI, there may be a shift of demand by this group to private physicians.

(4) Although the aggregate supply of private practitioners appears sufficient to meet new levels of demand, other factors, chiefly the predominance of specialty practice, will significantly limit their capability to produce the kinds of medical services which will be sought most by consumers.

New York City has a relatively large supply of physicians. In 1973 the American Medical Association reported 21,647 active physicians in New York City, of whom 8,754 (40 percent) were in hospital-based practice and 10,544 (49 percent) were in office-based practice (Table 7). There are no service data relating specifically to office-based practitioners in New York, but if national metropolitan averages for visits per week and regional averages of weeks worked per year are applied to the local supply, the potential volume of private ambulatory care is substantial

Table 7
Distribution of Physicians in New York City, 1973

	Number of physicians	Office based	Hospital based Full-time staff	Hospital based Residents	Hospital based Interns	Other activities	Inactive or unclassified
General practice	1,993	1,799	121	28	0	45	N.A.
Internal medicine	4,397	1,795	387	1,245	453	517	N.A.
General surgery	2,057	792	178	774	218	95	N.A.
Obstetrics-gynecology	1,399	751	118	416	18	96	N.A.
Pediatrics	1,656	617	211	549	122	157	N.A.
All other	10,145	4,790	1,314	2,216	386	1,439	N.A.
Total	21,647	10,544	2,329	5,228	1,197	2,349	2,858

N.A. = Data not available
Source: Unpublished data supplied by the American Medical Association. We are indebted to Edward Bennett, statistician, Center for Health Services Research and Development, American Medical Association, for extracting this information from the physician masterfile.

(Table 8). The office-based physicians could handle more than 46.8 million visits annually, or six for each New Yorker.

Of course, these are aggregate statistics and they do not indicate possible imbalances between the type of medical services sought by the public and the supply of physicians. It is difficult to estimate with any degree of precision the distribution of services that will be demanded by a population for whom there are no historical data. However, we have accepted the utilization rates of HIP clients as a first approximation of normal demand by a population with no financial barrier to care (see Table 9). An analysis of the utilization of HIP ambulatory services by

Table 8
Estimated Service Capability of Office-Based Physicians in New York City, 1973

Specialty	Number of physicians	Average No. of office visits per week	Average weeks worked per year	Annual service capability
General practice	1,799	131.6	47.3	11,198,000
Internal medicine	1,795	83.6	46.8	7,023,000
General surgery	792	78.4	46.9	2,912,000
Obstetrics-gynecology	751	99.0	48.8	3,628,000
Pediatrics	617	137.2	47.6	4,029,000
All other	4,790	80.0	47.0	18,010,000
Total	10,544	94.0	47.2	46,800,000

Source: Unpublished data from the American Medical Association and *Profile of Medical Practice*. Chicago, Amer. Med. Assoc., 1973, pp. 56,62. In the absence of precise data for average visits and weeks worked for the "all other" category, we have made our own estimates.

specialty indicates that nearly half of the services (47 percent) were provided by family practitioners; an additional 12 percent were provided by pediatricians. This is in marked contrast to the estimated distribution of the total capability of practitioners, only 25 percent of which consists of general practitioner services and 10 percent of pediatrics. These estimates suggest a shortfall in those private medical services which are likely to be in the greatest demand. Even if some proportion of the services provided by internists are regarded as essentially family practice, the imbalance still exists.

The discussion of the capability of private physicians thus far has been based on existent factors of supply, assuming the continuation of present patterns of practice. The initiation of NHI, however, may alter this, particularly if a fee schedule is imposed which favors selected procedures. A study of professional practice in Montreal before and after the implementation of Medicare—the Canadian NHI, a compulsory universal health-insurance plan covering the cost of all physician services under a uniform fee schedule—revealed a 15 percent decrease in the average length of the physician's work week. This decrease resulted from the sharp reduction in the number of house calls and telephone consultations as well as of hospital visits by general practitioners and the concentration upon office visits, presumably in response to more liberal payment for the latter.[4] While this precise constellation of change may not occur in New York, where house calls already have been virtually eliminated, a redirection of professional practice from less to more economically rewarding activities may be anticipated, with, perhaps, a consequent diminution in hours of work.

(5) Geographic imbalances also will limit the available supply of privately produced medical services, particularly among the poor and

Table 9

Analysis of the 1972 Utilization of HIP Ambulatory Services by Specialty and the 1973 Estimated Capability of New York Office-Based Physicians by Specialty

	HIP visits		Estimated office capability	
	No.	%	No. of visits	%
General practice	107,505	47.3	11,198,000	23.9
Internal medicine	7,574	3.3	7,023,000	15.0
General surgery	7,160	3.2	2,912,000	6.2
Obstetrics-gynecology	12,109	5.3	3,628,000	7.8
Pediatrics	26,389	11.6	4,029,000	8.6
All other	66,457	29.3	18,010,000	38.5
Total	227,194	100.0	46,800,000	100.0

Source: The American Medical Association (see Table VIII) and special tabulations prepared by the Research and Statistics Department, Health Insurance Plan of Greater New York (HIP).

near-poor minority population living in segregated neighborhoods which have been drained of private practitioners.

The location of office-based practitioners will limit their capability to meet new demands. A crude analysis of physician to population ratios based on the distribution of office-based practitioners by borough (Table 10) reveals a heavy concentration in Manhattan versus a sparse supply in the Bronx and Richmond. Within boroughs there is considerable further variation by neighborhood. Although the city's extensive transportation system permits easy interborough utilization of physician services (most significantly between Manhattan and the Bronx), people prefer a physician close to their place of residence, particularly for their more common complaints.

Most seriously deprived of easily accessible private ambulatory care have been the black and Hispanic minorities concentrated in the ghetto areas of Harlem, Bedford-Stuyvesant, South Bronx, and South Jamaica. The heavy post-war inflow of these populations was not matched by a commensurate increase in the number of physicians practicing in these communities. The combination of financial barriers to care during the decades before Medicaid, racial segregation, and the unattractive physical conditions within these areas served to deprive these people of medical personnel by the attrition of a preexisting physician supply and the failure of younger doctors, of any race, to replace them. The collection of data by community health-planning boards is under way, but in the absence of complete statistics on the availability of medical care to this population, some facts regarding central Harlem may be assumed to be typical. A survey by the Center for Community Health Systems and the Department of Pediatrics of the Faculty of Medicine, Columbia University, found that of 227 pediatricians and general practitioners with offices in upper Manhattan (which has a population of 650,000 persons), an area comprising three health districts (Riverside and Washington Heights, each 70 percent white, and central Harlem, more than 90 percent black), 57

Table 10

Population of New York City per Office-Based Practitioner, 1973

	New York City	Bronx	Brooklyn	Manhattan	Queens	Richmond
General practice	4,386	5,548	4,665	3,263	4,229	6,783
Medical specialties	2,375	4,422	3,733	949	3,182	3,220
Surgical specialties	2,772	5,695	4,038	1,070	4,256	3,795
All other	3,062	8,542	8,723	842	6,577	7,970
Total	748	1,430	1,184	287	1,066	1,181

Source: American Medical Association: *Distribution of Physicians in the U.S.*, Chicago, Amer. Med. Assoc., 1974, pp. 270-73.

percent were located in Riverside, 39 percent in Washington Heights, and a bare 4 percent in central Harlem.[5] The physicians in central Harlem are well advanced in age, and there are no newcomers to succeed them. The attrition of private providers is reflected in the climbing clinic-utilization rates at Harlem Hospital; pediatric visits alone increased by 44 percent between 1968 and 1971, half of these being ER encounters. The impact of expanded financial entitlement on a virtually nonexistent traditional private sector can only generate new entrepreneurial endeavors in the style of Medicaid mills to fill the vacuum. Accordingly, innovative efforts by existing institutions offer the most desirable response to meet the new demand in these neighborhoods.

(6) The shortfall of private practitioners rendering family care will lead to a rationing of services either by physician-determined selection of patients or by increased waiting time.

If an NHI plan uses different fee schedules or different payment principles for different groups, this would lead to physician-determined selection of patients. For example, the Nixon administration bill mandated a statewide fixed reimbursement schedule for the no-liability and sliding-liability groups, but permitted the collection of higher fees from the maximum-liability group. Such a difference in permissible fees will act as a financial barrier for the poor and near poor in obtaining the services of private practitioners.

If a uniform-payment principle is applied to all groups, the collection mechanism may become critical. Requiring the physician to collect either full fees from the patient or partial fees from the carrier (in the form of insurance benefits) and the balance from the patient (in the form of the deductible and coinsurance charges) will cause physicians to be more selective in accepting patients. Doctors will avoid poorer patients who lack the available cash to pay fees out-of-pocket. The alternative, granting physicians full payment from the carrier with the government periodically collecting the coinsurance and deductible charges, usually takes the form of proposals for a NHI credit card which assures full payment to the physician. Under such a scheme a patient's income should make little difference to the physician. However, physicians may still impose a supplemental cash payment above the basic scheduled fee, as in fact some participating GHI physicians have done. Thus, even the adoption of the most equitable payment mechanism—uniform fees with a national health-credit card—does not guarantee a nondiscriminatory physician response. Too many unknowns—the level of fees, the enforcement efforts, the willingness of consumers to pay additional fees—make prediction impossible.

If an equitable and well-monitored payment system is established, the newly entitled consumers will secure greater access (limited by geographical constraints) to private services which traditionally have been enjoyed by the maximum-liability group. The resultant competition would increase waiting time, with some consequent diminution of demand among upper-income patients, particularly for less serious ailments, and eventually would lead to some redistribution of services in favor of the lower-income groups. Such a scenario is suggested by the experience in Montreal. After the introduction of the Canadian NHI, the average waiting time both for a doctor's appointment and in the doctor's office increased, with the largest increases in the higher income groups. As a result, the average number of physician visits per person per year remained constant (five), but these shifted markedly from high- to low-income groups.[6]

(7) A large proportion of the ambulatory services which are now provided in institutional settings still will be required, but NHI funds will permit expansion and improvement of existing facilities.

Even under the most equitable NHI provisions, it is obvious that private practitioners will not be able to absorb the full volume of demand. Moreover, geographic maldistribution will operate to retain near-present levels of hospital-based care.

NHI, particularly if the federal government assumes responsibility for collecting copayments, will eliminate or significantly reduce the deficits which now arise in the operation of OPDs because hospitals cannot or will not refuse service to the large number of patients who lack resources to pay the full cost of their care. Consequently, hospitals will not face serious financial obstacles to improving their ambulatory services. When Medicaid was first enacted, the liberal New York State eligibility criteria afforded hospitals a similar opportunity, and many began to take action. However, the cutbacks in Medicaid soon caused these hospitals to abandon their plans. The Department of Health of the City of New York also developed plans to use Medicaid to finance improvements in its ambulatory-care facilities, but the initial plan for a network of Neighborhood Family Care Centers (NFCCs) also was curtailed eventually because of Medicaid cutbacks. Thus, NHI may revive the efforts of municipal agencies to establish independent ambulatory-care facilities.

If municipal and voluntary facilities simultaneously seek to expand, shortages of manpower among all health-care sectors are likely to arise. The municipal agencies, historically in the least favorable competitive position, would experience the greatest difficulty in staffing new facilities; contractual arrangements with voluntary institutions for staff would probably continue to be a primary source of physician manpower.

(8) Potential increases in the costs of ambulatory care will be related more to rising unit prices than to greater utilization.

Expenditures for ambulatory care have been a minor share of total health-care expenditures. One estimate[7] is that ambulatory medical and ancillary care account for 20 percent of all health expenditures in the United States. (This percentage may be increased by shifts from inpatient to ambulatory care when both are insured equally, but such estimates are outside the scope of this paper.) The increase in the volume of care under NHI which was projected earlier—two to three million visits—would engender some cost increase. However, in a system of the magnitude of New York City's, this would constitute a relatively small percentage increase.

A more significant cost factor is the potential inflation of physician fees. Fee changes will be dependent upon the payment principle or principles written into the NHI program. A law permitting "customary and reasonable" fees or permitting charges in excess of scheduled rates to some patient groups would engender a substantial inflation of fees. The marked increase in prevailing fees during the years immediately following the implementation of Medicare certainly suggests such an outcome.

Probably the greatest threat to the containment of costs will come from hospital-based ambulatory care. Under the present system of cost-related payments, even with prospective rates, unit costs have risen rapidly. Even if this is partially a function of present accounting practices, the applicable costs under NHI still will exceed prevailing private physician's fees. Since the costs of hospital ambulatory care are closely linked to the costs of hospital inpatient care, containment of either will depend upon a tightly monitored regulatory system.

One alternative suggested to limit the costs of institutional ambulatory care is the separation of outpatient from inpatient services in the computation of costs. The 1974 Medicaid rates from several facilities which have been established independently of a hospital indicate that this approach does not necessarily lead to economies. The Martin Luther King, Jr. Health Center's cost per visit ($51.78) exceeds that of Montefiore Hospital's outpatient clinic ($46.19); the cost of St. Luke's Hospital's neighborhood health-service program ($48.00) exceeds that of its OPD ($33.98); and the cost of the Department of Health's Bedford Health Center ($34.27) is about equal to that of the St. John's Episcopal Hospital clinic ($34.00). If a larger share of ambulatory care is rendered by reorganized and improved hospital-sponsored programs consequent to NHI, then total expenditures inevitably will increase.

(9) Under an NHI permitting free choice, consumers probably will want to retain their options in selecting a source of ambulatory care, so capitation arrangements are expected to experience limited growth.

There is no evidence to suggest that capitation arrangements will grow if both patients and physicians have the option to choose between group practice financed by capitation payments and the free choice of independent physicians. New York has had only one major prepaid group practice (HIP) since 1947 and it has not experienced rapid growth in recent years. A review of HIP enrollment (excluding Medicaid) indicates little or no increase each year between 1968 and 1974. Moreover, among the largest group of potential clients—municipal employees—the portion selecting HIP rather than an alternative free choice arrangement has declined from 40 percent in 1970 to 35 percent in 1974.

Within the past year an attempt by the Connecticut General Life Insurance Company to establish a prepaid group practice to serve an employed population in parts of Brooklyn, lower Manhattan, and Staten Island failed to attract sufficient subscribers to assure financial viability. Although the sponsors contend that this may be attributed to the uncertainty surrounding federal regulations for group contracts, the fact remains that the plan evoked little consumer enthusiasm.

An effort to convert the Martin Luther King, Jr. Health Center to an HMO serving a Medicaid and near-poor population encountered similar marketing difficulties. Although the center had built up a stable constituency of patients, these patients were reluctant to relinquish their freedom of choice. It also failed to negotiate an acceptable capitation rate with the state government.

(10) There are serious gaps in our knowledge and data which are required to anticipate the impact of NHI.

This analysis of the provision of present-day ambulatory services today was impaired by the lack of recent local data on (1) demographic characteristics of the New York population relevant to the demand for medical care, such as age, sex, and race in relation to income and family size; (2) the total magnitude of services produced by office-based private practitioners in family practice and the various specialties; (3) the extent to which specialists are a source of general care; and (4) the intraborough location of private practitioners and the way in which location relates to the utilization of their services. Moreover, many of the findings of this study were derived from data on payments in the absence of more precise service statistics for different income groups. The collection and analysis of more refined information in these areas are prerequisites for effective planning for NHI. Finally, any insurance plan that is implemented must be accompanied by the collection of comprehensive statistics on utilization.

Summary

Based on recent national proposals, it may be assumed that an initial NHI plan will provide universal coverage, contain income-conditioned copayments, and continue the principles of free choice and fee-for-service in the selection and payment of physicians. The implications of such a system for ambulatory services in New York City are:

(1) The extended entitlement to health-care financing provided by NHI will effect little change in the volume of care sought by persons at the upper and lower ends of the income-distribution scale.

(2) The near poor will significantly increase their utilization of ambulatory services.

(3) Much of this new demand will be directed toward private practitioners, the preferred source of care among all income groups.

(4) Despite an adequate aggregate supply of office-based physicians, the high proportion of specialists will cause shortfalls in the supply of primary care.

(5) The shortage of primary care by private physicians consequent to the vanishing supply of practitioners in low-income black and Hispanic neighborhoods will be intensified by increased demand among newly entitled groups.

(6) The general shortage of primary-care physicians will lead to a rationing of services either by physician-determined selection of patients or by increased waiting time. Under a differential payment scheme, poorer patients will be discriminated against; with a more equitable payment mechanism there will be some redistribution of services in favor of low-income populations.

(7) The shortage of private sources of primary care will perpetuate institutionally based ambulatory services; these institutional services may be enhanced by the availability of new revenues.

(8) The cost of ambulatory care, now 20 percent of all health expenditures, may increase, depending upon the payment principle or principles incorporated within NHI, with hospital unit costs potentially the most serious inflationary threat.

(9) HMO and other capitation schemes are unlikely to undergo significant expansion.

(10) Further studies of (a) the demographic characteristics and present patterns of ambulatory care of the different income groups in New York City and (b) of the magnitude and characteristics of office-based private practice are necessary to anticipate more accurately the impact of NHI and to plan for optimal implementation.

Appendix A. Method of Estimating Population Groups

The data used in estimating the size of the population groups were drawn from the 1973 Current Population Survey (CPS) conducted by the U.S. Bureau of the Census. Special tabulations from the survey relating to

Table 11

Three Out-of-Pocket Liability Groups Defined in Terms of 1973 Current Dollar Family Income and Family Size

Family members (No.)	Family income		
	No liability	Sliding liability	Maximum liability
1	0 — $2,400	$2,400 — $6,400	$6,400+
2	2,400 — 3,600	3,600 — 7,600	7,600+
3	3,600 — 4,200	4,200 — 8,200	8,200+
4	4,200 — 4,800	4,800 — 8,800	8,800+
5	4,800 — 5,200	5,200 — 9,200	9,200+
6	5,200 — 5,600	5,600 — 9,600	9,600+
6+	5,600 — 6,800	6,800 —10,800	10,800+

Where income cutoff points for defining the three groups differed from income cutoff points in the 1973 Current Population Survey, linear interpolations were made to estimate group size.

the population of New York City were purchased from the Bureau of the Census by the Center for New York City Affairs of the New School for Social Research. These data were made available to us through the cooperation of Blanche Bernstein, Director of Research, and Arley Bondarin, Research Associate, of the Center for New York City Affairs.

The CPS data provide information on income by family size for families and unrelated individuals. This information was converted from family units to population counts by multiplying by the appropriate number of family members, assuming that families in the more-than-six-member group averaged nine persons.

The population estimates were converted into the three out-of-pocket liability groups by defining each group in terms of family income as shown in Table 11. Where income cutoff points for defining the three groups differed from income-cutoff points in the CPS tabulations, linear interpolations were made to estimate group size.

Appendix B.   Method of Estimating Services

Hospital OPD and ER services

The total number of visits to OPD and ER facilities of voluntary, municipal, and proprietary hospitals in 1973 were supplied by Leonard Schrager, associate executive director, Health and Hospital Planning Council of Southern New York.

The total visits were allocated to the population groups on the basis of data relating to the method of payment for hospital ambulatory services which were gathered as part of the Survey of Hospital Ambulatory Care, June 3–June 21, 1974 conducted by the Research and Special

Table 12

Percentage Distribution of Hospital Ambulatory Care Visits
by Method of Payment

	Municipal ER	Municipal OPD	Voluntary ER	Voluntary OPD
Blue Cross	4.6%	3.0%	20.2%	4.1%
Medicare	4.5	12.2	6.7	14.9
Medicaid	36.2	33.2	33.4	41.3
Self-paying*	45.3	43.9	22.0	29.8
Other	9.3	7.8	17.7	9.9
Total	100.0	100.0	100.0	100.0

*This term refers to all patients who have no third-party coverage. Payments range from nothing to part of the charge; a very small number of visits are paid in full.

Source: Health and Hospital Planning Council of Southern New York and "Survey of Hospital Ambulatory Care, June 3-June 21, 1974," Special Projects Department, Blue Cross-Blue Shield of Greater New York.

Projects Department of the Blue Cross-Blue Shield of Greater New York. Special tabulations from the survey relating to hospitals in New York City were made available by Anne Cugliani and Jerome Jaffe of that agency.

The survey yielded data on the percentage distribution of method of payment for voluntary and municipal hospital OPDs and ERs. These figures are presented in Table 12. The methods of payment were associated with population groups as shown in Table 13.

Services of the Department of Health

Figures for the total number of services for each Department of Health Program were taken from the departmental publication, *Service and Vital Statistics by Health Care District, New York City, 1972.* The

Table 13

Association of Population Groups with Methods of Payment for Care in
Outpatient Departments (OPD) and Emergency Rooms (ER) of
Voluntary and Municipal Hospitals

	Municipal ER*	Muncipal OPD	Voluntary ER*	Voluntary OPD
Blue Cross	Maximum	Sliding	Maximum	Maximum
Medicare	Maximum	Sliding	Maximum	Maximum
Medicaid	None	None	None	None
Self-paying†	Sliding	Sliding	Sliding	Sliding
Other	Maximum	Sliding	Maximum	Maximum

*All visits to proprietary emergency rooms were assigned to the maximum liability group and were totalled with the voluntary ER visits assigned to this group.
†This term refers to all patients who have no third-party coverage.

total for "other services" includes visits to all Department of Health clinics except those to dental and child health clinics.

The total services were divided among the population groups according to estimates of the share of services provided to those who are eligible for Medicaid by the Bureau of Child Health for child-health stations (33 percent) and by the Bureau of School Health for the school-health program (37 percent). No estimates were available for the distribution of the remaining category of visits, so it was assumed that the percentage of visits by those eligible for Medicaid was similar to that for other departmental services (35 percent).

HIP enrollment and services

Enrollment and service statistics for the HIP groups located in New York City (the two groups in suburban counties were excluded) were supplied by Marilyn Einhorn, Research Director of HIP. The enrollment figures were drawn from a 1972 midyear count. The service statistics are drawn from a count of services provided during 1972.

The enrollment was divided among the Medicaid and maximum-liability groups based on the same data. Services were allocated to the two groups in proportion to the size of their enrollments.

Union health centers

All figures relating to the total eligible population, the population using these centers, and the services provided are drawn from a survey of union health centers by Sanford Lenz of the New York State School of Industrial and Labor Relations. The findings of this survey are being prepared for publication, but preliminary data were made available for this paper.

Free-standing facilities

A complete listing of all facilities is contained in the New York State Department of Health *Health Facilities Directory, 1974*, vol. 3. Service statistics for 1973 for 36 facilities providing medical services exclusive of methadone maintenance were made available by the Bureau of Health Care Reimbursement, Division of Health Economics, New York State Department of Health. These 36 facilities are the largest free-standing clinics in New York City; the total for these facilities is the one used in Table 2. The services were allocated to the population groups in a 50 percent–50 percent ratio on the basis of method-of-payment data from one of the larger facilities, the Martin Luther King, Jr. Health Center.

Table 14
GHI Enrollment and Services, 1974 (Excluding Type E Coverage)

Type of service	Number of services	Estimated number of ambulatory visits*	Average membership	Estimated utilization rate
Surgery in hospital	58,547	117,094	1,415,774	0.0827
Surgery out of hospital	111,980	223,960	1,415,774	0.1581
Maternity	18,045	198,495	1,415,774	0.1402
Medical in hospital	32,092			
Consultation in hospital	16,474			
Home and office visits	2,833,001	2,833,001	1,328,718	2.1321
Consultation out of hospital	141,495	141,495	1,328,718	0.1064
X rays	227,961			
Laboratory	636,942			
Anesthesia	53,543			
Visiting nurse	805			
Radiation therapy	5,458	5,458	1,415,774	0.0038
Ambulance	1,965			
Total	4,138,308	3,519,503		2.6233

*Ambulatory visits per service are based on estimates in Avnet, H.: *Physician Service Patterns and Illness Rates,* New York Group Health Insurance, Incorporated, 1967, pp. 47-48.

Group Health Incorporated

Enrollment and service statistics for GHI come from unpublished data made available through the cooperation of George Melcher, president, and Lynn Doctor, vice-president of GHI. Total enrollment in 1974 for all GHI plans was 1,753,218. A survey by GHI in 1971 indicated that 55 percent of all GHI clients resided in New York City. The recent availability of GHI type E coverage for municipal employees increased this proportion to 60 percent in 1974, according to estimates by GHI; thus, we estimated that 1,051,930 GHI clients now reside in New York City.

Statistics on services for those with regular GHI coverage were used to estimate the volume of visits to physicians by this group. GHI service figures were converted to estimates of the number of physicians' visits and rates of utilization as indicated in Table 14. The combined rate of utilization (2.6233 visits) was applied to the estimated total New York City resident enrollment (1,051,930 members) to yield the estimated total volume of GHI's private practitioner services included in Table 2.

Medicaid private physician services

Data on the total number of physician services paid for by Medicaid during the last three quarters of 1973 and the first quarter of 1974 were made available by the Department of Health of the City of New York with the cooperation of Dr. John Gentry and Fran Nojovitz. Ambulatory services were defined to include all home and office visits by physicians exclusive of methadone-maintenance and psychiatric visits, abortions, and maternity care.

References

[1] K. Davis, "A Decade of Policy Developments in Providing Health Care for Low-Income Families," *Conference on a Decade of Federal Antipoverty Policy, 1975*, Racine, Wisconsin. Unpublished.

[2] Union Family Medical Fund of the Hotel Industry of New York City: *Annual Statistical Report for the Year Ended May 31, 1974*. Unpublished.

[3] M.S. Mueller, "Private Health Insurance in 1973: A Review of Coverage, Enrollment and Financial Experience," *Soc. Sec. Bull.* 38:21 (1975).

[4] P. Enterline, J.C. McDonald, A.D. McDonald, L. Davignon and V. Salter, "Effects of 'Free' Medical Care on Medical Practice—The Quebec Experience," *NEJM* 288:1152 (1973).

[5] "A Proposal to the Robert Wood Johnson Foundation for a Child Health Care Project, October, 1973," Center for Community Health Systems and Department Pediatrics, Faculty of Medicine, Columbia University. Unpublished.

[6] P. Enterline, V. Salter, A.D. McDonald, and J.C. McDonald, "The Distribution of Medical Services Before and After 'Free' Medical Care—The Quebec Experience," *NEJM* 289:1174 (1973).

[7] Nora Piore, "Problems and Opportunities for Community Hospitals in Primary Care," *Community Hospitals and the Challenge of Primary Care*, Center for Community Health Systems, Columbia University, New York, 1975.

Proposal for City Action in Dealing with Ambulatory Medical Care under National Health Insurance

GEORGE A. SILVER

The customary procedure for opening a position paper considering the consequences of legislation not yet in force is to prepare a graceful justification for the possibility of miscalculating the future direction of the legislation. I have no such intention. In my opinion, the state of the economy, previous unfortunate governmental experiences with open-ended health expenditures, mistrust of physicians' charging habits, lack of confidence in official regulatory bodies and the formidable size of current health and medical care expenditures all point in one direction: ceilings on appropriations; ceilings on expenditures for medical care. This paper undertakes to examine the consequences of such an outcome and suggests actions that might be taken to reorganize and improve medical care services on the assumption that no matter what health insurance act is passed (a) the larger part of the funds to be spent for medical services will be under official control; and (b) these funds will be limited by law.

Let me deal with some definitions first. "Funds under official control" means just that. Either the Social Security Administration or a parallel Health Security Administration will be responsible for collections and disbursements. (Obviously, if "Medicredit" is the only piece of legislation that passes the Congress, there will be no ball game.) The positive assumption made here is that the legislation will make it possible for the city to obtain control of such funds coming into New York City.

If it is argued that the introduction of carriers (intermediaries) would nullify this official control, I must reply that this need not be the case. Current Medicare legislation, for example, contains language making it possible for official agencies to be carriers, thereby saving the overhead and pre-empting the commercial carriers. Although no state (except for Oklahoma on behalf of public assistance clients) has undertaken to be such a carrier, we know that it is possible, and we should make use of the information to ensure that official agencies will exercise official control over the funds.

"Funds limited by law" means that total expenditures will be controlled by the budgetary ceiling imposed by the legislation. It is not impossible to control total expenditures even though the official expenditures represent only a part of that total. Unless specifically prohibited by law, the official agency can specify by how much and to what extent it will participate in payments. It may choose to set fee scales, to reimburse client as well as provider or to select only certain organized forms of treatment as eligible for full reimbursement. Indeed, this is possible now, within limits, in Medicare and Medicaid, except that providers have been allowed greater leeway in setting charges and in reimbursement scales by both the federal agency and by the carriers. These allowances have been based on the P.L. 89-97 sections of the law prohibiting interference with current methods of practice and have been interpreted to mean "methods of reimbursement" instead of "methods of medical treatment" alone. Furthermore, in view of the relatively lesser portion of the population covered by these bills, the risk of antagonizing both the medical profession and hospital groups has been too great.

The Logic of the Assumption that Budget Ceilings Will Be Imposed

—The serious nature of the present national economic crisis and the recurrent argument as to whether it has "bottomed out" or not, is one reason why it can be assumed that any congressional action will have a ceiling on expenditures.

—The crisis in New York City underlines the point.

—The experience of the various congressional committees that have undertaken to estimate costs of Medicaid and Medicare expenditures in the past, and the outspoken criticisms of physicians, hospital administrators and insurance companies emanating from these sources indicate a distrust of "self-policing" of costs in these groups.

—The recent report from the Nader group on the "toxic" effect of cost-plus financing is only a ripple of the strong current of feeling among consumer groups, which will become increasingly articulate as NHI becomes a current agenda item.

—The recognition and the reluctant quasi-acceptance among physicians themselves of the need for ceilings, which is expressed, however, as an acceptance of the possibility of standard fee scales in reimbursement— not quite the same thing as acceptance of budgetary ceilings, I admit—but a step along the way.[1]

—The proposed federal regulations enabling community health centers to provide the same minimal services as family health centers were published in the May 16, 1975 Federal Register.

—P.L. 93-641, the National Health Planning and Resources Development Act, is a powerful indication of the direction of thinking at the national level, not only among legislators, but judging from the regulations, among officials of the executive branch as well.

When there is legislation which covers the majority of the population and when funds will be in official hands, the negotiations as to reimbursement methods and quantity will take on new significance. It has always been recognized that physicians, hospital officials and other providers feared compulsion, which was usually taken to mean that patients were *compelled* to accept certain kinds of treatment, or that doctors would be *compelled* to apply certain kinds of treatment—the compulsion was always visualized in professional terms. Under a budgetary ceiling, however, the compulsion will take on a new form; it will compel rigidity of reimbursement mechanisms and will require doctors and hospital officials to work within financial limits. It may be argued that this will force restrictions upon kinds and scope, or quantity of treatment, since less money will buy less service or products of whatever kind. Again, this is not necessarily so. Ceilings will limit the income of the provider, compelling more efficient and more productive behavior, and what has been urged for years will suddenly become necessary.

We will address in this discussion the confrontation between physicians (wishing to retain their income levels and the freedom to charge as they see fit), and the agency responsible for paying for medical care; so, too, the parallel confrontation between hospital officials and the agency on the issue of reimbursement levels without diminution of service.

Issues

What has to be done to (a) retain access for patients to ambulatory medical services they may receive; (b) improve and expand ambulatory care for those not now achieving satisfactory access; (c) reimburse providers in a manner satisfactory to them, and (d) stay within budgetary limits established by law?

The impact of these issues can be lessened by making better use of available funds through moves to reduce current costs or render current operations more efficient.

Separation of In and Outpatient Services

Hospital operations are the most expensive of all medical care service activities because of the "readiness to serve" necessity imposed upon the hospital. Every bed has to be ready to take care of the sickest patient who might be admitted. As a part of the hospital operation, outpatient services suffer the consequences of the massive overhead imposed by the hospital's pattern of staffing and service. *Removing the outpatient department from under the hospital's wing and setting up free-standing services will reduce costs to the ambulatory care sector.*[2] Essentially this proposal recommends breaking up the clinic system long ingrained in New York City's (and other cities') medical care delivery system. What are the objections to it?

—Teaching institutions will lose control of the hospital population basic to undergraduate and graduate medical education.

—Physicians in practice no longer work in clinics; it is a house staff activity. Separate the clinic from the hospital and you lose the medical staff needed to run the service.

—Without hospital supervision these free-standing units will degenerate into the poor quality "Medicaid clinics."

—It would be cheaper to put the patients into doctors' offices and the results would be no different.

—Building a thousand clinics would be time-consuming and costly, and the eventual overhead just as great as that in hospitals.

The objections can be met as follows:

—Existing hospital clinic space can be used, but administered independently so that costs and charges represent services performed and do not reflect hospital overhead. In other words, existing clinic facilities within, or associated with, hospitals do not have to be dismantled or phased out. What is needed is a separate outpatient operation and service function which is reimbursed at its cost, not at hospital cost. Primary care would be separated from consulting services, which could remain as part of the hospital costing structure. Hospitals then would be reimbursed for consulting services on the basis of the physician-cost of consultation sessions provided.

—Primary care would be mediated through physicians plus trained nurse-practitioners or physician assistants. In addition to hospital outpatient departments converted to primary care, the city health department clinics, as well as rented office space in neighborhoods, would be used to provide primary care facilities, although not the consultant services. Given the continued use of hospital and health department offices, only a relatively small number of facilities would have to be built or rented. Physicians working in primary care units would be reimbursed on either capitation, session or salary basis. House staff would not provide primary care (except perhaps under special circumstances, as part of a pilot teaching-center activity).

—Supervision would be arranged through the health department for on-the-spot evaluations, plus hospital staff evaluations where feasible.[3] In addition, a system of consumer boards, a city ombudsman for health and district grievance committees would offset the possibility of "Medicaid factories," poor quality, or poor satisfaction.

—Private practitioners who wish to undertake to see patients in their own offices may, provided they allow themselves to be evaluated and supervised as their colleagues are in the centers.

74

—A complete emergency care service has to be established independent of (though related to) the primary care centers, hospital clinics and other services, both for outreach (ambulance to home), emergency room (outpatient) and inpatient emergency care. This has to be staffed around the clock.

So much for the arguments against the feasibility of the proposal. What about the fact that (a) the hospitals will not be willing to give up their control over the space; (b) the doctors will not be willing to accept either the reimbursement or the working conditions and supervision in the center; (c) sufficient paraprofessionals to man the primary care units do not exist; (d) community boards and consumer participation in New York City has led to one unholy row after another on the basis of race, religion or economic groups (look at the school boards!); (e) travel between primary centers and consultation centers is probably non-existent in many areas; (f) isn't this just another of those idealistic, academic, castles-in-Spain projects without any foundation in reality or possibility?

Proposal 1

Eli Ginzberg's associates have produced an excellent document and illustrated it with useful and important data.[4] With added data along with their figures, I would like to make different points: The NHI bill may, and probably will, have language allowing "free choice of physician," and it may be that the language will be so unambiguous and emphatic that it cannot be circumvented. Let us assume, then, that the clientele of the city will be the clients who now use the municipal clinics; that is, the patients who use the voluntary hospital clinics will continue to go there, while the ones who use the municpal clinics will continue to go there. What can be done, under such circumstances, to make most efficient use of the funds available to the city for its clinic clientele?

An annual fee per client should be set, based on a projected cost derived from estimates for a specified type of organization and a particular location for the delivery of primary care medical service. The city can adjust its performance to meet this fee, while voluntary hospital clinics not choosing to modify their performances accordingly will probably close, and the city must then undertake to provide care in their place. Private practitioners will also be paid the same fee, provided the criteria set for performance are met. Where this is refused, the city will again have to move in, as indicated above.

Let us take the smallest option: city clinics for patients now using city services. Of the 1.4 million Medicaid enrollees, 364,000 use voluntary hospital clinics; 266,000 use city hospital clinics; 770,000 use private physician offices.[5] For primary care, including home and office, but *not* hospital services, 1,000 adults (over age 6) would use perhaps 3 visits a year. The number is hard to pin down because Blue Cross and Ginzberg data cannot be sorted out on that basis. Ginzberg says overall utilization (including specialists' visits) is 7.5 percent and Blue Cross indicates that about 20 percent of visits to clinics are "general" or "walk-in"; so 2–3 is a good guess (chart attached). As for children, the likelihood is that, except for well-baby care (possibly 5 visits a year) children would be seen as often as adults in primary care settings, except as emergencies.

Nurse screening would offset one visit at least, so that the 3,000 services for 1,000 adults would require the services of 1 nurse and 1 physician. (Child medical services are more likely to be 4 nurses and 1 pediatrician for 2,000 children.)[6] This is based on a 38-hour week, 48 weeks a year, for district center units serving 15,000 people, with separate emergency services based on a self-contained unit of specially located emergency rooms, ambulance teams, etc.

I'd like to define a few terms I'll be using in the following discussion:

Unit: a team of 1 or 2 doctors and a nurse or nurses to provide care for 1,000–3,000 people (adults and children).

Center: a physical location for primary care. It may serve one or more units up to 15,000 people.

District center: a service unit which may include one or more physical "centers" and a federation of functional units.

Federation: clusters of units associated with a district center—the functional staff for the geographic location.

Team: see *unit.*

Firm: the team or teams working out of an operational center.

For the city, it will be necessary to provide 18 such centers, which should be visualized as "federations" rather than single institutions. That is, the doctor/nurse team may be one unit, although two or three units may operate together out of a single center location, each with an independent case load, but related to the other members of the unit administratively—through a central telephone and call system, exchange of time and office for illness or vacation, etc. Each of these units would be located in an existing health department clinic or rented space and advantageously situated to accommodate the patients in that area. (A comprehensive review of clinic address files will be made to ascertain the optimal geographic location of clinics.)

We are talking, then, about 270 physicians divided between family practice/internists for adults on the one hand, and pediatricians on the other. If there is some question about the willingness of general practitioners to participate in such a scheme, note that at present, 2,662 general practitioners participate in the Medicaid program, and 266 of them receive 65 percent of the Medicaid money. It happens too, that 2,662 "general practitioners" (from Ginzberg, from data supplied by the New York City Health Department, Chart II) is 963 more GPs than the AMA says there are in New York City (Chart III). This means that at least 963 internists in office-based practice (of whom the AMA says there are 1,795, almost exactly as many as there are GPs) are participating in general medical care under Medicaid. It means, too, that a significant number of GPs and internists receive so much of their income from Medicaid that they could probably be induced to work on salary for the city in the primary care program.

Pediatricians participate even more extensively in Medicaid than family doctors/internists. Of the 617 that the AMA says there are in New York City, 532 receive Medicaid reimbursements. They do share more widely than the others, however, so that 53 pediatricians take away only 57 percent (rather than 65 percent) of the total Medicaid reimbursement to that class of physician. It seems not unlikely, then, that a significant number of pediatricians could be induced to work full time for the city under a NHI program of this kind.

Operational costs for a firm of 12 doctors and 16 nurses (estimated average for a "center") with secretarial help and overhead costs of supplies and equipment, should not come to more than $1.3 million; 18 such centers, then, would cost $23.4 million, or in the neighborhood of $90 per person per year for primary care. (Since hospital costs will be set at perhaps $150 per day, and the expectation of hospitalization at 500 days per 1,000 persons per year, the hypothetical firm above will have the funds available [$1.125 million] to incur 7,500 days of hospitalization.) If the overall allowance per person is fixed at last year's expenditure rate of $480 per person, the firm will have available $4,775 million additional for *all other costs*, including specialized consultations, inpatient medical and surgical services, drugs, appliances, nursing home care and dentistry, as well as the public health costs. Current Medicaid expenditures for ambulatory care run to $365.6 million (Ginzberg, Chart IV), which is more than $265 per person on Medicaid!

Put differently, the city of New York now spends Medicaid money in unlimited fee-for-service reimbursement for primary care to clinics and private physicians. By establishing a standard of medical service delivery in a team structure in a fixed reimbursement *not* related to fee-for-service, this cost can be reduced significantly.

If voluntary hospitals operating clinics find that they cannot organize and arrange for provision of services in a manner consistent with the criteria described above, and at a cost equivalent to that being used to reimburse the city's organized services, the city should be prepared to augment its resources and provide the added units of personnel and locations to meet the needs of patients who would otherwise attend voluntary hospital clinics. Assuming that the same staff needs would obtain for the 365,000 people who use the voluntary hospital clinics, each cluster of 15,000 would mean that an additional 24 "firms" would be required; again, appropriately apportioned geographically. It might be more useful, however, to enlarge the "federations" from 15,000 to as many as 25,000 patients served and retain the structure of 18 sets (district centers) for as long as possible. There is something lethal about size, and the responsibility for more than 25,000 people may lead to impersonality and the kind of bureaucratic neglect that most people find so distasteful about group and clinic practice. The same would hold true for the administrative units (district centers); if there are too many more than 18, they may get lost in the bureaucratic shuffle at headquarters. A balance needs to be struck between these requirements.

Proposal 2

The former plan envisioned a situation in which absolute freedom of choice is imposed by the NHI legislation; in which the city is prevented by legal barriers from imposing discipline upon providers by means of differential reimbursement; and in which the city, then, is unable to encourage grouping of physicians for primary care without itself entering into administrative arrangements. If, on the other hand, the NHI legislation permits, or encourages, the recipients of federal funds to form HMOs, for example, or allows the city to choose salaried or per-session reimbursement in preference to fee-for-service, the accomplishment of the desired result will be easier. Then physicians may be persuaded, if they are to be reimbursed at all, to adapt themselves to team practice according to standards established by the administrative agencies.

Recruitment of needed physicians for supplementing the teams in existence, or for the addition of new teams, will be increasingly difficult as the number of physicians required surpasses the few hundred that may be easily recruited for the city-type program. However, the need for a physician pool may be diluted by the use of increasing numbers of specially trained nurses. The economic press resulting from loss of patients may bring in physicians who would otherwise have continued in private practice.[7]

Proposal: Specialized Consultations

Existing voluntary hospital clinics can be utilized for specialty consultations in accordance with a formula that provides reimbursement for square footage of space used, secretarial help, laboratory and X-ray or other diagnostic equipment and fee-for-service or fee-per-session for the physicians. The hospital overhead will not be used in calculation of costs. If this cannot be done, then office buildings can be rented or constructed as space for clusters of specialists ("Polyclinics") for specialty consultations. Each of these specialty clinics would be expected to serve several "federations" of medical team units—perhaps as many as 100,000 people. It may not be necessary to have more than five such polyclinics to a borough. Thus teaching institutions would retain their valuable load of specialty "teaching material."[8]

Proposal 3

While a NHI law that will undertake a transform medical practice directly is hardly likely, it is not impossible that such legislation will be considered and perhaps even passed. If so, restructuring the municipal and voluntary hospital clinics as independent entities separate from hospital operations may actually be encouraged by financial incentives of the HMO type.

The arguments put forth here should allow thoughtful planners to consider whether under such circumstances they would not consider dividing up in and outpatient responsibilities as outlined here, and encouraging the separate development of primary care centers and specialist centers to which primary care centers would relate. In other words, the specialized centers would be a resource for many primary care centers, instead of each HMO being structured to include both a primary care activity and specialist services.[9]

If this cannot be done for bureaucratic reasons, or out of simple inertia, I hope that some effort at least could be devoted to experimenting with the form suggested here. The idea of a "comprehensive group practice center," although not really popular, has captured the imagination of most people, particularly planners and legislators. Size continues to preoccupy me as the ultimate villain, obstructing as it does the provision of humane, patient-oriented, sympathetic care. I would like to see the system concentrate on creating hundreds of "units," teams of nurses and doctors (never more than 5 or 6 people) combined in "federations" that serve 15,000 to 30,000 people and related to a specialist center that serves as many as 100,000.

Among the many advantages that such a system would promote would be the possibility of supervision, professional education and control, without the artificial "continuing education" farce of meetings and lectures. A primary care doctor associated with a specialist center would have a particular internist or pediatrician as his preceptor and consultant; he would meet with him at regular intervals, and call him

79

about difficult cases; the consultant, in turn, would visit the primary care doctor in his office, review records with him there and perhaps even see patients. This two-way flow would do more to maintain and improve the quality of practice than all the expensive audiovisual tools yet invented.

Proposal: Emergency Care

While this paper is not intended to deal with the emergency care network required, it is essential that the network be considered since without it the primary care structure described cannot work and will be no better than the present inefficient three-tier medical care delivery system.

Each borough should have designated emergency care centers to which ambulances will bring the injured or sick, and from which medical care advice, telephone service, ambulance and medical services will flow 24 hours a day. The walk-in patients who now crowd the hospital emergency rooms will be expected to go to their own doctor of record (or city team center or voluntary team location) for care. The ambulance and emergency set-up will be independently sprung and separate from the primary care system, even though both may be under the administration of the city health department.

Proposal: Surgicenter

It is tempting to think of the primary care center as a potential "surgicenter"—a center designed and equipped to offer maximum opportunities for outpatient surgery that reaches out to perform many of the procedures now regarded only as inpatient. The temptation should be resisted. Hospitals should be encouraged to create outpatient surgical centers sufficiently sophisticated to match their inpatient facilities, and staffed accordingly. Without the incentive, there may be no stimulus for hospitals to experiment with outpatient surgery at all, thereby increasing the inpatient surgical load, perhaps adding to days of stay, and making concomitant demands on the budget. As for primary care centers, staffed as indicated, they would be ill-equipped to undertake extensive surgical procedures, and the immense potential of the surgicenter would be lost.[10]

Proposal: Mental Hospital and Ambulatory Care for the Mentally and Emotionally Ill

The model for ambulatory care should be the Amsterdam first aid system. Primary care centers will make this possible. The existing Community Health Centers (CMHC) can do the emergency calls and provide back-up, consultation and support. After triage from the CMHC, the patient will be sent to a general hospital, mental hospital, or referred back to his primary care center with instructions for follow-up. Ambulatory care will be carried out in primary care centers, while Community Mental Health Centers will continue to provide needed psychiatric care where the primary care physician needs the added support.

Discussion; Timing

Strategically, this is an excellent time to make a break with tradition. The plan sounds a lot bolder than it is. In fact it is in the mainstream of American medical practice and returns, at a somewhat higher level, to what was the "golden age" model of medical practice—the family doctor, a one-to-one, small-scale operation. At the same time, it plugs into the latest in medical care in its use of specialists and the hospital. It takes place at a time when the national economic crisis and the plight of the city cry out for solutions that will simplify and contain the inflationary trend. The proposal represents a radical break only in the sense that it offers something "different"—team operation—and this aspect can be used to appeal to the young and alienated physicians, particularly to women and minorities. It can call forth added support from nurses, pharmacists and other health workers who will see themselves in more visible and useful roles.

Hospital Overhead

There may be some argument with hospital administrators on the issue of the transfer of costs and the imputation of unrealistic overhead in outpatient operations. Let us examine the question seriatim: Hospital operations are geared to provide service to the sickest patient. This means that staff, equipment and supplies have to be kept at a level consistent with this philosophy. Any part of the hospital that is operated as a part of this process has to share that overhead—the OPD being a case in point. Even laboratory and X-ray facilities, designed as they are for inpatient activities, may slow up, confuse and perhaps inflate the cost of the OPD process. If the laboratory or X-ray is run as a part of the inpatient department, even if it is physically separated and designed to fit OPD needs, it will still be charged the composite overhead.

The simplicity of the space and equipment needs of a primary care center will, of necessity, create a lower cost than that same facility under the hospital umbrella. One economist has argued that this line of reasoning only transfers social cost and not actual operational costs. I believe the above approach refutes this argument.

The Team

One important aspect of this design, if it is not already evident, is that the emphasis is not on the individual physician as provider, but on the team. While the patient and the administration may see the physician as the carrier of the ball (recall the experience of the Family Health Maintenance Demonstration at Montefiore Hospital in which no matter how much we emphasized team, the patient always saw the doctor as the "captain" of the team) the use of a team and the encouragement of the team structure as the mainstream of medical care delivery is very important. It makes it possible to mount flexible attacks on delivery when the service demands are heavier than the physician can carry; if the load is such that a physician cannot be obtained, or if there is a "job action" in which the physicians withhold their services and jeopardize the success of the development of the program. Further, if the occasion arises and the program has to be enlarged quickly and physicians are not available, the dilution of the existing structure by adding team members (not doctors) may keep the program afloat. The team, however, has to be educated to work as a team, and this may require a period of orientation both before and during the early days of operation.[11]

Licensing

The power of the city to license ought not to be underestimated. Where the law allows, licensing power should be used to cajole physicians into participation in the program; that is, it should be taken for granted that all physicians will participate if they are to be paid from the common fund. Therefore, if the law assigns the funds to the city for distribution, those physicians who do not pull their weight in helping the program to move ahead will be excluded from reimbursement altogether. However, if the law allows "free choice" in the sense in which we have discussed it, "negative direction" might be utilized—that is, licensing closed for certain areas of the City and open for others—but this avenue needs to be explored carefully.[12] Licensing does offer an opportunity; how much is difficult to estimate without having a law in hand. Certainly, if city people have any hand in designing the law, they should ask for language that permits the city to impose the burden of participation on every physician.

Licensing has to be seen as a flexible tool to be used either as a deterrent or stimulant; as reward or punishment. The state could play a powerful role in this, e.g., state licensing could be predicated on a minimum time of involvement for each physician in some community health activity, somewhat along the lines of HEW regulations of hospital services for the poor. Doctors, after all, are educated at public expense, as hospitals are built with public funds.

Other possible suggestions are: All licenses in the state to be good for only one year in the city and to be renewed annually; all new licenses in the state agree to serve in areas of service needs for the poor; all graduates of New York City medical schools have to serve one year in city-sponsored programs; elimination of special licensing for hospital staff as it is presently practiced, unless the hospital participates in city programs; or, additionally, unless the accredited staff participates in them—thereby making the hospital responsible for appointing to staff only those who serve in city programs. Alternatively, the hospitals might be made responsible for furnishing a quota of physicians out of house staff, or attendings, or both, to fulfill city needs for primary care physicians.[13]

The Consumer: Preparing for the Change

There are two important elements in getting such a program off the ground: (1) to persuade the authorities (and I include here the jaded sophisticates among the professional hierarchies) that it ought to be done, it can be done, and it is feasible within the framework of law, authority and tradition; and (2) that the eventual consumers will understand the program and accept it enthusiastically. The enthusiasm, I may add, may be necessary to persuade the officials to get started!

Once the planning decision is made and steps are being taken to flesh out the pattern, a campaign to educate the public has to be mounted. Representatives (elected or appointed or selected) of the patients to be served must take part. The emphasis has to be on function and not structure. Once people have been made fully aware of the intention of the exercise—then the precise design of the structure of units, federations, specialized consultation centers and emergency service will be elucidated. It would be a serious mistake to go to the people with a "plan." The approach must be through the service rendered. The elements of the plan as described here—and it should be plain that it is an outline; bare bones to be fleshed out in P.L. 93-641 planning bodies—must be communicated with considerable help from consumers as well as professionals, if a real structure is to come out of the pattern.

An Agenda of Issues for Further Exploration Prior to Implementation

1. *Quality control measures and the role of the Health Department:* Record examination by itself is a weak reed and yet records must be

reviewed. It is suggested that the health department perform periodic reviews, but that a particular specialist in a specialist center have a continuing assignment to meet with, visit and consult on cases with each primary care physician.

2. *Worker participation in control and decision-making of unit and federation operations:* Here I am concerned not with policy decisions to be made at the higher administrative levels, and what part the trade unions will play in this, but with the day-to-day operating problems in which workers should have a say along with physicians, and in a partnership of some kind with the patients.

3. *Maximum size of "federations."*

4. *Selection of locations.*

References

[1] 70 percent of doctors expect a fixed fee schedule or forced assignment of fees. *Patient Care*, January 1, 1975.

[2] ". . . to prevent the use of the general acute hospital with its extensive facilities by those who do not need those facilities. . . ." B. Abel-Smith, "Value for Money in Health Services," *Social Security Bulletin*, July 1974, p. 23; see pp. 17–24.

[3] A.E. Miller, "Remodeling the Municipal Health Services for a Unified System of Ambulatory Medical Care in the Central City," *Medical Care*, September–October, 1972, 10:395–401.

[4] Eli Ginzberg et al., "The Implications of National Health Insurance for Ambulatory Care Service in New York City," Task Force on the Impact of National Health Insurance, Regional Medical Program, New York, 1976.

[5] *Ibid.*

[6] P. Andrews, A. Yankauer and J.P. Connelly, "Changing the Patterns of Ambulatory Pediatric Caretaking," *AJPH*, May 1970, 60:870–879.

[7] "Moreover, home nurses and public health nurses increasingly work from doctors' premises—both those that are owned by the practitioners and those that are not." Abel-Smith, "Value for Money," p. 23.

[8] "In each region, one or two regional teaching hospitals are the sole providers of the rarer specialties." *Ibid.*

[9] ". . . . world experience has shown, as the U.S. experience is also beginning to show, the paradox underlying attempts to preserve the free and independent practice of medicine." *Ibid.*, p. 22.

[10] ". . . . in more and more countries it has been accepted that the use of hospitals depends upon the extent and coordination of provisions outside hospitals." *Ibid.*, pp. 24, 25 et seq.

[11] Wise et al., *Making Health Teams Work*. Cambridge: Bollinger, 1974.

[12] "One use of regulation that would at present be unacceptable in the United States but is found in several European countries is restriction on the number of doctors who can practice in a particular area." Abel-Smith, p. 22.

[13] L.C. Ferrow, "Types of Hospital Appointments Held by Physicians in Various Socio-Economic Areas of New York City," *Medical Care*, July-August, 1972, 10:310–322.

Restructuring Maternal and Child Health Services in the City of New York

BETTY J. BERNSTEIN

To prepare this paper data was assembled on: (1) special groups—pregnant women, infants and pre-school children, school-aged children, adolescents; (2) special health needs—family planning, abortion, ambulatory and inpatient care, primary and specialty care, dental care. (Extensive supporting data were included and are in the author's possession).

After analysis of the data, serious deficiencies in the system were found, not the least of which is the lack of accountability. As Mayer noted in 1971, no one agency in the city is responsible for knowing which children are receiving care—of what kind, at what cost, or where—even when public funds pay for it.[1] Not even preventive measures, such as immunizations, are required until children enter school, which is very late. Other major and critical deficiencies are: (1) lack of comprehensive care providing diagnostic and treatment services for every age group except for proportionately few individuals in special programs (the health department's program under the Bureau for physically handicapped children, the Children and Youth [C&Y] projects and pregnant women in the Maternal and Infant Care [MIC] projects); (2) for all age groups and specific services—deficient referral and follow-up mechanisms; (3) no relation between resources in the neighborhoods and boroughs to population needs; (4) absence of reliable cost and other information including little accurate information on numbers of services provided, the amount of manpower and other resources deployed for specific individuals or conditions or their unit costs.

Data are lacking on how many or which children are receiving medical care, or whether it is emergency care only or comprehensive care. For some groups, i.e., those using private practitioners, no New York City statistics are available. For others, such as hospital outpatient clinics, data is mainly kept on visits, not patients. Medicaid can not yet give figures on the numbers of children receiving care, what kind, how much, or at what cost, because data until recently was kept on a head-of-household basis. Thus, an estimate for even the public costs for children's medical care—let alone total costs—would be unreliable.

There is great fragmentation in the system: multiple sources of care; duplication in some cases; misuse of emergency rooms—all wasteful in manpower and money. What is more, it is known from school entrance examinations that many children are not receiving necessary care in pre-school years. The two systems of health care—one for those who can pay and use private practitioners and the other a clinic system for those who cannot pay, are both inadequate—in ensuring quality, comprehensiveness and cost control. We must use restructuring to create one good system of care for all.

A Brief Outline—MCH Services and Government Financing

These gaps in data and in services in New York City exist in 1975 despite the fact that maternal and child health services have a history both in the United States and in New York City of more and earlier governmental-sponsored and financed preventive, diagnostic and treatment programs than any other groups (except the armed forces and veterans). New York City led the way in 1908 when it created the first municipal unit in the world devoted to the health protection of mothers and children.[2]

Through the years the United States Children's Bureau (created in 1912) developed, sponsored, encouraged and financed MCH programs with quality standards throughout the country.[3] The Emergency Maternity and Infant Care Program (EMIC), established during World War II for pregnant wives and infants of servicemen, was successful in requiring standards of care through MCH units in state health departments.[4] MCH and crippled children's programs were encouraged in all the states. With the expansion of Title V of the Social Security Act, the Children and Youth (C&Y) projects, sponsored by medical schools or teaching hospitals, provided comprehensive care to children in defined geographical areas.

Cost Effectiveness of MCH Services

The extensive development of public MCH services is no doubt based on several factors—the humane considerations in assisting helpless children and pregnant women and the cost-effectiveness of preventing, or minimizing, infant disability simultaneously with promoting optimal growth and development of the children.

In 1968, Henry K. Silver stated that, "between 20% and 40% of all children suffer from one or more chronic conditions, and about 30% of these handicapping conditions could be prevented or corrected by comprehensive care during the first five years of life; comprehensive care which was continued to the age of 18 would prevent or correct 60%."[5]

Kessner et al in studying New York City infant mortality data, found that more than 95 percent of the pregnant women with risks can be identified during an initial evaluation. Their data lend support to the concept that prenatal health services do influence pregnancy outcomes. In the mothers in the study with "inadequate" prenatal and maternity care up to 2.82 times higher infant mortality rates occurred than in those with "adequate" care.[6] Maternal and child health services are probably the most cost-effective of all health services since prevention and treatment will affect the future health of the children and thus their capacity for social usefulness. A child allowed to develop a communicable disease (possibly causing an epidemic), or to become blind or incapacitated due to lack of early identification and treatment becomes an unnecessary burden to society.

Primary Prenatal and Pre-School Care—the Priorities

The need to restructure outpatient care for pregnant women, pre-school children and dental services is becoming ever more urgent. New York City data show that the child-bearing population is increasing as the proportion of non-whites and Hispanics (whose fertility rates are higher) increases in the population; similarly, the prematurity rates are higher for non-white and Puerto Rican groups. Evidence of the maldistribution, inadequacy and fragmentation of infant and early childhood primary health resources compared to population and need were assembled by the author. In most areas, there is an inverse correlation between need and resources.

School-aged children and adolescents are not classified as a key risk group since this is a relatively healthy group in which the major problems are psycho-social. The need for some screening and follow-up on school children with known disabilities is accepted. For this group other reports have outlined possible school, health department and community health roles.[7] Family planning and abortion services are omitted because data revealed that only if NHI does not cover abortion or family planning drugs will there be major financial impact. It is presumed that the maternity service proposed will provide family planning services which, if expanded, will meet the unmet family planning need.

Assumptions of NHI Benefits

(1) A NHI law will cover pregnant women and all children with no coinsurance or deductibles. Services to them will have a direct relevance to the future health of the child, which cannot be said for coverage of

some other groups and health services that are being advocated. (In New York City, in the absence of NHI coverage, health services for children will be cut, as is now happening because of the city fiscal crisis.) (2) Parents will be required to provide basic health services for their children, just as is true in compulsory education. (3) The goal will be to organize primary MCH services which will be easily accessible, of high quality, efficient in the use of manpower and with controlled costs. (4) The city will be permitted to set higher standards than those of the federal or state governments, and to provide and monitor primary services in public, regional, or other approved centers. (5) Cost ceilings of some kind will be established. A primary care capitation payment will be mandated or else encouraged. (6) Dental care for children will be included.

Proposal: A Publicly Planned and Monitored Primary Health Program for Prenatal Care and for Pre-School Children to Age Six

In reviewing available data, it seemed to the author that if NHI, with its universal entitlement, is to provide quality, comprehensive services which are accessible and with costs controlled, it will first be necessary to restructure the MCH system in the city for all pre-school children and pregnant women.

The basic recommendation is that the Department of Health of the City of New York be given responsibility, working with New York State and the HSA and its subdivisions, to determine the need for maternity and early childhood primary medical centers in each region; the need to be based on population, age groups, socioeconomic status, etc. The health department would create regional child health centers where each child under six would be registered, using a new medical identification number. The department would be responsible for establishing provider standards, assisting in the creation of primary centers and approving and monitoring them. The primary maternity or child health centers could be either expanded child-health stations, MIC projects, neighborhood family care centers, hospital units established or reorganized for the purpose, HMOs, or new units. Team responsibility for the patients would be encouraged, with follow-up an essential ingredient. Non-emergent and non-urgent visits to other than the primary provider would be discouraged in a variety of ways. Financing on an annual capitation basis is recommended. If, for political reasons, it is necessary, fee-for-service practitioners would be included if they agreed to the standards and to being monitored as other providers.

Difficulties encountered in implementing these proposals will include philosophical differences with the overall concept or with specifics recommended; practical problems in having them implemented; the necessity for cooperation from the state, professional medical groups, hospital associations and consumers; and the need for development of mechanisms to control the system. Revamping of education in health professional schools will be necessary, with emphasis on continuity of care and delivery by teams. Students must be taught how to work as part of a team. Mechanisms must be developed for gathering operational research data and determining the cost-effectiveness of these programs. Comparison of differing pilot programs would be a first step.

It is not now proposed to incorporate these centers into comprehensive family care centers, although this will be possible. The problems in accomplishing the latter are greater and seem less likely of achievement within the near future; furthermore, there has been a far longer history in MCH of organization of services, standard setting and cost controls than in other areas. It would also seem logical to encourage methods of identifying and treating the most vulnerable groups, where future cost-effectiveness is more certain and where reorganization can curtail costs drastically, while improving quality.

1. Health department responsibilities will include: Planning MCH Services—The city will be divided into regions—either using the existing 22 health center districts, combinations of HSA districts or some other combination. Each region will be surveyed for population groups—numbers, ages, ethnicity, socioeconomic status—which will determine the amounts and types of medical and auxiliary (counseling, outreach, follow-up) services needed, available services, and gaps. Areas deficient in specific medical services will be identified. The goal will be the establishment of a sufficient number of diversified prenatal and pre-school primary health centers to meet the needs of each particular neighborhood. Details regarding structure, financing, staffing, and linkages follow. Identification of existing non-profit and public services which are willing to organize in accordance with the standards, organizational features and recommended financing will be made. Areas with no, or few such sources of care, will also be identified and will probably require public services.

2. Setting standards and monitoring them: for all providers, standards will include professional quality medical standards, plus requirements regarding record-keeping, reporting each baby born and its primary provider to the regional center, follow-up, referrals to approved specialists or specialty centers only and affiliation with an approved back-up hospital in pediatrics or obstetrics as the case may be. Approved primary care centers will have additional requirements concerning administration as well as linkages with the emergency service, specialty and inpatient facilities, coverage of its case-load for non-trauma cases at all times and utilization of a consumer advisory board.

The standards will encourage a team approach, utilizing board-certified or eligible pediatricians, obstetricians, and family physicians; certified nurse-midwives and pediatric nurse-practitioners; public health and registered nurses; social workers, nutrition and health education counsellors, psychologists, translators where necessary and auxiliary staff (laboratory, X-ray). A patient ombudsman—full or part-time—should be included, as well as a process for patient grievances.

In-service training at periodic intervals for all staff, particularly all medical staff, will be required so that they may keep abreast of latest developments in their fields. This will occur in part as a result of the inter-site visiting by primary and secondary staff and through case conferences. However, periodic in-service training sessions should be an integral part of the program.

Referrals for consultation for children would be made only to approved specialists, who would be required to send a report back to the primary center prior to reimbursement, if feasible. For certain categories of diagnosis and treatment, reimbursement will only be made to approved centers as is now done under the city health department's handicapped children's program, which requires quality and comprehensive team evaluation and treatment. This should cut down on the unnecessary sub-specialty hospital clinics. Many hospital specialty and sub-specialty clinics are now continued—at great cost—for research, teaching, or prestige value—even though they may not have sufficient patient load to provide good quality care. An option would be to require that each specialty referral be reimbursed only if made by the primary care center, limiting shopping around. It would also curtail the patient's right to more than one opinion.

For certain procedures, the possibility of prior approvals can be explored. A community advisory board should be required to meet city health department guidelines with at least 55 percent of the membership consisting of actual consumers or parents of the children. For the prenatal centers, former patients might be substituted. Linkage with the sub-area councils of the HSA will be developed. Hours, outreach, patient amenities, costs, parent and public information will be prime concerns, although medical care issues will *not* be excluded. The boards should be represented when health department and other auditing takes place. Their advice on unmet needs and patient grievances can be most important. Experience with the city's Consumer Advisory Boards for ambulatory care in voluntary hospitals and clinics and with the Hospitals Corporation Community Boards has shown that they contribute meaningfully and that hospitals can live with them. When all children, as in the schools, are involved, such boards will be more attractive for participation. Prenatal, infant and pre-school health care all have large components of consumer behavior and preventive care factors. Thus consumer input and active involvement are essential in a structured, meaningful way. Since cultural patterns differ regarding use of medical care, it is particularly important to have local area involvement.

Monitoring will include all facilities—public, non-profit, and other. This should include all components—comprehensiveness, quality, staffing, consumer board participation, record review, plant and physical equipment and follow-up. (This is now being done by the health department PSRO teams for the EPSDT and other programs.) Additional features will include notation of non-cooperation by specialists, as well as by other approved primary providers and hospitals, in promptly forwarding summaries of referrals. Such non-cooperation might result in the elimination of the specialty teams or hospitals as a referral source or for NHI reimbursement.

An essential part of the standards and monitoring will be record-keeping, to assure that there is follow-up on all necessary preventive and treatment measures. Computer tracking systems, publicly sponsored but not necessarily publicly operated, could generate risk categories and individuals needing care. For a city with 750,000 pre-school children, where mobility is high, the problems in setting up such a system seem too great at present. Thus, identification of patients and follow-up will be dependent on the regional networks, while experimentation with computerized regional systems can proceed.

To lessen objections to standard-setting and monitoring by the health department, it is suggested that the American Academies of Pediatrics and Family Physicians and the American College of Gynecologists and Obstetricians and their local subdivisions have an active role both in standard-setting and monitoring.

Structure

Regional Centers

Each regional center will be responsible for overall supervision of the facilities in its region and for record-keeping, particularly of the children in the area.

Identification System

Every infant born in the city when given a birth certificate will also receive a medical identification number which will make possible later medical tracking. The health department will establish procedures whereby the child's record is sent to the appropriate regional health

92

facility. The medical number, differentiated from the Social Security number recently required for all Medicaid recipients, will alleviate the risk of jeopardizing confidentiality regarding income and non-health information to health providers. The parent will be given a card with the child's number and the number of the primary provider of child health they have chosen, if known at that time. If not, the latter will be inserted when the child is registered. Since payment for primary care will, optimally, be on a capitation basis, unless the mother changes the child's primary provider (restrictions on numbers of changes may be necessary), other providers will refer the child back to the primary provider, except for emergency care. Such a numerical system will make possible the tracking of children's health care; the assurance that each child receives necessary preventive care, while hopefully reducing or eliminating duplication and fragmentation of care; and elimination of misuse of emergency facilities. Better care and lower costs will result. Also made easier by such a system will be research on delivery, manpower, organization, utilization and costs, as well as health outcomes.

Regional high risk registers for pregnant women and pre-school children would facilitate checking on services, though probably not at the beginning. Thus, care to high risk cases would be monitored as the primary centers are audited. For school children, a risk registry is even more essential, since no recommendations are made here for their primary care. This problem should be addressed by the health department.

Primary Centers

Primary centers can include expanded child health stations and MIC projects, existing or new NFCCs or HMOs, or reorganized facilities operated by approved hospitals. They will provide primary care, with both preventive care and treatment having formal linkages with secondary and tertiary providers. A back-up hospital approved in that specialty will be required. These centers could be operated by the city health department, the New York City Health and Hospitals Corporation (HHC), non-profit hospitals, HIP centers, NFCCs, HMOs or newly formed groups—all within a regional and city plan. Hours and days of service will be flexible to meet community needs. In areas where there are many working mothers, a flexibility in hours and some possible week-end hours will be required. Consultation during evenings and weekends, and phone consultations, must be provided to prevent unnecessary emergency visits. Within each center, a team approach will be encouraged. The physician will supervise the medical care and provide consultation and some direct care, especially for the high-risk patients.

Enrollment of each infant in a child health center will be mandatory, just as school enrollment is for older children. Since it is hoped that most children will be enrolled in a center, each primary care center will have a roster of children for whom it is responsible for primary care, plus those referred for diagnosis or specialized care. Follow-up and outreach will be the responsibility of the center or of other specified agencies. For example, a child needing continued specialty care may receive it from the specialty source, but either the latter or the primary care center must be responsible for the basic preventive measures. The source of care for those not being served directly in the network will be noted in the regional center, which will also maintain and audit more thoroughly the roster of high-risk children, particularly infants.

At present, many of the early childhood centers—family day care, group day care, Headstart, among others—have their own health programs, either on-site or with an outside health provider. Arrangements will have to be made with these centers to accept the evaluation and care of the child's primary center; to require each parent to indicate the child's primary center for reference; and to develop liaison between the two centers. The early childhood centers can easily perform the outreach and follow-up for children enrolled in their centers. This will reduce the duplication of health services now provided for some of these children. Mandatory registration early in pregnancy cannot at this time be required in the United States. However, inducements for early prenatal care can be used as is now done by MIC (e.g., the MIC free pregnancy testing program tested 18.8 percent more women in 1974 than in 1973, directly related to a 30.5 percent registration for prenatal care during the first trimester). Another incentive is the Women, Infants and Children (WIC) supplementary food program available to pregnant women.[8]

Basic to the sound functioning, consumer acceptance, and cost control of prenatal neighborhood centers is the greatly expanded use of certified nurse-midwives as part of the obstetrical team. This is an approach now used by eleven MIC projects, hospitals and ambulatory care units. In other countries—Holland and Denmark, for instance—nurse-midwives are handling 90 percent of the deliveries. England uses them extensively. Midwives can handle most normal, spontaneous deliveries and, up to the last trimester, can care for some of the risk categories. All risk categories noted in the ACOG guidelines would be referred for consultation or treatment by the obstetrician or the hospital specialty service.[9] Nurse-midwives must be graduates of an approved midwivery program, of which there are two in New York City; they should be on the staff of the back-up hospital, so that they may handle their own deliveries; they should be affiliated with a university-sponsored program. Since salaries of nurse-midwives are now about $16,000–$22,000, there would be a large saving in physician cost. Wherever they are used, patient satisfaction is great. The problems will arise in expanding clinical training programs for nurse-midwives and in hospital and physician acceptance of them.

As nurse-midwives relieve the burden of the obstetrician, so well-trained pediatric nurse-practitioners (PNPs) can provide good care and help to solve the problem of pediatric manpower. Many hospital pediatric clinics do not now provide well-baby, i.e., preventive, care. As the attitudes of pediatricians towards providing such care change, so must the pediatric residence training programs encourage interest in such care and train pediatricians to work with nurse practitioners. Yet preventive child health care is essential, and PNPs have shown their ability to perform well. Henry K. Silver, after a year's experience in one Denver child health station, noted that trained pediatric nurse-practitioners could care for 82 percent of the children themselves, with only 18 percent requiring referral to a physician or medical facility.[10] Andrews et al. also demonstrated their use in a primary pediatric ambulatory care setting, as have De Angelis and others.[11] The key to the optimal operation of nurse-practitioners seems to be in their relationship with supervising pediatricians during their period of internship.

While our first choice would be to require parents to enroll their children only in those facilities approved as meeting all the standards (similar to the approval of schools licensed by the state), this may not be politically feasible. Care, then, could be allowed by other certified family practitioners, pediatricians and obstetricians, but only if the provider agrees to send to the regional health center the data that the city requires (such as immunizations and other preventive measures for children and a list of high-risk children and pregnant women).

Monitoring hundreds or thousands of non-center primary providers will undoubtedly create problems, but cases might be monitored on a sample basis, using the data sent to the regional registrar. The issue of "decertifying" for reimbursement those who do not report or whose care does not meet standards will have to be addressed.

Linkages

Noted under "Standards" are the affiliations which will be required in each primary center-specialty services, community hospital, secondary and tertiary care facilities and other agencies such as social agencies and early childhood centers which might do outreach and assist in follow-up. In order to make these linkages real rather than theoretical, specific formal agreements should be encouraged and in some cases mandated. These will be enhanced by mechanisms such as joint staff appointments, case conferences, supervisory responsibilities, some joint staff meetings, and on-site visits in both directions. The new Health Systems Agency and its sub-area councils should assist both in developing and implementing linkage systems for specific committees. One of the major problems now, a very costly one, is the lack of such linkages and the resulting duplication of tests, procedures, and even immunizations. (As a Columbia University study showed in only 18 percent of hospital OPD cases reviewed was there transferral of information back to the child health station).

Emergency Services

George A. Silver, in his ambulatory care paper for the task force,[13] has recommended an emergency service in each borough to which ambulances would bring trauma cases 24 hours a day. In addition to this, for prenatal cases and young children, more specific telephone advice and walk-in service is necessary and will need to be developed for each center and region. When primary care centers are closed coverage will be available within each region or even in the primary center. Patients enrolled in a center or with a primary provider will be referred back to them for non-urgent or non-emergent care. Within each regional center and perhaps each primary center where necessary, use of special patient counseling programs for those who misuse the ER will be possible.

Specialty Care

The health department's Bureau for Handicapped Children now establishes standards for the diagnosis and treatment of children with various types of handicaps and chronic diseases. It also operates certain free diagnostic clinics. This program, which includes comprehensive standards, has operated successfully to assure quality diagnosis and treatment for children with suspected or actual conditions. Though specialty care is not the subject of this paper, standards and methodology of this program should be utilized where possible in eliminating poor quality and non-comprehensive care.

Outreach and Consumer Behavior will be integral to the success of the proposal. Patient motivation to utilize facilities correctly must be encouraged by a variety of means, including provider education.

Financing

An annual capitation fee set according to formula, including cost for the primary health care of each child, would be set for each center. George Silver has recommended that if hospitals choose to operate a primary center, their reimbursement should not include hospital overhead, since hospitals exist primarily for the seriously ill who require esoteric, expensive equipment, staffing and services.[14] Primary care does not require these services and therefore their costs should not be included. Similarly, a fee for maternity care, including pre and post-partum care should be set. This would not include hospital costs or specialty care. Centers would reimburse physicians and some other personnel on a salary, capitation, or session basis. One positive aspect of the capitation fee would be reimbursement for service by non-physicians. Most federal, non-profit and commercial insurers do not reimburse for such care now. Follow-up and health education costs will be included in the capitation amount, if federal and state law and regulations allow. It is unlikely that outreach will be so covered. Therefore, some city or state funds will be necessary for this vital component.

Since one of the objectives of the plan would be to discourage solo private practice and inadequate care, such as that provided in many "Medicaid mills," and since required standards for these providers might be lower than for primary centers, the capitation reimbursement would also be lower. Fee-for-service payments, only if required by the NHI law, will be allowed. It is hoped, however, that the financial incentives of the capitation formula and the required standards will serve to discourage solo practitioners and "Medicaid mills."

Constraints, Questions and Possible Answers

1. Should the city be given broad responsibility to mandate registration, establish standards of primary care for each child under six and for pregnant women, and to monitor this care? There is need for assuring good, basic preventive and treatment services for pregnant women and young children in New York City, and for one agency to be responsible for this function and to monitor its services. The city health department has had extensive experience with direct provision of MCH services, standard-setting and monitoring, and would seem to be the most logical agency to assume the new function. A new agency would seem wasteful in view of the experience of the health department. This expanded responsibility will require the cooperation of the New York State Department of Health, HSA, providers—both institutional and professional—and consumers. Unless the type of registration and monitoring outlined is carried through, there will be no assurance that the large amount of additional funds which will be available through NHI will result in essential services being provided to each child and pregnant woman, with quality assured, and cost controlled.

The New York City Health Department has a Deputy Commissioner for Professional Standards and Review, whose teams audit health department services, including EPSDT, as well as the services of outside providers. The department's Bureau of Ambulatory Care Evaluation and Institutional Review Unit has also been monitoring and evaluating ambulatory services in voluntary and municipal hospitals, HIP centers and free-standing units. The EPSDT experience has shown that in-depth audit can be made and tabulated, and steps taken to upgrade deficient centers. However, as outlined here, the increased number of centers to be audited may create difficulties, especially if private practitioners are included. Problems will also arise from the increased bureaucracy necessary to monitor, and from possible conflicts and duplication with PSROs, professional bodies and state and federal agencies. The alternative would be a multitude of private monitoring bodies in which case accountability would vanish. Having one agency responsible, however, will make possible the continuous evaluation of the organizational arrangements, standards, utilization, costs and health care outcomes.

2. Is the city the most effective resource to establish neighborhood networks of prenatal and pre-school primary health services and to operate some of them? Yes. The new HSA and its sub-area councils—all representing government, providers and consumers—will be intimately involved in the planning and implementation of neighborhood networks, but the primary centers should remain under one organization. Different auspices are possible as long as standards are met. The city health department now operates child health stations including pediatric treatment centers and, by contract, the MIC centers. The HHC operates some neighborhood family care centers.

New York City bureaucratic problems (finance and civil service are but two) are real and must be addressed. While recognizing the need for one umbrella organization, it would be possible to approve voluntary primary care centers, with the city limited to planning, organization, standard-setting and monitoring. What will happen in the case when no group will organize a center where the need is great? Since financing will be from the federal government, it should be possible to overcome city budget and civil service restraints and to establish centers where they are needed.

The health department's Bureau of Child Health has lately been able to attract young, well qualified pediatricians. Staffing may be a problem, but with free-standing, hospital-affiliated neighborhood centers, the incentive for physicians to join would be there. Inducements for physicians to associate with publicly operated centers will include: a higher salary or session payment than now paid by the city (which will be possible under NHI); the physician's desire for linkage with secondary and tertiary medical facilities; regular in-service training and possible appointment in hospitals.

With the team approach, the physician will be relieved of many of the routine functions which many of them consider boring. If certified nurse-midwives and pediatric nurse-associates are used, it is estimated that they can care for about 80 percent and 82 percent respectively, of the normal prenatal and primary child health care cases, with physicians available. Thus the physician's status as supervisor or consultant, with the benefits outlined above, will be attractive. He or she will also be relieved of some of the pressures which pediatricians and obstetricians must now endure, such as long hours on call and difficulties of admininstering an office, among others. Some of these considerations will also apply to non-profit centers and will act as inducements to private practitioners to affiliate with such centers.

3. Can total free choice be eliminated and team care mandated? If the goal is to assure quality and control cost, complete free choice and shared health facilities should be discouraged in different ways. The main problems will occur with those who now utilize solo practice private physicians. It is hoped that the pressure to obtain NHI reimbursement (and to control costs) together with the assurance of accessibility, availability, comprehensiveness and quality will convince consumers to give up total free choice. A choice, then, would be made among physicians and other personnel within a group, and between approved groups in each region. (As noted earlier, if not politically feasible, approved private practitioners could be used, as long as they meet standards, including child registration.) Since capitation payments would not cover all auxiliary costs in individual settings it might mean the approval or reimbursement of shared health facilities, if they are not otherwise controlled. One option would be to require all such groups of physicians to meet the primary center requirements. It is doubtful, however, that shared health facilities would accept either the capitation payments or the other requirements.

Team care can be mandated only for centers. Some physicians and institutions may object to the use and roles assigned to pediatric nurse-practitioners and certified nurse-midwives. The lack of licensure in New York State for PNPs is a restraint. Hopefully, additional training programs, licensure and proper internship will lead to acceptance. Other elements of the team concept such as the use of public health nursing service, social work and nutrition counselling and staff for follow-up are essential to yield the desired health-system results.

4. State vs. City: standard setting, capitation, and reimbursement. Until 1971 (Section 228, Public Health Law), the city was exempted from the New York State Sanitary Code although in many instances the city's

standards were higher and their programs more extensive than the state's. The present language of subdivision (3) allows for local regulations which comply with minimum standards of the state or are not in conflict with state regulations. There may need to be legislation allowing the city specific powers to establish its own standards no lower than those of the state. Recent experience with state standards and enforcement for nursing homes and with city standards and enforcement for EPSDT providers would seem to indicate that the city is capable of setting and monitoring standards.

Some fee-for-service for children may, regretfully, be necessary but cost ceilings seem inevitable. Any fee-for-service reimbursements should discourage their use, especially since the center capitation payment will cover a broader range of services. Federal and state cooperation and negotiation will be essential in setting the variable reimbursements for children, either through fee-for-services or capitation payments through the centers. For infants, pre-school children and pregnant women there has been experience with team approaches and capitation payments— MIC, EPSDT, EMIC. EMIC paid on a total maternity case rate for pre and postnatal care and delivery, no matter what the complications. Thus it can be done. In these two areas of primary care, standards of care exist, as do estimates of cost.

In light of the general escalation of medical care costs, financing problems must be faced. There are two areas of primary care—for pregnant women and for infants and pre-school children—where preventive care is an essential, large component of the service, and where standards of care and estimates of cost in organized settings already exist. This is the obvious place for the city to begin adjusting to the law as needed in order to accomplish specific goals for these two groups. Free-standing clinics, operated by hospitals, but without hospital overhead, could be reimbursed on a capitation basis, if approved. It is probable that an NHI law will allow, or even prefer, capitation payments. The capitation formula could be calculated by the state. A constraint here is that the New York State Health Department has so far been unwilling to set differential rates for various parts of the state. This would be desirable for New York City in order to attract teaching-hospital physicians with higher salaries to the centers.

5. Will these proposals inhibit the family care objectives? Coordinated family care is a goal which has not yet been attained for the majority of New York City families in either private or public sector. For those groups most at risk, where extensive gaps in service and accountability exist in New York City, and where cost-effectiveness is great, the primary prenatal and pre-school primary centers are a beginning. They could be a part of neighborhood family care centers if the latter were to

meet the previously established standards and accept the capitation grants. There will be pressure for them to do so as part of their comprehensive care.

6. Hospital opposition to these proposals? Providers, private practitioners and institutions may object, as most of us do, to efforts to reorganize or to control them. As noted, independent, free-standing providers will be reimbursed as long as they meet standards and keep records on a regional and center basis. Hospitals which now operate general pediatric and obstetric clinics, and which need the patient load to maintain specialty accreditation, may have problems if they are not designated as approved centers. However, the concept here is that primary prenatal and pre-school health services must be accessible and available in the neighborhoods where people can easily use them, and they must be organized to meet patients' needs.

The hospital power base centers in the chiefs of service who are primarily concerned with complicated cases, research and training. Patient needs and cost control are secondary. This power base must be shifted to the public-interest sector if we are to reform the system. As Abel-Smith notes, the present nature of the free health market can lead not only to excessive, unnecessary costs, but also to loss of quality and lessened promotion of social values.[15] Asnes and Novick have stated that the functions of the pediatric outpatient clinic remain primarily determined by institutional orientation, tradition and constraints; such clinics are not suitable for training future physicians. They recommend a restructuring of the clinics with patients offered enrollment within a modular practice.[16]

If hospital clinics are reorganized to meet the standards, they, too, could receive the capitation fee for pregnant women or children. Specialty services could remain in hospital centers, but there would be fewer of them reimbursed and on a new, non-hospital cost basis. Some hospitals could be contracted with to operate or provide supervision or neighborhood primary care centers and some would be the back-up hospital for primary centers.

7. Mandatory registration, and record-keeping: is it possible? The medical identification number which will be available only to medical authorities, and which lists only the child's name, primary care resource, and possibly, his risk group, would protect major requirements for privacy. There will be problems in establishing an efficient numerical system for each child with the health provider in order to allow for changes in the latter. A major problem may arise from the mobility of families, particularly in the low income groups. However, unavailability of walk-in emergency services will discourage non-registration when families move. Records in each primary center will yield valuable data on

quality, services, needs, health problems, utilization, manpower and costs—data which are now not available anywhere.

8. Problems concerning certified nurse-midwives and pediatric nurse-practitioners: nurse-midwives as an integral part of hospital obstetrical teams may not be accepted in some hospitals. Six of the MIC affiliated hospitals do not now accept them. Until sufficient numbers of nurse-midwives can be trained this will not be a major problem. Obstetricians themselves, however, are generally enthusiastic about being relieved of the routine cases, but if the birthrate continues to decline, resistance may come from the obstetrician-gynecologists in New York City—896 office-based and full-time hospital staff in 1973.[17] New York State education law should be modified to allow nurse-midwives to prescribe from a circumscribed list of medications. Sections 6521, 6902, 6909 and 6512 of the state education law define the practice of medicine to include prescribing and make it a crime for nurses to practice medicine. Some foreign countries allow midwives to prescribe certain drugs, including narcotics, which are frequently necessary in delivery. Since the expanded role of midwife—including delivery—is stressed, legal change is necessary.

Pediatric nurse-practitioners are not yet licensed in New York State. There is a lack of clarity as to physicians' or institution's liability for their work, and PNPs cannot sign prescriptions. In some set-ups, they operate under "standing orders." The Academy of Pediatrics and American Nurses' Association are now considering standards for licensure of PNPs. The New York City health department school and child health programs as well as some hospitals and free standing clinics are utilizing such personnel now. After training, highly competent supervision for PNPs is essential, as is the on-going close relationships with pediatricians and hospitals if they are to make the greatest contribution possible.

In reviewing available data, it seemed to the author that if NHI, with its universal entitlement, is to provide quality, comprehensive services which are accessible and with costs controlled, it will first be necessary to restructure the MCH system in the city for all pre-school children and pregnant women.

The basic recommendation is that the Department of Health of the City of New York be given responsibility, working with New York State and the HSAs and its subdivisions, to determine the need for maternity and early childhood primary medical centers in each region; the need to be based on population, age groups, socio-economic status, etc. The health department would create regional child health centers where each child under six would be registered, using a new medical identification number. The department would be responsible for establishing provider standards, assisting in the creation of primary centers and approving and monitoring them. The primary maternity child health centers could be either expanded child-health stations, MIC projects, neighborhood family care centers, hospital units established or reorganized for the purpose, HMOs or new units. Team responsibility for the patients would be encouraged, with follow-up an essential ingredient. Non-emergent and non-urgent visits to other than the primary provider would be discouraged in a variety of ways. Financing on an annual capitation basis is recommended. If, for political reasons it is necessary, fee-for-service practitioners would be included if they agreed to the standards and to being monitored as other providers.

Difficulties encountered in implementing these proposals will include philosophical differences with the overall concept or with specifics recommended; practical problems in having them implemented; the necessity for cooperation from the state, professional medical groups, hospital associations and consumers; and the need for development of mechanisms to control the system. Revamping of education in health professional schools will be necessary, with emphasis on continuity of care and delivery by teams. Students must be taught how to work as part of a team. Mechanisms must be developed for gathering operational research data and determining the cost-effectiveness of these programs. Comparison of differing pilot programs would be a first step.

Conclusion

As Yankauer state, "Children are not little adults. They have special needs stemming from their growth and development and their future human resource potential."[18] They need preventive and health-related services, not merely a "simplistic medical model" for the future protection of all children. The author believes that the proposals are reasonable, possible and would be cost-effective.

References

[1] Shirley A. Mayer, "Child Health Issues in New York," *City Almanac*, Center for New York City Affairs, The New School for Social Research, October, 1971.

[2] Leona Baumgartner, "One Hundred Years of Health: New York City, 1866–1966," *Bulletin of the New York Academy of Medicine* (second series), 45:6 June 1969, pp. 555–586.

[3] For an excellent history of the U.S. Children's Bureau see Dorothy E. Bradbury, *Five Decades of Action for Children* (revised edition 1963) U.S., H.E.W., Social Security Administration, Children's Bureau.

[4] Nathan Sinai, *E.M.I.C., A Study of Administrative Experience*, University of Michigan Bureau of Public Health Economics: Research Series No. 3, 1948.

[5] Henry K. Silver, "Use of New Types of Allied Health Professionals in Providing Care for Children," *American Journal of Diseases of Children* 116, November 1968, pp. 486–490.

[6] David M. Kessner, Project Director, *Infant Death: An Analysis by Maternal Risk and Health Care*, National Academy of Sciences, Institute of Medicine, 1973, pp. 6–7, Tables 1–2.

[7] *Change is Overdue*, Citizens' Committee for Children of New York, April 1974.

[8] *Progress Report 1974* and data submitted by staff, New York City Department of Health, Maternity, Infant Care-Family Planning Projects.

[9] *Standards for Obstetric-Gynecologic Services, 1974*, American College of Obstetricians and Gynecologists, Chicago, Illinois.

[10] Henry K. Silver, "Use of New Types of Health Professionals."

[11] See Priscilla Andrews, Alfred Yankauer and John P. Connelly, "Changing the Patterns of Ambulatory Pediatric Caretaking: An Action-Oriented Training Program for Nurses," *American Journal of Public Health* 60:5 May 1970, pp. 870–879 and Yankauer, Tripp, Andrews and Connelly, "The Outcomes and Services Impact of a Pediatric Nurse Practitioner Training Program—Nurse Practitioner Training Outcomes," *American Journal of Public Health* 62:3 March 1972, pp. 347–353.

[12] Karen R. Dickinson, Russell S. Asnes and Lloyd F. Novick, *"The Referral Process: An Indicator of the Relationship Between a Child Health Station and Urban Hospital"* (Columbia University Faculty of Medicine, Center for Community Health Systems, September 1974).

[13] George A. Silver, "Proposal for City Action in Dealing with Ambulatory Medical Care Under National Health Insurance" (Task Force on the Impact of National Health Insurance, New York Regional Medical Program, June 1975).

[14] Silver, "Proposal for City Action in Ambulatory Care."

[15] Brian Abel-Smith, "Value for Money in Health Services," *Social Security Bulletin* 37:7 July 1974, pp. 17–28.

[16] Lloyd F. Novick and Russell Asnes, "The Urban Pediatric Outpatient Clinic: A Changing Role" (Columbia University Center for Community Health Systems. Unpublished, undated).

[17] Charles Brechner, Karen Brudney, Miriam Ostow, "The Implications of National Health Insurance for Ambulatory Care Services in New York City" (Task Force on the Impact of National Health Insurance, New York Regional Medical Program, April 1975, Table 6).

[18] Alfred Yankauer, Statement before Sub-committee on Oversight and Investigations, Committee on Interstate and Foreign Commerce, U.S. House of Representatives, October 8, 1975. Unpublished.

Nursing Home Care in New York

FREDERICK O'R. HAYES

Nursing home care occupies a peculiar place in health care, beset by more anomalies and ambiguities than any other health care component. The nursing home, in virtually all of its varying forms is, first of all, not so much a health care facility as an institution for the aged. Its most important services are the supervision and physical assistance it provides for those with limited capacity for autonomous functioning due to the physical and mental infirmities of old age. Health care and treatment are secondary. The nursing home, in fact, bears a stronger resemblance in its service structure to the infants' home than it does to the acute care hospital.

The nursing home also has a unique place in the current system of public financing and in the various proposals for national health insurance. Nursing home care is the only service for which Medicaid now provides nearly universal coverage. On the other hand, a review of the various health insurance bills proposed to date provides strong evidence that long term care is the health service most likely to be omitted from whatever national health insurance bill is ultimately enacted. This has important fiscal implications for state and local governments since the cost of nursing home care under Medicaid is already very substantial and has been increasing more rapidly than any other health care component.

Despite numerous exceptions, it is not unfair to say that the nursing home in America has historically and traditionally been substandard. The typical nursing home has been housed in a structure converted from residential or other uses, often inappropriate for institutional use, and usually with serious structural and safety deficiencies. The services provided were minimal, and the health care limited largely to medication and diets prescribed for those patients under regular attendance by a physician. The underlying cause was, of course, economic. The barely acceptable nursing home would require an annual outlay per patient in 1976 dollars of perhaps $4,000 to $6,000, an amount beyond the means of most patients or their families. Still, it is less than half the average current cost of skilled nursing home care in New York State today.

Medicare and Medicaid changed that situation by providing, for the first time, a substantial flow of public dollars to support nursing home care. The initial Medicare policies were later revised to limit support to those patients needing convalescent care after discharge from a hospital for only a limited time period. The burden since has fallen almost entirely on Medicaid, which now supports about 80 percent of the patients in New York State's nursing homes.

Although Medicaid applied the same income standards to determine eligibility for nursing homes as for any other type of health care, a far larger proportion of the elderly than of any other age group has come under the prescribed ceilings. In addition, the elimination of responsibility by law for the support of the aged by their offspring meant that the aged would be judged on the basis of their income and resources. For those who entered nursing homes as private patients with the income or resources to pay the bill, the high cost of care (now averaging about $15,000 per year in New York State) would exhaust the resources of most, often in a matter of months.

With the stimulus of Medicare and Medicaid, the effective demand for beds exceeded the available supply. The state initiated a program of low-interest loans to non-profit institutions for the construction of nursing homes. With the known factor of Medicaid support for patients, operators of proprietary nursing homes were then able to obtain loans for the construction of new nursing homes from commercial sources, both with and without FHA loans. In the ten year period, 1965–1975, the number of skilled nursing home beds in New York State increased by about 65 percent.

At the same time, the state established policies that were certain to increase both the quality and cost of nursing home care. Instead of the flat, low maximum rate for nursing home care used in most states, New York elected to use a cost-based reimbursement system and to couple that with new minimum requirements, e.g., hours of nursing care per patient day under Article 48 of the hospital code.

Ten years after Medicaid, New York's nursing homes are everything that money will buy. They are by far the most expensive nursing homes in the nation; the most richly staffed with the highest paid employees and, coincidentally, with the highest proportion of rip-offs and abuses by operators of nursing homes of any state in the union. The average quality of care should be, and in fact probably is, the best in the nation, but in the worst institutions it is undeniably bad despite its cost. While the state opened its coffers to the most generous Medicaid nursing home plan in the nation, it has never devoted the resources nor developed the attitudes and the analytical thinking which are needed for the surveillance and control that would make the new system honest and effective.

It should be emphasized that Medicaid solved some of the historic problems of nursing homes by closing inadequate and unsafe structures and by beefing up underfinanced service levels. A large proportion, probably most, of the current problems of abuse and substandard performance are new ones, often occurring in facilities built since 1965 and owned by persons new to nursing home operation.

In addition to the problems of cost and quality, there are also the problems posed by the difficulty of developing and applying consistent standards for admission to nursing homes and for determining which of the two categories of nursing home is appropriate in each case. There is considerable evidence of misplacement, with more patients in nursing homes, and more in the highest service-skilled nursing facilities than patient condition would warrant.

The New York metropolitan region can be regarded as the center of the state's problems. Over half the suitable nursing home beds are in New York City and the three northern suburban counties. Within this region and the Nassau-Suffolk region costs are by far the highest, projected bed needs (according to the Moreland Commission) most questionable, and abuses most rampant.

The Classification of Nursing Homes

The Skilled Nursing Facility

Federal law on Medicaid and Medicare has specified the categories of nursing home care. These categories are carried through in state law and regulation under Article 48 of the hospital code.

The Skilled Nursing Facility (SNF) was defined for both Medicaid and Medicare by the Social Security Amendments of 1972 as an institution providing those services ". . . which are or were required to be given an individual who needs or needed on a daily basis skilled nursing care (provided directly by or requiring the supervision of skilled nursing personnel) or other rehabilitation services which as a practical matter can only be provided in a Skilled Nursing Facility on an inpatient basis."

The purpose of the amendment was to impose a stricter definition, not merely on the nursing facility, but also on the patients eligible to be admitted to such facilities. The expectation of the Congress was that this provision would reduce Medicaid nursing home costs through the relocation or reclassification of SNF patients not requiring that level of care. The patients not requiring SNF care would be relocated in less expensive intermediate care facilities. At the same time a medical audit provision was added to insure that SNF patients would not be placed in intermediate care facilities. In addition, the Professional Standards Review Organizations (PSROs) were given the authority to review the appropriateness of a patient's admission to an SNF, as well as his length of stay.

Intermediate Care Facilities (Health Related Facilities)

The best working definition for an intermediate care facility (ICF) (in New York State called a health-related facility (HRF)) is a nursing home that does not meet the requirements for skilled nursing facilities. The ICF was first defined in the 1967 amendments to the Social Security Act which made the ICF a benefit for the recipients of public assistance but not for other Medicaid patients. The apparent purposes of the legislation were two-fold: (1) to provide a less expensive alternative to the skilled nursing facility; and (2) to provide a means of retaining facilities unable to meet the about-to-be imposed standards for skilled nursing facilities. The ICFs, under this provision, literally became "everything else." They were brought into Medicaid as an optional benefit and made subject to Medicaid regulation by P.L. 92-223 in 1971. That legislation defines the ICF as providing on a regular basis health-related care and services ". . . to individuals who do not require the degree of care and treatment which a hospital or skilled nursing home is designed to provide but who because of their mental or physical condition require care and services (above room and board) which can be made available to them only through institutional facilities."

The ICF-HRF is what might be called a "barely health-related facility," but the still recent Medicaid regulations treat it, perforce, as a health care institution. There are requirements for physician supervision and for registered nurses and pharmacists to oversee and consult with ICF staff. Social services, activities programs, and standard dietary services are required, but may be provided by contract rather than in-house.

Domiciliary Care Institutions

A third category, the domiciliary care institution, is, in effect, a home for the aged with no pretensions to status as a health institution. It is not eligible for Medicaid reimbursement. For those in these institutions eligible for such assistance, the federal government pays $386.70 per month under the Supplemental Security Income program, with all but the federal contribution of $157.70 shared between the state and local government. Most of these institutions are private proprietary homes for adults (PPHAs). The differences between PPHAs and HRFs are often minor. Inclusion of the PPHAs completes the spectrum of residential institutions devoted primarily to the aged.

How Many Beds?

There can be little doubt that, in 1965, at the initiation of Medicaid and Medicare, there were far too few nursing home beds of adequate quality in New York State, in the New York metropolitan area or in the nation. There had been a huge increase in the total population age 65 and older between 1950 and 1960. By 1975, the elderly in New York City numbered 980,000 compared to 605,000 in 1950. In the three northern suburban counties, they had increased from 62,000 to 126,000 and in Nassau-Suffolk, from 68,000 to 204,000. Moreover, the economic support for nursing home care had not been sufficient even before the surge in our older population to build enough beds or beds of sufficiently high quality.

During the last decade, the situation has changed drastically. The rise in the over-65 population has slackened. In New York City, the total elderly population is expected to actually decline after 1980. At the same time, the supply of beds has been greatly expanded with the support of Medicaid-financed patients and the additional help of a state loan program for voluntary institutions.

The planning estimates of the state health department call for substantial further expansion to provide 53,802 skilled nursing facility and health-related facility bed needs to meet New York City's 1979 requirements. This may be compared with the average 1974 census of 30,029 in New York City nursing homes.

Control on admission to nursing homes has been inadequate and, here and elsewhere, almost every probe into patient characteristics identifies some significant proportion of patients in nursing homes that do not require nursing home care, as well as skilled nursing facility patients who would be more properly placed at the lower level health-related facility. Nor is it likely that there is any substantial number of elderly persons living at home who need the services of a nursing home; surveys of the elderly population in both Rochester, New York, and Durham, North Carolina, reached that conclusion.

These data suggest that even current usage of nursing homes is likely to overstate needs. They cast even more substantial doubt on the validity of the health department estimates for 1979. The issue is an important one. Nursing home beds, like hospital beds, tend to be occupied if they are available. Each 1,000 additional beds increases annual expenditures at current occupancy rates by $15 million per annum. A nursing home population of 50,000 would represent at 1974 rates an annual carrying cost of about $750 million, 90 percent of which would be borne by Medicaid.

The Moreland Act Commission has applied factors from the Rochester survey to each of the state's counties. The results for New York City suggest that the current bed inventory is likely to be sufficient without further expansion to meet 1979 needs.

Any estimate of needs under current conditions must be regarded as something of a guess dependent upon assumptions with respect to key facts in the characteristics of the population at risk. Over the longer run, unnecessary nursing home care can be minimized and the data developed to supply better planning factors. A central admission and control referral service for each county, perhaps built upon the Monroe County model, is probably the best means of doing this. It demands more clearcut criteria for placement and a superior, standardized patient assessment form. With more rigorous and consistent admission standards, the data resulting from these operations would be a major input into the planning operations of the new Health Systems Agencies.

The Cost of Nursing Home Care in New York State

The New York State Department of Health sets rates of reimbursement for nursing homes annually by applying an inflationary factor to the reported actual costs for the second prior year. For example, the 1976 rates are based on reported 1974 costs with an upward adjustment for the estimated effect of inflation between the two years. Some base year costs may be disallowed by virtue of not being reasonably related to patient care. In addition, if a sponsor incurs added costs through the elimination of a deficiency identified by the department's survey teams, or more commonly, if higher wage rates result from a collective bargaining agreement, then the rates for individual homes may be adjusted upon the sponsor's application.

Homes are grouped by ownership, region and size. About 35 groups are used. The state will not include in the reimbursement base that part of overall per diem costs (excluding property costs, return of equity, drugs and therapy) over 13 percent above the group average. Similarly, costs for administration and dietary and housekeeping services taken together are not allowed to the extent that they exceed the group average by 10 percent.

The use of a cost basis for reimbursement has marked effects upon costs. From 1967 to 1975, average Medicaid rates of reimbursement increased by 165 percent for proprietary homes and by 146 percent for voluntary homes; over the same period the consumer price index for the New York State area increased by 64 percent while, nationwide, acute hospital costs went up 133 percent.

The average cost per diem in 1974 in a sample of 145 skilled nursing facilities was $40.62; in a reduced sample of 52 homes, per diem costs ranged from a low of $21.16 to a high of $72.85. This may be contrasted with a maximum rate during the same period of $18.42 in California under the MediCal program, and of about $21 under the Connecticut Medicaid program.

There are three factors contributing to the difference in costs between New York and other states. The first is real property cost. This is higher in

New York, partly because of the high costs of the metropolitan region, but more probably due to the debt-service costs on the number of new nursing homes built in New York under the stimulus of cost-based Medicaid reimbursement. The average property cost is $5.02 per patient day, but the reduced sample shows a variation from a low of $1.09 to a high of $12.40. The former is presumably a fully depreciated older facility and the latter a recently constructed home reflecting high recent construction and interest costs. (The issues in property cost reimbursement are complex; the Moreland Commission has devoted Volume 2 of its report to that issue.)

The second factor is the average level of wages. The minimum weekly wage for unionized health workers in New York City is now $183 per week or $9,516 per year. This is approximately $2\frac{1}{4}$ times the minimum of a decade ago. That increase is significantly in excess of the rise over the same period in the consumer price index. Differential rates of unionization are probably responsible for the fact that wages for health workers in the highest wage county are 86 percent above those in the lowest. It is clear, then, that one important result of New York's cost-based reimbursement system has been a major improvement in real wages of nursing home workers. Certainly, increases of this magnitude cannot have occurred in states which have low per diem ceilings. Indeed, the most likely effect of the ceiling approach is that nursing home workers in the affected states received wage gains somewhat less than the cost-of-living increases during that period.

The higher wage level may have had some impact upon patient care by attracting personnel of higher quality. This is an arguable proposition, more likely to be true over the long run than in the short term. However, the overall range of increases raises some serious questions. The wage-rate increases were negotiated between nursing home operators and unions, with an awareness on both sides that the reimbursement policy of the government, the industry's major customer, would cover the cost of the settlement. The government, for its part, has taken a passive stance in accepting the fiction that the negotiations took place between two private parties on the basis of the economics of private sector business. This contrasts with the tough attitude the state has taken in negotiations with its own employees. (The state's recent decision to freeze nursing home rates has led nursing home operators to argue that scheduled wage increases under existing collective bargaining contracts could not be met. In one case, an arbitrator has held against the operators.)

The third contributor to New York State's higher costs is in the richer staffing and service in its nursing homes. This is most evident in the size of the nursing staff in relation to the number of patients. New York has imposed a requirement that skilled nursing homes provide at least $2\frac{1}{2}$

hours of nursing care per patient-day or, alternatively, 4 hours per bedfast patient, 2 hours per semi-ambulatory patient, and 1 hour per ambulatory patient. It has accepted for reimbursement even substantially higher nurse-patient ratios, especially in the voluntary homes.

The average cost per diem of the nursing staff (excluding fringe benefits) in 145 skilled nursing facilities in 1974 was $13.93, or just about one-third of total costs. The reduced sample shows a variation among 52 homes from a low of $5.87 to a high of $23.34, a variation that must reflect differences in staffing as well as in average salaries. Staffing patterns confirm this conclusion. If we convert each reported member of the nursing staff to annual man-hours of work on the basis of 230 eight-hour days per year, the calculated number of nursing hours per patient-day varies from 0.2–2.5 hours in the lowest quintile to 4.1–8.7 hours in the high quintile. The median is 3.1 hours per patient day. Hence four-fifths of New York State's SNFs provide more nursing staff than the $2\frac{1}{2}$-hour requirement.

There is little doubt that more is better. A nursing home with 4 nursing hours per patient per day will, almost certainly, provide better service to patients than one with only $2\frac{1}{2}$ hours in daily nursing time per patient per day. Yet the end result is to create several classes of skilled nursing facilities without corresponding classification of patients' needs for different levels of service. A statistical analysis showed no correlation between the average hours of nursing time per patient and the proportion of patients who were either bedfast or quasi-ambulatory, and who thus presumably needed more care than ambulatory patients. It is worth carrying the relationship between patient needs and nursing resources one step further and noting that, even if nursing hours per patient were identical in all facilities, there would still be great imbalances because of the large variations in patient mix. The average proportion of non-ambulatory patients in the reduced sample was 33 percent, but the standard deviation embracing two-thirds of all the cases is approximately ±16 percent—the range, hence, extending from 17 percent to 49 percent. The issue is important. The New York State Department of Health alternative formula suggests that a bedfast patient requires four times as much nursing time as an ambulatory patient and twice as much as a quasi-ambulatory patient.

The matter is also important because it is a major public expenditure policy issue. If the median figure of 3.1 nursing hours from our sample is assumed to be an average, the six-tenths of an hour per patient per day over the required $2\frac{1}{2}$ hours represents, at the minimum New York metropolitan rate, about $1,000 per patient-year and over $70 million annually in program costs.

The level and variation in dietary costs casts a somewhat different light on the cost issue since differences are less related to concepts of nursing home operation. Average costs per patient-day were $5.54 and the range, in the reduced sample, was from $2.79–$11.85. Even the costs of raw food varied from $1.09–$7.15 per patient-day with a median of $2.17. One might doubt the nutritional adequacy of the diet provided at the lowest cost figures, particularly since the cost of meals provided employees is included in the expenditure figures. The high figures, on the other hand, suggest extravagant or wasteful performance, or possibly accounting peculiarities.

There is a more systematic pattern in the variation of nursing home costs than the above discussion would indicate. The dominant pattern is readily apparent when costs are compared by region, by number of beds and by ownership (Table 1).

Table 1
Average Cost per Patient Day: 1974
(Sample of 145 institutions)

By Region		By No. of Beds		By Ownership	
Albany	$34.76	0–50	$27.00	Voluntary	$50.70
Buffalo	32.05	51–100	33.19	Proprietary	34.99
Rochester	32.31	101–200	39.58	Government	41.81
Syracuse	32.11	201–300	38.69		
White Plains	43.79	over 300	46.89		
New York	44.66				
All	40.62		40.62		40.62

These data show some marked patterns in cost variation. Average costs are remarkably constant in the three regions of central and western New York, slightly higher in the Albany region, and substantially higher in the downstate regions of White Plains and New York. The average for White Plains is 37 percent and for New York 39 percent above that of Buffalo. The second pattern is the sharp increase in average costs as the number of patient beds increases. The average cost for homes with over 300 beds is nearly 74 percent higher than the average for homes with 50 or fewer beds and 41 percent above the average for homes with 51–100 beds.

Lastly, the data show that the homes operated by voluntary non-profit organizations are far more expensive than those operated either by governments or profit-making proprietors. The average for voluntary homes is 45 percent higher than the average for proprietaries. That difference is widely recognized and usually attributed to the inclusion in rates for voluntary institutions of services—especially of physicians and therapists—that are billed separately for patients in proprietary institutions. As shown in Table 2, this is not borne out by a comparison of costs for each major function.

113

Table 2
Average 1974 Costs per Diem
(Sample of 145 skilled nursing facilities)

	Voluntary	Proprietary	Government
Nursing	$16.02	$12.78	$14.12
Dietary	7.21	4.69	5.47
Administration	3.90	2.83	2.99
Housekeeping	2.79	2.07	2.03
Property	5.77	5.42	2.49
Repair and maintenance	3.92	1.80	3.34
Fringe benefits	4.54	2.59	6.55
Social services	0.59	0.17	0.18
Therapists	1.27	0.59	0.98
Physicians	1.21	0.10	0.83
All other	3.48	1.95	3.63
TOTAL	$50.70	$34.99	$41.81

The differences between voluntaries and proprietaries in the costs of physicians, therapists and social services account for only $2.21 or about one-seventh of the $15.71 difference in average total costs between the two types of institutions. The voluntaries are more expensive because they operate at a higher level of quality or at lower efficiency with respect to virtually every functional cost center.

A multiple correlation analysis of a reduced sample of institutions found factors that explained a large part of the variance in costs among institutions. The difference in institution size, as measured by gross square feet, explained 41 percent of the variance; differences from county to county in average salaries of health workers accounted for another 12.8 percent; the proportion of patients in one- and two-bed rooms contributed 7.3 percent to the variance, and patient turnover rates an additional 4.8 percent.

The correlation analysis can identify the statistical factors associated with cost differences but offers no causal explanation or justification. It does not indicate, for example, that large institutions are inherently more costly or that they provide more or better services. Rather, the analysis suggests that the state, as a prudent purchaser of nursing home services, should determine that it is getting its money's worth. This is even more true of homes with high costs that are not fully "explained" by the multiple correlation.

Costs in the reduced sample of 52 nursing homes vary from $21.16 to $72.85 per diem. Much of the variation is "explained" by the regression equation—high costs attributable chiefly to location in the high-cost downstate area or to large facility size. The "unexplained" deviation ranges, nonetheless, from (−) $6.96 to (+) $24.21. Twenty-three of the homes show "excess" costs; nine of them $3 per diem or more.

The cost comparisons raise some difficult policy questions. Despite the great variations within each group of nursing homes, it is clear that there is a two-track system in which the patients in the voluntaries are traveling first-class and those in the proprietaries second or third-class. Moreover, the group system of controlling increases keeps all institutions in their established tracks. A proprietary institution that wished to emulate the higher service levels of the voluntaries could not do so without breaking out of the limit imposed by the group average.

The situation poses excruciating policy issues. The state tolerates, and indeed tends to perpetuate by its policies, a gross inequity among Medicaid-supported nursing home patients. If an upgrading in the service level of the proprietary homes was warranted, the state budget problem would clearly make its implementation impossible. On the other hand, to cut back reimbursement levels for the voluntary institutions would mean attacking the best and most humane nursing homes, while the problems of deficiencies, fraud, callous operation and neglect exist almost entirely in a handful of homes in the proprietary sector.

The state is now spending $1 billion annually on nursing home care, excluding the support it provides through its share of Supplemental Security Income for payments to residents of private proprietary homes for adults and other homes for the aged. This amount exceeds every other component of Medicaid except payments to hospitals, and it can only continue to increase under current policies. Even with federal sharing, the state and its local governments are each contributing about $300 million annually to nursing home costs. The missing ingredient was the failure to decide how much was enough. A cost-based reimbursement system demanded a far more sophisticated policy structure than would the flat-rate systems of most other states. The state simply did not contend with many of the issues involved.

The Quality of Nursing Home Care

The reports of the Moreland Act Commission and, before it, the Stein Commission, provided convincing evidence of the state's failures in enforcing adequate quality standards. The problem has several causes:

1. The health department has long attempted to pursue a consultative rather than a regulatory posture toward deficient homes.

2. The health department's surveillance operations have been chronically understaffed.

3. The major inspection activity, the HEW-designed Facility Survey, is concerned largely with "paper" requirements, such as the existence of adequate written policies, staff credentials, clear assignment of responsi-

bilities, the establishment of required committees and the like—that were more concerned with the *capacity* for sound operation than with the quality of actual operations.

4. The second annual inspection, the Periodic Medical Review, is potentially far more relevant to the determination of operational deficiencies, but has been grossly under-designed and understaffed.

5. Enforcement machinery was inadequate and cumbersome.

A final reason is the difficulty of designing an adequate surveillance system, especially if its findings must be sufficiently documented to survive due process administrative hearings and judicial review.

The on-site inspection of nursing homes is very effective in identifying deficiencies in structure, plant and equipment. Nursing home operating characteristics are, however, far more transitory; conditions observed during the two days of the annual survey may not be representative; indeed, are likely to reflect a "heads-up" approach simply because the state's surveyors are there. Moreover, the deficiencies easiest to observe tend to be in areas, such as housekeeping, where the effect upon patient care is limited.

The Periodic Medical Review, under which every patient and his medical record must be examined, is not subject to the same limitations. In New York State, however, the review is very limited and performed by nurses without a physician on-site. It can identify a few treatment deficiencies, e.g., weight changes not reflected in the medical record and physician's instructions, but little more.

There has been no tabulation and comparison among homes of deficiencies identified in either the survey or the PMR—and some question as to whether the results of either inspection are sufficiently worthwhile to warrant the effort.

A revised and expanded surveillance system should rely heavily upon statistical comparisons of performance among homes. Any sufficiently comprehensive survey will identify deficiencies in virtually any nursing home. The only way in which these deficiencies can be meaningfully calibrated is against the performance of other nursing homes. To say, for example, that the PMR identified 23 serious deficiencies in treatment in one 300-bed nursing home has very limited significance. If, on the other hand, we can say that the 7.67 deficiencies per 100 patients (23 ÷ 300) is double the median for all nursing homes and would place the particular home in the highest and worst quintile, a case has been established for more frequent and intensive health department surveillance and for strong support provided for departmental enforcement action. The effectiveness of such comparative analysis depends, of course, upon the application of the same issues and the same standards to every nursing home. This is eminently possible.

Medical care is perhaps the most important aspect of nursing home care simply because therapy, most medication, therapeutic diets and special nursing care are usually provided only on physician's instructions. An unusually objective review of adequacy of medical care is possible for patients with conditions for which the appropriate form of treatment or protocol is relatively fixed and not significantly dependent upon the judgment of the physician. Diabetes and hypertension, which afflict perhaps one-fifth to one-fourth of nursing home populations, are of this character.

A protocol-based review may also proceed the additional step of determining whether the prescribed treatment is actually being followed. Protocol violations can literally be identified in checklist form, and comparisons among nursing homes in the incidence of aggregate violations, or in the incidence of particular and more serious violations can be readily made. Jane Heidt's work with the Fund for the City of New York has indicated that violations are likely to be common, and that incidence rates tend to vary widely.

Protocol-based reviews could be effectively supplemented by a structured physician review of patient condition and record as part of the PMR. Data could, with the proper structure, be used in the same comparative fashion as that developed from protocol-based reviews.

There should, in addition, be a routine reporting and analysis of certain patient conditions that arise primarily or solely from inadequate nursing care. Decubiti, contractures, pneumonia, urinary tract infections, malnutrition and dehydration are all, more or less, of this character. The incidence of all of these or any one of them per 100 patients provides indication of where there are serious problems.

A parallel approach makes sense in a number of other areas of nursing home care. A random sample of menus should be reviewed for nutritional adequacy and variety and, if possible, supplemented by samples of patient opinions on food. Inter-home comparisons of the extent, range, and degree of patient participation in activity programs would provide stronger indications of under-performance in this area than would any other method. A similar statistical analysis of the provisions of physical and occupational therapy would identify homes where the data gave strong indications of underuse of therapies. Social service assistance and even dental care lend themselves to similar approaches. In many of these areas, there are not established norms for the provision of service, and little is known systematically about the range in current practices. Where low level performance carries no certain connotation of deficiency, it identifies those homes that warrant special surveillance.

The review of the quality of medical and nursing care would be greatly advanced by use of a standard patient assessment system that made it possible to follow, from the record, changes in patient condition and capacity for autonomy.

One still neglected area is the need to develop and enforce standards of professional accountability. Every home has a medical director (usually part time) and a director of nursing. Every patient must (with few exceptions) be examined by a physician once a month and there are doctors who serve as attending physicians to 100 or more patients in a single nursing home. No one seems to have raised the question of responsibility and accountability of these professionals, even in nursing homes where adverse conditions and their impact upon patients has reportedly been clearly evident to lay reviewers. The matter deserves serious exploration.

The Possible Impact of National Health Insurance upon the Health Budget of New York City

In attempting to define the probable range of effects that national health insurance (NHI) might have on New York City's funded health services, and on the municipal budget, this paper will first discuss the present budgetary costs of health programs funded by the city. There follows a "static" analysis of the possible impact of NHI provisions on the city's health budget and, finally, more "dynamic" considerations for budget changes. Because there is a basic lack of information about New York City's health care system (as well as uncertainty over the dimensions of a future NHI plan) there are no final conclusions and plans here; rather, it is hoped, a contribution is made to the long-range discussion of national health insurance and city budgets.

Expectation of Continued Rapid Growth in Expenditures

New York City spending on health programs has increased dramatically in recent years. A comparison of the data in Table 1 with earlier data developed by Piore and Lieberman indicates that New York City's expense budget appropriations for health programs roughly doubled in the period from FY 1971 to FY 1975.[1] The proportion of municipal expenditures accounted for by city tax funds has remained relatively constant during this period.

There are a number of reasons why the city's expenditures on health programs can be expected to continue to grow quite rapidly in the near future. (In view of the upward pressures on the amount the city spends for health care, it is likely that tough budgetary measures by the city during the next five years will be necessary to hold the average annual rate of increase in city health care expenditures to 10 percent or less [as compared to an average annual rate of 14 percent for the past four years]. If the city's expenditures on health increased 10 percent per year for the next five years, the city would be spending about $2 billion in city tax levy on health care by 1980.)

1. Prior to the recent explosion in commodity and raw material prices, the prices of health services increased more rapidly than consumer prices generally—especially in New York City where the claims of health services unions are powerful.

Table 1

City of New York Funding Support by Agency or Program for Health Services, 1974–1975 Executive Budget*
(Millions of Dollars)

Agency or Program	Total Budget	City Funding	State & Federal Funding	Direct Payments	Misc.
N.Y.C. Health and Hospitals Corporation (HHC)	921.9	457.1	381.0	66.7	17.1
Department of Mental Health & Mental Retardation	148.8	56.7	76.5	—	15.6
Department of Health (including employee fringe and debt service)	143.6	78.4	62.6	0.1	2.5
Medical Examiner	3.2	1.6	1.6	—	—
Executive Management—HSA	5.0	2.5	2.5	—	—
Department of Education	12.0	6.0	6.0	—	—
Addiction Services	81.0	25.0	56.0	—	—
Department of Social Services— Medicaid assistance less payments to HHC	1122.6	353.2	769.4	—	—
Employee health including "welfare fund"	262.0	196.0	70.0	—	—
Miscellaneous departments	6.4	1.9	4.5	—	—
TOTAL	2710.5	1178.4	1430.1	66.8	35.2

*Estimated from various sources by J. H. Weiss.

120

2. The population of New York City appears to be aging more rapidly than the population of the United States as a whole.[2] In 1973, about 12.8 percent of the population of the City of New York was over age 65 as compared to 10.2 percent for the United States. Since the elderly demand and require more health services than the population generally, a continuation of this trend will tend to increase the demand for municipally-funded health services.

3. The per capita income of New York City appears to have increased less since 1971 than per capita incomes nationally, while at the same time the proportion of poor persons in the city population has increased.[3] Since a high proportion of the municipal budget for health programs is used to provide health care to the medically indigent, a continuation of the relative economic deterioration of New York City could lead to further increases in the demand for city-funded health services.

4. Pension costs in the city's expense budget are growing rapidly as the city incurs increasing liabilities due to its enormously generous pension system; this will put further pressure on the cost of municipal health care services. (I estimate that the city allocated about 33 percent of each wage dollar for fringe benefits in FY 1974–75.)

5. The amount of city debt service attributable to health care facilities is expected to double in the next three years (to at least $100 million) as a number of new health care facilities for the New York City Health and Hospitals Corporation (HHC) become operational.[4]

6. The added start-up and operating costs to the city associated with the opening of new municipal facilities (e.g., Lincoln Hospital, East New York, NFCC, etc.).

The Present City Budget for Health Programs

The FY 1974–75 New York City budgetary costs for health programs are summarized in Table 1. Municipal funding for health programs in FY 1974–75 will be about $1.2 billion in city tax levy (CTL). About 15 percent of the total tax collections of the City of New York (for capital and expense budget items) is used to fund health programs. Planned health expenditures in the city expense budget account for $2.71 billion out of a total expense budget of $11.1 billion, or about 24 percent of the city's expense budget for FY 1974–75. (On a per capita basis, the City of New York spends more than twice as much as any other major city on health programs.)

The largest share of city funds for health programs in FY 1974–75 is accounted for by HHC (Table 1). A special HHC cost study in 1973 indicated that more than three-fourths of HHC costs that year were accounted for by inpatient services. It is worth noting, moreover, that the City of New York subsidizes a much higher proportion of HHC's costs for outpatients than for inpatients.

The Medicaid program costs city taxpayers 27 percent of each Medicaid dollar expended in New York City (as estimated by NYC Bureau of the Budget). (The range of services provided, and the gross Medicaid expenditures for NYC in FY 1974–75 are summarized in Table 2.) The highly complex rules for determining Medicaid eligibility in New York State, and the existence of a shifting population where individuals move in and out of eligibility for Medicaid as their economic and health circumstances change, make even a rough analysis of the implications of NHI for the New York City–New York State Medicaid program difficult, if not impossible. To further complicate matters, there is a lack of data on the exact amount of Medicaid expenditures for specific types of services. For example, there seem to be no data on the amount spent on Medicaid specifically for voluntary hospital outpatient services.

The health benefits provided by the City of New York for its employees are the third most costly item in Table 1. In FY 1974–75, the city will spend an estimated $160 million on "basic" health insurance for its more than 300,000 employees (as estimated by NYC Budget Bureau personnel). The basic health insurance provided by the City of New York

Table 2

Projected Expenditures for Medicaid for New York City by Type of Service, FY 1974–75*

Service	Gross Expenditures (Million $)
Hospitals—Public	$346.0
Hospitals—Vol./Prop.	383.5
Nursing homes	329.0
Public home infirmaries	43.0
Intermediate care facilities	63.0
Clinic and emergency room care	
Public	74.2
Other	127.0
Physicians	106.8
Dental Care	27.3
Other practitioners (podiatrists, etc.)	18.7
Drugs	57.0
Home health care	9.9
Homemaker/home health aids	5.0
Personal care aides	15.0
Prepaid insurance	16.2
Other medical care (Labs, X-rays, Prosthetics)	30.0
Child health assistance	3.0
Children's institutions	17.4
TOTAL	$1671.8

*Source: Internal State Department of Social Services Reports.

122

contains more generous benefit provisions than those contained in the Nixon Administration's NHI proposals (H.R. 12684) or the Mills-Kennedy Bill (H.R. 13870). Furthermore, in addition to the "basic" health insurance plans provided by the city, the city contributes roughly $100 million (about $300 per employee) to so-called "welfare funds" which are used primarily to provide health services for municipal employees. (Although it is believed that these funds are primarily used to purchase supplementary health insurance benefits for city employees, an unknown portion of these funds is used to purchase other fringe benefits. Thus, city funding for employee health benefits is probably somewhat less than the $196 million shown in Table 1.)

Possible Impact of NHI

In order to analyze in detail the impact of particular NHI provisions upon items financed by the health budget of New York City, it is necessary to have certain types of data which are generally nonexistent, such as data on the distribution of health expenditures by income, age and health insurance status. It is also necessary to have some precise information concerning the characteristics of the population that uses HHC inpatient and outpatient facilities (e.g., their income, health insurance status, age, residence, etc.). The data describing the Medicaid population in New York City are totally deficient.

If the prime objective is to provide New York City policy-makers with some general insights about the type of NHI program that might be preferable for New York City, from the point of view of minimizing the city's budgetary costs for health, a number of useful observations can be made without undertaking detailed analyses.

New York's basic position with respect to national health insurance should be quite simple: *The more the better!* This is so because New York City, as compared to other large cities, spends a disproportionate amount of its own tax levy funds on health services; most of it going for health services to benefit the medically indigent segment of the population through HHC programs and Medicaid. Since those persons who pay most of New York City's taxes do not notably benefit from the city's role in health services (except for municipal employees who benefit greatly from the generous city-funded health insurance plans), New York City's substantial expenditures on health services tend to make it, for those persons, a relatively less desirable place to live. Consequently, the New York City government and its principal taxpayers clearly should be in favor of any NHI provisions which would force taxpayers in other parts of the country to pay through whatever financing mechanism for those health services for which New York City's taxpayers presently pay.

Static Analysis

In this and the subsequent section of the paper I am assuming that the provisions contained in the Health Security Act (Kennedy-Griffiths Bill, S. 3 and H.R. 22), the Comprehensive National Health Insurance Act (Kennedy-Mills Bill, H.R. 13870 and S. 3286), and the Comprehensive Health Insurance Act (Administration Bill, H.R. 12684 and S. 2970), are representative of the type and range of benefit provisions which are likely to be contained in a NHI bill which eventually passes the Congress. Also, all cost estimates of the impact of NHI upon the amount of the city tax levy (CTL) required to support city-funded programs are based upon the assumption that NHI was in effect throughout FY 1974–75. *Future cost inflation and changes in the composition of programs are ignored.*

It is perhaps easiest to begin by discussing the types of health programs that are currently financed by New York City which are not likely to be covered, or to be only partially covered, by any future NHI act. The most costly type of services that are likely to be only partially covered by any future NHI bill are extended care services. Further, the growing demand for extended care programs implies that this component of the health services presently financed by the city is likely to grow rapidly relative to the expected increase in total cost of health services in the city.

Comprehensive dental care for all citizens is another category of expenditure which is unlikely to be covered by national health insurance. Some of the health insurance bills provide dental care for children, but it is not known what proportion of the dental care services funded by the city are provided to children. Hence, one can only guess that dental care services for the medically indigent are likely to remain an area of potential municipal responsibility, with an unknown cost which is presently probably in the range of $10–20 million.

The health insurance bills which have been proposed typically provide limited or no home health services or homemaker/home health-aid services. These programs under Medicaid presently require $7 million in city funding. It is unclear (but probably unlikely) whether NHI will cover health services provided in certain institutions like prisons, schools and children's institutions. Funding by the city for health and mental health services provided in these institutions will be about $18–20 million this year. Some form of limited payment for outpatient drugs is likely to be provided for under NHI. Funding by New York City for outpatient drugs will be about $15 million under Medicaid this year, and I estimate that the portion of HHC outpatient drug expenses subsidized by the city (from the 1973 HHC cost study) will be about $12 million in FY 1974–75.

Under any conceivable NHI plan the city will still have to pay for the

124

city health department's epidemiological, regulatory and quality control, management, statistical, inspection, etc. functions. At the maximum about half of the CTL funding for the health department could be construed to be for personal health services of the type that would be covered under NHI. Consequently, the city would continue to spend about $39 million in tax levy on health department programs if the Kennedy-Griffiths plan became operational.

The amount of funding by the city for its employee health plan would depend very much on the nature of the financing mechanism of a future NHI plan. If NHI were to be financed by a tax on payroll (e.g., the Administration Plan), then it is likely that the CTL cost for health insurance for employees would remain substantially unchanged. It is highly unlikely that the municipal unions would agree to greater contributions by employees for health benefits, since their general position is that the city should pay for the total cost of these benefits. Also, if the city's health insurance benefits are more generous than the benefits provided by a future NHI plan, the city will, of course, have to supplement the NHI provisions. This would be necessary so that present city funding for municipal employees could represent a "floor" for future CTL funding for health insurance benefits for city employees (assuming city employment does not decrease sharply). In contrast, if the Kennedy-Griffiths plan were to be enacted, the city funding for a portion of its employee-health plans might be reduced to the extent that the plan was financed from federal general revenues, (i.e., 50 percent). If this were the case, the amount of CTL required to finance health insurance for city employees would be reduced to nearly half of the estimated $196 million for this year.

Most NHI plans are unlikely to pay for a high proportion of the addiction services now financed through the city budget. Since a substantial portion of the city funding for addiction services in FY 1974–75 went to provide *long-term* methadone or therapeutic services for addicts, the city would probably have to continue to pay for a high proportion of these services in the future.

A national health insurance bill is unlikely to pay for the entire cost of the programs funded by the city's Department of Mental Health and Mental Retardation. In fact, all three of the health insurance bills mentioned above limit the number of days of insured psychiatric care for outpatients, and either provide no mental health services for patients or a limited number of days of such services (e.g., 30 full days or 60 partial days under the administration's proposal). Although precise data on the distribution of the number of visits by outpatients to voluntary hospital and municipal hospital mental health programs were not made available to me, it is known that a high proportion of the patients served by these institutions do not utilize more than 30 outpatient visits. Thus it can be

125

expected that NHI would probably cover an unknown, but reasonably high percentage of the $16 million in city tax levy spent on voluntary mental health contracts and community mental health centers in FY 1974–75. There seem to be no data on the distribution of mental health expenditures between outpatient and inpatient services in HHC hospitals, or on the distribution by length of stay of mental health patients in HHC hospitals. Therefore it is impossible to make a fair estimate of the possible impact of NHI upon the magnitude of CTL expenditures for mental health services presently provided by HHC institutions. My educated guess is that between $20–37 million in present city funding for mental health and mental retardation services would not be covered by a relatively "generous" program.

The data in Table 3 are based upon the preceding discussion plus "educated guesses" about the "high" and "low" funding responsibilities of New York City for the health programs that are not likely to be covered, or only partially covered, by NHI plans. Assuming that NHI was in effect during FY 1974–75, it is quite possible that CTL of $484 million would be necessary to finance the programs listed in Table 3. On the other hand, the most generous NHI program is unlikely to reduce city funding obligations for these programs below the level of $266 million. The maximum savings in city tax levy for the programs listed in Table 3 is $250 million (i.e., the difference between the amounts in columns 1 and 3).

Most of the likely NHI programs will probably cover a high proportion of the costs of inpatient hospital services, as well as the costs

Table 3

New York City Funded Health Programs Not Covered or Partially Covered by Likely NHI Plans

Programs	Estimated City Funding FY 1974–75 (Millions $)	City Funding Obligations* After NHI (Millions $)	
		High	Low
Extended care	$122	$122	$ 80
Dental	20	20	10
Home care	7	7	3
Institutional care			
(e.g., prison health, etc.)	19	19	5
Outpatient drugs	27	20	5
ASA programs	25	20	0
Employee health	196	196	100
Management & Medical Examiner	4	4	4
Mental health & retardation	57	37	20
Health Dept. programs			
(exclusive of health services)	39	39	39
TOTAL	$516	$484	$266

*Assuming NHI was in effect in FY 1974–75. High and low estimates based on "educated guess" by J.H. Weiss.

of physician services, other independent health professionals (e.g., podiatrists), equipment and supplies, X-ray, laboratory, ambulance services, etc. These services account for the balance of the health services (i.e., those not listed in Table 3) supported by New York City funds.

The most generous possible health insurance plan (e.g., Kennedy-Griffiths) would cover the entire cost of hospital services. Under this plan, the city might save a maximum of about $270 million for the subsidized inpatient services of the HHC. In addition, I estimate that the city might save about $103 million in city-funded Medicaid expenditures for inpatient hospital costs at voluntary and proprietary institutions. Thus, the maximum possible savings for the city in city-funded inpatient hospital care services would be about $373 million.

Under the Kennedy-Griffiths bill, funding by the city would cease for physicians and other professional services, as well as for such related current costs as Medicaid expenditures for therapeutic devices and for prepaid health insurance for the medically indigent. The city would save an estimated $155 million for city-funded HHC outpatient and emergency room costs and an estimated $29 million for city-funded private physician costs under Medicaid. (The savings in CTL for Medicaid programs are based upon the CTL share of the costs in Table 2.) Moreover, the city would not have to spend the previously estimated $39 million on current health department programs which provide health services directly or which fund voluntary hospital OPDs. The city would also save about $31 million in Medicaid-funded clinic and emergency room care for other than public institutions. Finally, the city might save as much as $18 million in the city-funded Medicaid expenditures for such items as "other practitioners" services, therapeutic devices, labs and X-rays and prepaid health insurance for certain Medicaid recipients. In summary, if the "most generous" NHI plan was in effect, the city might save an additional $272 million in CTL for these health services programs.

The maximum savings in CTL under these assumptions for both inpatient programs ($373 million in CTL) and the programs listed above is $645 million. Thus, an "upper-bound" for reductions in New York City funding for health programs (in FY 1974–75 terms) is this figure plus the $250 million in maximum savings in CTL for the programs listed in Table 3, or a total of $895 million. (These calculations assume that the HHC will not be able to recover all of its capital outlays through NHI rates. If all of the HHC's capital outlays were reflected in NHI rates, the $895 million figure would be $15–20 million higher.)

There are several reasons why it is unlikely that the projected savings in CTL used to support inpatient, ambulatory care, physicians and other health professionals, and related costs, will reach the "upper-bound" of $645 million:

1. It is quite possible that NHI will not cover all segments of the medically indigent population.

2. Most NHI proposals contain substantial deductible and coinsurance provisions for both inpatient and outpatient services. For instance, some plans include the possibility of a "Health Card" system under which covered individuals would charge the costs of covered services. The plan would pay providers on the basis of those charges at the applicable rate of reimbursement. The deductible and coinsurance amounts paid by the plan would be billed to the covered individual, and thus the NHI plan, rather than health services providers, would bear the initial and primary financial risk for collecting coinsurance and deductible amounts. This is clearly the kind of administrative provision that the City of New York ought to be in favor of if a NHI plan is enacted containing coinsurance and deductibles provisions.

3. All NHI bills contain various limitations on the types of services covered.

4. Cost containment provisions in many NHI proposals will limit allowable patterns of utilization and rates for reimbursement and fees. One potentially important provision is the distinction between participating and non-participating providers. For instance, under the administration plan, "full-participating" providers would agree to accept reimbursement through the "Health Card" as payment in full for all patients. "Associate-participating providers" would agree to accept reimbursement through the Health Card as payment in full for certain categories of patients, while the physician would be allowed to bill the remainder of his fee to certain other categories of patients. "Non-participating" providers would not be reimbursed by NHI for services provided. If the professional fee schedules and ambulatory care rates under this plan were not in line with market conditions in New York City, it is quite possible that a substantial portion of providers would either be "non-participating" or "associate participating." This would tend to continue the "two-class" system of care, and the city might be forced to subsidize HHC physician costs in order to retain the requisite number of capable physicians.

Some Dynamic Considerations

The nature of the cost-containment rules and administrative mechanisms associated with any future NHI plan will clearly have considerable impact upon the potential tax levy savings to New York City from NHI. Because the upward pressures on the costs of health services in New York City are very strong compared to those in other areas, the city government should, in principle, be in favor of strong cost-containment provi-

128

sions and administrative mechanisms. The city's health care personnel are well represented by several powerful unions and professional employee associations. These unions and their counterparts in other sectors of the city's economy are one important reason why New York City's cost of living is one of the highest in the country, and why the cost of publicly provided services (including health services) is high compared to those of other areas. Since New York City (and New York State) government officials have had difficulty in the past in resisting union demands, these officials should be in favor of externally imposed strong cost-containment measures which shift the onus for resisting unreasonable demands by health care employees' unions and associations from city officials to other administrative authorities.

On the other hand, the city's tax levy savings from NHI could be limited by overly aggressive local cost-containment measures which hold institutional and provider fees below levels generally determined by market forces. If this were the case, the quality of health services in New York City would gradually deteriorate as key health care personnel left for other locations more financially desirable—unless the city or state supplemented the rates and fees allowed under the NHI Plan.

In recent years, the average daily inpatient census in HHC hospitals has been declining steadily. After a sharp one-time shift in inpatient days from the municipal to the voluntary sector following the enactment of Medicaid and Medicare in 1966, the average daily inpatient census in HHC has declined steadily from 12,388 days in 1969 to 10,627 days in 1974. The enactment of NHI would certainly encourage further reductions in the average daily inpatient census of HHC hospitals. Since more than 60 percent of HHC patients are presently Medicaid and Medicare patients who, under NHI, presumably could choose voluntary hospitals if they wished, these "city charge" patients would be the group most likely to change their patterns of utilization in response to more comprehensive inpatient and ambulatory care insurance coverage.

It is not clear how NHI might affect the shift in demand for OPD services between the voluntary and private and municipal hospital sectors. On one hand, a very generous plan (e.g., the Kennedy-Griffiths Bill) would induce some shifts to voluntary and private services from HHC facilities. On the other, a NHI bill with substantial deductible and coinsurance provisions might have little influence on the current patterns of utilization of OPD services. In this case, the enactment of NHI would still leave the HHC with a tremendous responsibility for the delivery of ambulatory care services to the medically indigent. This would also, of course, indirectly influence inpatient rates of occupancy since extensive ambulatory care services tied to HHC hospitals affect HHC inpatient rates of utilization.[5,6]

An important factor affecting potential shifts in the demand between the HHC and the voluntary and private sectors is the availability of competitive voluntary or private services in proximity to HHC facilities. For example, it would be anticipated that a health facility like the new Lincoln Hospital, located in a relatively economically depressed area with no major voluntary facilities in the immediate vicinity, would not find its inpatient rate of occupancy or level of outpatient visits substantially altered by a generous NHI plan. In contrast, a facility located near other potentially competitive services in Manhattan (e.g., Metropolitan Hospital) might experience short-term shifts in demand for its services. Similarly, private practitioners are not likely to provide much competition for organized ambulatory care facilities which are located in economically depressed, high crime areas, regardless of the nature of any NHI plan which is enacted.

The city should be in favor of a NHI plan which helps to promote the maximum rationalization of the health care system by providing incentives for patients (and their physicians) to utilize the type of care and services most suitable for their particular problems (e.g., intermediate care vs. short-term general hospitals, etc.).

The impact upon the city budget of any potential shifts caused by NHI in the utilization of various types of health services will be unclear until the NHI plan has been in effect for several years. This is because the cost-control policies and mechanisms associated with any NHI plan are the key factors linking changes in utilization patterns to fiscal impacts. A tough cost-control program (through the regulation of rates and utilization) could force the HHC either to close health care facilities or to experience much higher cost factors—which could push costs above allowable rates, thus necessitating a larger city tax levy subsidy. (This would not necessarily be larger than before the enactment of NHI, but larger than after the enactment of NHI in the absence of tough cost controls.) In contrast, relaxed regulatory policies and procedures could allow the HHC, through marked increases in rates, to pass on the increased costs stemming from reduced inpatient utilization.

One further point is worth mentioning. In the long run it is certain that a NHI plan with a broad range of benefits combined with reasonably tough cost-control policies and procedures will force some HHC facilities either to improve the effectiveness of their services or to lose large numbers of patients (with a new and greater range of possible choices) to competitive voluntary and private services.

On the basis of the preceding discussion, I would give the following guidance to municipal policy makers who are concerned about how NHI might reduce the fiscal burden of municipally-supported health services upon city taxpayers:

1. If NHI had been in effect in FY 1974–75, the tax levy savings attributable to reduced city funding for health services programs would be a maximum of $895 million, or about three-fourths of the CTL now spent on health programs. Under the most generous possible NHI plan, substantial municipal funding responsibilities would still remain for employee health insurance plans, health department programs which do not provide personal health services, the financing of extended care programs and certain mental health services. While it is conceivable that NHI will not substantially reduce the CTL for health services, it is more likely that the city will, at a minimum, save $300 million or more, since a high proportion of inpatient costs will be covered by almost any NHI plan. Therefore, an NHI plan is likely to reduce CTL expenditures by an amount equal to 4–12 percent of the city's total tax collections (in terms of FY 1974–75 budgets).

2. The city should obviously push for the most generous package of benefits possible in any future NHI plan.

3. In particular, the city should urge that the specific benefit provisions in any future NHI plan allow for the complete reimbursement of alcoholism programs, drug programs and other institutionalized health and mental health services provided by the city (e.g., prison and mental health).

4. If the future NHI plan is likely to contain coinsurance and deductible provisions, the city should take a strong position on the need for administrative arrangements which put the burden for collecting coinsurance and deductibles on the financial intermediary and the NHI plan.

5. The city should favor strong cost-control provisions in any future NHI plan with the proviso that the final responsibility for cost controls rests with institutions exogenous to the city government.

6. The city might favor the financing of NHI from general federal revenues (as opposed to a tax on employers) since this would shift part of the burden of financing health insurance for its employees from CTL to general federal revenues.

There are at least two tasks pertaining to the development of better data that the city and the HHC might contemplate undertaking in preparation for NHI. First, the city and the HHC might improve their cost-accounting systems in the health department and in HHC institutions so that they could more accurately ascertain the total costs of health services programs which might be reimbursable under NHI. (There are clearly many reasons why this might be useful even in the absence of NHI.) Second, the city and the HHC should learn more about the socioeconomic characteristics of those patients using HHC institutions. Regardless of the possible advent of NHI, the HHC ought to have data on its maximum potential collections from third-party payers under current conditions, and on the socioeconomic characteristics of its "city pay" patients.

Finally, unless the HHC's governance and legal and social responsibilities are changed, the advent of NHI will not relieve the city of the responsibility for promoting and supporting a greater HHC capability for more effective management and patient care. The advent of NHI is likely to increase rather than decrease the demand for such a capability through the creation of a tougher competitive and regulatory environment. While fiscal pressures on the city for the improvement of the HHC's management and patient-care capabilities may lessen in the short term with the advent of NHI, the need for the HHC to provide efficient, good quality health services should not diminish especially since in many areas of the city (and for many specific types of services) it will remain the prime provider of health services.

References

[1] Nora Piore and Purlaine Lieberman, "*Changes in the Scope, Characteristics, and Role of Public Expenditures for Personal Health Care, New York City, 1961, 1966 and 1971,*" Center for Community Health Systems, Columbia University, October 1973.

[2] Blanche Bernstein and Arley Bondarin, "*New York City's Population—1973,*" Center for New York City Affairs, New School for Social Research, November 1974.

[3] *Ibid.,* p. 7.

[4] Source, New York City Budget Bureau personnel.

[5] Irving Leveson and Brian Richter, "*Effect of Ambulatory Care Policy on a Hospital's Occupancy Rate,*" New York City Health Services Administration, May 1972.

[6] Alan Leslie and others, "*A Study of Long-Stay Patients Unnecessarily Hospitalized in Municipal Hospitals,*" New York City Health Services Administration, March 1971.

Some Implications of National Health Insurance for New York City's Health System

IRVING LEVESON

Some Potential Impacts of National Health Insurance

The introduction of NHI is likely to increase the share of costs which is covered by insurance and to bring some services under insurance coverage for the first time. The reduction in the consumer's out-of-pocket costs will raise demand. This can be expected to lead to increases in unit costs as well as utilization.[1]

Increases in unit costs can be generated by many different mechanisms. Prices may rise as a way of allocating available resources. Greater inefficiency may be tolerated where costs can be passed on to third-party payors. The services included in the average day in the hospital or visit to a clinic may increase along with other increases in utilization. There may be heightened pressures for wage increases under collective bargaining once a larger share of the costs of wage increases is paid for by all persons who pay insurance premiums, rather than by those who become ill. Union pressures for wage increases may be encouraged by the growing demand for services since job security will be less affected by increases in costs when job shortages exist.

The importance of these factors will depend upon the means by which reimbursement rates are set. Any rise in demand would be expected to lead to increases in utilization in those services and among those groups of the population which would experience the greatest declines in out-of-pocket cost. NHI is expected to exert particular pressure on ambulatory care for this reason. The expansion of coverage can also prevent reductions in utilization which would otherwise occur in response to such factors as rising costs and increased availability of lower-cost alternatives. New services and higher-cost methods of treatment may be in greater demand when the costs of greater use by one patient are borne by a larger population. Pressure for new facilities is also increased because of the effects of insurance on capital financing. The costs of paying off a mortgage are passed on to a general population and the steady income which insurance provides makes it easier for institutions to borrow. Greater insurance coverage for out-of-hospital care may make it possible to reduce reliance on hospitalization, but the resulting availability of beds, equipment and staff tend to assure that the beds will fill up with new patients even when insurance coverage for ambulatory care has increased.

Some Issues of Cost and Utilization: Bed Need

A number of developments have combined to greatly reduce the number of general-care hospital beds needed in the City of New York. A study examining data through 1970 found that the average length of stay in all hospitals in New York City was more than one-fourth above the national average; that the occupancy rate of the voluntary hospitals was unnecessarily low and that the municipal hospitals were operating with an average occupancy rate 10 percent below the voluntary hospital rate. The study concluded that *"By reducing the average length-of-stay by one-half of the excess over the national average as nursing homes become available and raising the average occupancy rate to 90 percent, the hospital system in New York City could admit the same number of patients as it does now with 20 percent fewer beds."* [2]

The size of the planned expansion of long-term-care facilities has been reduced since 1970. However, the number of nursing home beds has expanded by one-third to 32,000, with 7,000 additional beds approved. In addition, 9,000 health-related-facility beds have come into operation, and 13,000 more are approved. The opportunities remain substantial for greater reduction in general hospital patient-days, both through the expansions in long-term care which have already occurred, and which may continue to take place, and through the more effective use of pre-existing long-term-care facilities. (The study was generous in its assumptions about length of stay because, with the role of medical schools in New York City, the tendency is to keep patients longer for teaching purposes. Had the national average been used as a standard, the number of excess beds would have been estimated at one-third.)

Little has occurred to change the earlier numbers. In fact, the population of New York City shifted from its stable level and declined by 200,000 between 1970 and 1973. [3] Yet the increase in the number of beds in the city has continued. Between 1970 and 1975 the number of general-care beds in upstate New York fell from 38,053 to 37,145 while population was growing. In New York City, however, with a declining population, the number of beds rose slightly from 38,320 to 38,520.

The difference between New York City and New York State patterns becomes more dramatic when approvals for further increases in numbers of beds are examined. In upstate New York approvals have been granted for the addition of about 4,000 general-care beds, commensurate with population growth. In New York City, with a smaller and declining population, 6,000 new beds have been approved; only one-fifth of them, however, are already under construction. (The Health and Hospital Planning Council of Southern New York is currently reviewing the status of those approvals. This review need not lead to a reduction in the

134

number of approved bed increases, but instead may result in new approvals to replace those that have not advanced in construction.)

The large number of bed approvals has special significance for the question of response to national health insurance. Most of the approvals came between the passage of Medicare and Medicaid in 1966 and 1971, when concern about the fiscal implications of further expansion became widespread. The implications of that kind of response for the ability to contain costs under even higher levels of insurance coverage are not encouraging. But it is still possible to reverse the pattern of unnecessary expansion. Approved construction has been delayed by a succession of factors: inflation; the Economic Stabilization Program; the tightening of rate-setting at the state level; administrative delays and recession. *As much as half of the expansion of general care beds in New York City can still be stopped.*

The Cost of Excess Beds

There has been a great deal of confusion about the social costs of building unnecessary beds. New York City's construction costs of over $200,000 per bed is added to by more than $50 per patient-day by the cost of a 30-year mortgage. (The $200,000 figure includes interest, administration and other indirect costs during construction. The cost is for voluntary hospitals; the figures for municipal hospitals are substantially higher.) The decline in population, potential improvements in hospital efficiency and shifts away from hospital use mean that in many cases this cost can be avoided entirely, since many older facilities that are retired need not be replaced. The construction cost figures are also relevant to the cost of facilities which are left idle when occupancy rates are unnecessarily low.

The major problem with unnecessary beds is not that they will not be used. The problem is that they will be. There is a vast literature which demonstrates that bed availability is perhaps the single most important determinant of the number of days of hospital care per capita in a system with substantial insurance coverage.[4] As a result, the excess cost of each unnecessary bed in New York City is approaching $200 per day, even after subtracting the costs of alternative sources of care. *Keeping the number of beds tight is an essential strategy for avoiding unnecessary hospitalization.*[5]

Collective Bargaining

A unique feature of the health care system of New York City is the extent of unionization. Local 1199 of the Drug and Hospital Employees

Union covers 60,000 workers in voluntary hospitals and nursing homes, and District Council 37 of the American Federation of State, County and Municipal Employees covers 20,000 employees of municipal hospitals. The rapid wage gains which unions have achieved have been one of the forces pushing costs up. The growth in wages for health care workers began from a position in which wages were inordinately low. With the introduction of Medicare and Medicaid, wages rose rapidly. Between 1966 and 1969, wages in typical health occupations in hospitals rose 15–20 percent faster than the cost of living. By contrast, the rise in wages for clerical occupations which are competitive with other industries exceeded the general rise in prices by only half as much.[6] In recent years unions have moved beyond the elimination of low wages due to inequities in the health system to establish wages which reflect social standards rather than productivity. In July 1975 the minimum wage in Local 1199 contracts reached $181 per week.

The introduction of national health insurance raises questions about the extent to which even faster wage increases will take place as the costs for them are more widely distributed through a broad financing base. There are some factors, however, which suggest that wage increases may not continue to be as great as in the past. "Catch-up" and establishment of "social minimum" wage have largely been achieved. Established unions tend to be less adamant in their wage demands than new unions. On the other hand, hospital unions with the advantage of broad federal reimbursement may still press for wage levels that are out of line with workers possessing similar skills in other industries. There are questions being asked increasingly about the effects of collective bargaining on the decision-making processes in the health system, and what its implications are for the delivery of services.

Union influence can have a strong impact on decisions about adjustments of resources and services to changing conditions. They can add to costs in agreements over wage rates and staffing patterns. They can be a major force against the closing of hospitals or the reduction of program levels because their desire to protect jobs may often supersede an interest in the efficient production of services. At present these problems are particularly serious in the municipal system, where the greatest changes are occurring. There, decisions are subject to political pressures, and subsidies for inefficient or under-utilized services are more likely to come out of public funds than private ones.

Private Physicians' Services

The number of physicians in New York City is about the same as it was ten years ago (rising and falling slightly during the period). There has

136

been a rapid shift to hospital-based practice. Hospital-based physicians accounted for 22 percent of all physicians in the city in 1959 and 32 percent in 1966, rising to 39 percent in 1970.[7] No direct data are available on changes in the number of physicians' private office visits since the introduction of Medicare and Medicaid. There are currently 30–40 million such annual visits accounting for 75–80 percent of ambulatory care visits to physicians. (This range is derived from the numbers in the New York City Population Health Survey for the years 1964—1969-70. The latter year shows a large increase which is unexplained. The 1964 data are consistent with data for the region from the National Health Survey and with national estimates of physician time-allocation, suggesting that the true figure is toward the lower end of the range.) The other ten million annual visits are almost entirely to hospital outpatient departments and emergency rooms, about half of them municipal and half voluntary.

Some indications of changes in the patterns of use of private offices can be obtained from observation of changes in utilization of hospital-based ambulatory care. In the first few months after Medicare and Medicaid were introduced, visits to municipal hospital outpatient departments declined by one-tenth as patients experimented with using private doctors' offices. In the period between 1965 and 1967, however, visits to municipal OPDs fell by only 5 percent and combined visits to OPDs and emergency rooms by less than 2 percent. At the same time visits to voluntary hospital outpatient departments and emergency rooms rose by 7 percent as treatment of the medically indigent became more profitable; thus the number of ambulatory care visits to municipal and voluntary hospitals combined grew by 2 percent.

Increases in the cost of ambulatory care can come about either because of increases in the cost of office visits, increases in the cost of hospital-based visits or shifts in service from physicians' offices to outpatient department and emergency rooms. Since the introduction of Medicare and Medicaid there has been a sharp increase in the cost of hospital-based ambulatory visits. By early 1970 the average Medicaid rate for an outpatient visit in New York City was already $26.64, double the average cost of a visit to a specialist's office, and the average rate for an emergency room visit was $21.21. Since that time the average cost per visit for hospital-based care has doubled. (Figures for municipal hospitals have not yet been made final by the New York State Department of Health. The average Medicaid rate for a voluntary OPD in January 1975 was $48.89 compared to $27.00 in the first six months of 1970. The voluntary hospital emergency room rates were $41.71 and $25.50 respectively.)

There is considerable disagreement about why a clinic visit should cost nearly $50 while a visit to a specialist's office typically costs one-third to one-half that amount. Part of the difference is attributable to the inclusion in the clinic cost of laboratory, pharmacy and X-ray services which are not included in the doctor's fee. Administrators of ambulatory care facilities frequently claim that one-fifth or more of a clinic's reimbursement pays for overhead charges for services performed in other parts of the hospital—an apparent dramatic change from a few years ago when many hospitals were in the position of subsidizing their clinics. This problem of cost allocation can be dealt with if third-party payors insist on better accounting.

Some studies have shown a greater time per visit spent by physicians in not-for-profit clinics than in physicians' offices, and some observers have suggested that this reflects the greater efficiency of physicians operating under the incentives of private practice. Others have suggested that clinics tend to give more service in their longer visits. It is impractical to monitor physicians' time. But instead *OPD and emergency room costs can be controlled if reimbursement is tied to a more detailed reckoning of services provided.*

The question of the mix of services between hospital sources and physicians' offices cannot be looked at independently of the question of how physicians' fees are determined and the way those fees affect physicians' participation in the program. In July of 1969 the New York State Department of Health cut the fee for a physician's office visit under Medicaid by 20 percent: between 1969 and 1971 there was a rise of 800,000 visits to outpatient departments and emergency rooms. Because of the high cost of hospital-based care, the cuts in fees cost more money than they saved, and we do not know how many persons went without care as a result.[8] When fees were later returned to their initial level and with an allowance for change in the cost of living, only a small number of physicians were willing to serve Medicaid patients.

There are three choices in the national health insurance decision which will have a strong impact on the way ambulatory medical care is delivered. First is the question of *whether coverage of patients by insurance is compulsory.* If it is not, some persons who are least able to pay for services or who have the least foresight will be thrust upon hospital-based sources of care at higher cost. Second is the decision regarding *whether or not all physicians must accept patients under the plan.* Medicaid made participation voluntary with the result that half the physicians in the city refused to accept Medicaid patients. It is not at all clear how these issues will be resolved.

The third question relates to the *method of fee-setting.* Medicare was able to rely on a usual and customary fee in an environment in which most services were provided under the influence of some market forces. As the health insurance system approaches universality, and if it is to use a fixed-fee system, there will no longer be a market standard to refer to. Medicare actually provides a mixed system, with a fixed fee for physicians when they accept assignment rates, and a market-related fee otherwise. While some regulation may be desirable, *it would be unhealthy for physicians to face controls over fees for out-of-hospital care which they do not face for hospital-based care and thus be squeezed out of providing noninstitutional services.*

Municipal Hospitals: Changes in Utilization

The introduction of Medicare and Medicaid produced a shift in demand away from municipal and toward voluntary hospitals. The number of discharges from municipal hospitals fell 10 percent between 1965 and 1967. However, because of the increased demand for service by the aged, the average length of stay rose 7 percent, with the result that the municipal census declined by only 3 percent. In the voluntary system the increased demand of the aged was added to the shift from municipals. The rise in the average length of stay of 10 percent was accommodated not only by a rise in occupancy rates but also by a fall in discharges of 4 percent. The declines in length of stay which began after 1969 have reduced occupancy rates in voluntary hospitals to 2 percent above pre-Medicare levels and have further reduced the municipal census.

After the initial effects of Medicare and Medicaid, the census in municipal hospitals continued to decline beyond even the results of the more general trend toward shortened lengths of stay. Several explanations are possible, but the relative importance of each remains unresolved.

Some further shifts from municipal to voluntary hospitals may have occurred as reimbursement of the aged and the indigent no longer depended on the use of the municipal system. The effects of free choice of provider may have been gradual as patients developed new relationships with physicians and institutions. The increase in collections of unpaid bills at municipal hospitals may also have induced patients to seek the services of voluntary hospitals once they were no longer able to receive free care.

In addition to these demand effects, it has been suggested that Medicaid reimbursement rates for voluntary hospitals became more favorable over time so that the hospitals accepted Medicaid patients more readily. It has also been suggested that under the affiliation contracts with medical schools and voluntary hospitals—which supply half of the physicians' services in municipal hospitals—the amount of service provided by physicians has declined. (This applied to changes which occurred before appropriations for affiliate services were reduced. It has also been suggested that city cuts in nursing and other support services made physicians less effective.)

The average census for general care beds in municipal hospitals in New York City fell from 6,884 in 1969 to 6,443 in 1973. Between the periods July 1973–January 1974 and July 1974–January 1975, the general care census fell 5 percent to 5,942. The census in other areas experienced even greater declines. The total census of municipal hospitals fell 13 percent between 1969 and 1973 and another 6 percent in the most recent year-to-year comparison. As a result, in July 1974–January 1975 the total census was below 10,000 for the first time (9,980). The closing of beds has not kept pace with these declines in census, and so rates of occupancy have declined. The new Lincoln, Woodhull and North Central Bronx Hospitals scheduled to open in the next two years contain more than 1,000 general care beds. A concentrated effort will be needed to assure that these facilities which were intended for replacement do not result in a further expansion of beds.

A large part of Medicare and Medicaid funding represented a replacement of public subsidies which were previously in effect in the budget of municipal hospitals as payments to voluntary hospitals under the Charitable Institutions Budget and under the Kerr-Mills Act. Replacement of existing funds will be important in future legislation but some expansion can also be expected to take place. As a result, the introduction of national health insurance can be expected to produce further decreases in the use of municipal hospitals and pressures for expansion of capacity.

The municipal hospitals still contain many medically indigent patients—persons whose incomes are low but still above the eligibility levels for Medicaid. This is primarily the result of the cutbacks in Medicaid eligibility which removed more than a million persons from coverage. Fifty-nine percent of municipal inpatients came from families with incomes below $6,000 in 1959–60 compared with 34 percent for voluntary hospitals.[9] A study of Brooklyn hospitals in 1971 showed that 60 percent of municipal patients were eligible for Medicaid compared with 29 percent for voluntary hospitals. Municipal patients, on the other hand, accounted for 16 percent in the municipal hospitals and 29 percent in the voluntaries.[10] Any change in financing which increased the benefits for the Medicaid population could result in a huge decline in the municipal census. A change which reproduced the Medicare pattern for Medicaid patients would cause a truly massive shift. But the history of Medicare and Medicaid does not suggest that shifts will be this large, at least in the beginning. An indication of the initial effects on the municipal hospitals of the introduction of national health insurance is provided by the size of the immediate change in admissions from 1965 to 1967 from

140

214,000 to 200,000. (Admissions is used rather than census since the rise in length of stay due to added utilization of the aged is not applicable for future changes in coverage.) This implies an initial decline in general care census of approximately 6 percent. Adjusting to this decline would require a reduction of approximately 500 beds.

The average daily census for general care in municipal hospitals fell more sharply and continuously than the number of admissions. Census declined from 7,497 in 1965 to 6,903 in 1867, or by 8 percent. By 1974 census had dropped to 6,074, a decline of 19 percent in nine years. However, after dropping from 214,000 in 1965, admissions remained roughly constant at around 200,000 from 1967 to 1974 excluding abortions. All of the decline in census after 1967 was attributable to a fall in the length of stay. This, in part, represented a continued shift of patients requiring longer stays to the voluntary hospitals and, in part, improvements in technology and efficiency. We conservatively assume that declines in length of stay will not continue, and that the average length of stay in municipal hospitals will continue at about one-tenth higher than in voluntary hospitals.

Projections of long-term adjustments can be obtained by asking what would happen if in the future, persons who presently have no hospitalization insurance were to use municipal hospitals as frequently as those who now have it. The figures for 1970 were as follows:

Percentage of New York City Inpatients in Municipal Hospitals[11]

Family income under $6,000	
With insurance	22.91
Without insurance	56.71
Family income over $6,000	
With insurance	9.51
Without insurance	25.01

With a rise in income as well as insurance coverage the use of municipal hospitals for inpatient general care would doubtless fall to the level of use of non-poor families with insurance. If one-tenth of the city's general care patients were served in municipal hospitals, allowing for the difference in length of stay, municipal hospitals would provide 11 percent of all patient days. This would imply 112,000 admissions (excluding abortions) and an average daily census of 3,500, a 42 percent drop from 1974 levels. If these were provided at 85 percent occupancy the number of general care beds required would be 4,100; 3,700 fewer than in 1974.

The projections of long-term adjustments are based on the assumption that persons with equal opportunity and with inpatient insurance are as likely to choose municipal as voluntary hospitals for inpatient care. To the extent that some families receive unequal treatment by medical care delivery or financing systems, or are unable to afford uninsured ambulatory care services which provide entry into voluntary hospitals for inpatient care, the long-term adjustment would be more modest. However, to the extent that services in the voluntary hospitals are considered more desirable, the adjustment could be even greater than indicated.

The Changing Role of Municipal Hospitals

As the financing of health insurance expands and the demand for municipal hospital inpatient services falls, it becomes necessary to go beyond considerations of adjustments in staff and facilities to re-examine the appropriate structure of medical care delivery. This requires a reconsideration of the role which the municipal hospitals play.

Part of the importance of the municipal hospitals in the past has stemmed from their provision of care to persons who faced unequal opportunities because of race. National data indicate that there is still a significant problem of racial discrimination in the pattern of hospital adminissions. A study showed that one-fourth of the nation's hospitals admitted no minority patients in 1969; yet the same study showed substantial improvement between 1966 and 1969.[12] Today the most serious of such problems are confined to a few areas. In large cities, where the range of alternatives is greater, changes in financing make it possible for those who face discrimination to seek other sources of care. In New York City the relatively liberal Medicaid coverage, the ethnic composition, public attitudes and the continued existence of some municipal hospitals can be expected to assure that problems of racial discrimination will not be serious.

At one time municipal hospitals played a significant role as sources of care during periods of economic distress. But during the recession in 1975 municipal inpatient use declined sharply rather than increasing as it did in the Great Depression. It is clear from recent pronouncements in the Congress that even the most restrictive NHI bill will give significant attention to the problem of insurance coverage of the unemployed. This will make it even more possible for those adversely affected by economic factors to receive care in other institutions. (The municipal hospitals are no longer active in the treatment of chronic diseases as they were in the heyday of tuberculosis and cancer hospitals. There may be some appropriate municipal role in the chronic disease area, but much more effort in program development would be needed to design a program around the problem, rather than around the availability of beds. It would also be critical to ascertain that the growing activities of the Veterans Administration hospitals would not be duplicated.)

142

There is a geographic maldistribution of hospital beds which in some cases has been improved by the location of municipal hospitals. For the most part, however, municipal hospitals tend to be distributed similarly to the voluntaries, rather than in such a way as to compensate for their distribution. In view of this, and of the possibilities for greater regional planning of *all* hospitals in the future, we will treat the question of whether hospitals are needed in certain areas as separate from the question of whether those hospitals should be municipal or not.

It is clear that municipal hospitals no longer fulfill their special roles to the same extent that they once did. Those special functions are expected to dwindle still further as the voluntary hospitals continue to take on more of the functions formerly handled by the municipals. The changing role of municipal hospitals, as well as the considerable changes in utilization, makes it necessary to examine a number of issues regarding the structure under which future activities will be carried out: this approach deals simultaneously with bed need and with other aspects of the way services and resources are handled.

At various times suggestions have been made that municipal hospitals should become self-sufficient in staffing, should admit private paying patients, should be transformed into separate subcorporations, or be sold off to, or as, voluntary hospitals. Let us examine some of the considerations which bear on these suggestions. The notion of self-sufficiency in medical staff would be furthered if municipal hospitals were allowed by the city to pay salaries which are competitive with the voluntary hospitals instead of relying on staff provided through affiliation contracts. Further, the combination of bureaucratic restrictions and the undesirability of the neighborhoods in which many municipal hospitals are located would still make it exceedingly difficult to find a sufficient number of good physicians willing to practice full time in those hospitals. The admission of private paying patients raises numerous questions: Would all patients receive equal treatment when some are served by physicians with a profit incentive and others by physicians who are salaried? Even if two groups of patients were to be treated on two separate floors, would not access to ancillary services, operating rooms, etc., create opportunities for substantial inequities? The problem of the morale of salaried physicians may also come into play. To convert municipal hospitals to voluntaries may not by itself provide the assurances of access to care that municipal hospitals now provide. Subcorporations established to bring about a greater local role in governance would leave unanswered the questions of staffing and of the need for service on a regional basis.

Perhaps the most basic problem with all these proposed solutions is that they are piecemeal. What is needed is an alternative that may draw on elements of them but that does so in a manner that will create a complete system of health care.

143

Alternative Approaches: The Consortium Idea

A particularly interesting approach is in the establishment of health services consortia. A health services consortium would combine groups of voluntary and municipal hospitals. *All physicians in the consortium would be allowed to admit patients into any of its facilities.* Shared responsibilities would be developed for underserved areas; the pooling of resources would allow improved utilization; services would be planned for and implemented regionally.

The Capital Area Health Consortium (CAHC) in Hartford has claimed some success along these lines. CAHC is a cooperative arrangement among eight hospitals. This consortium goes significantly beyond the sharing of services. The 2,000 physicians are allowed to treat patients in any of the 3,000 beds in all of the hospitals, thereby making it possible to economize on costly capital equipment.[13] *A health services consortium model combining groups of municipal and voluntary hospitals could have great advantages for New York City*, which is, in fact, in a unique position to provide the initiative for its development. New York City presently contributes approximately $220 million toward the budget of the Health and Hospitals Corporation to cover the costs of: (1) persons who are legally required to pay their bills but do not do so; (2) bills which are the obligations of third-party payers but go uncollected, often because the patient's insurance coverage is unknown; (3) specific subsidies for services which are not reimbursed by other parties; and (4) fees for outpatient care that are calculated on a sliding scale according to income.

Under a properly designed and administered comprehensive national health insurance system, the need for payment under the first two of these categories would disappear. The city would be in a position to use these new-found funds, together with the $150 million presently spent on purchases of staff through affiliation contracts, to provide the incentives of strong financing for health services consortia. Furthermore, cost savings achieved under consortia can be used to increase service intensity or to expand services rather than merely to reduce costs. This choice and its responsiveness to public desires will depend upon the nature of regulation at the state and national level as well as on the city's influence.

As the details of a national health insurance program become clear it will be necessary to consider the appropriateness of other subsidy policies. At present the city should seek greater flexibility in its mandate so that it will be permitted to give funds for hospital care under a wider range of legal and institutional arrangements than it is presently able to, and to make those funds depend on how well performance criteria are met. Any changes in the nature of the city's contribution to the Health and Hospitals Corporation would require changes in legislation at the state level. The New York City Health and Hospitals Corporation Act states that: ". . . the city shall include in its expense budget an appropriation of tax levy for the services provided by the corporation and pay the corporation an amount which shall not be less than one hundred seventy-five million dollars; provided however, that for the fiscal year beginning July first, nineteen hundred seventy-two and thereafter the amount shall be adjusted annually to take account of increases in the cost of health care as reflected in increases in the average rates of reimbursement set by the state pursuant to section twenty-one hundred seven of the public health law for health and hospital services in New York City, and changes in the volume of services rendered by the corporation and required by the city for which no reimbursement from third-party sources is available." [14]

The legislation appears to require revision whether or not the city seeks to use its contribution for consortia. The last phrase is ambiguous and should be replaced by a more explicit statement that the city's contribution will be *reduced* when greater reimbursements from third-party sources become available, whether or not the volume of services changes.

As municipal hospitals and voluntary hospitals become more like each other it is proper that they be treated more alike in terms of capital financing. The interest and amortization payments included in the hospital reimbursement rate would then go directly to the Health and Hospitals Corporation. At present they go to the city with undesirable consequences.

When the state floats bonds for the construction of hospitals, the interest on the bonds becomes a current operating expense. In this and in other cases where external financing has been permitted, the city has taken advantage of the ability to float bonds outside its debt limit to pyramid its loans. Unlike a voluntary hospital, the city pays, not only the amortization, but also the interest out of the capital budget. Normally the city would pay perhaps two and one-half dollars for every dollar it spent (depending on interest rate and term of the bonds) when interest on the bonds is included. But if the city were to use long-term bonds to pay for interest costs in the newly built hospitals, it would spend 4 or 5 dollars for every dollar of service it received. Being aware of this, and in order to avoid these large increases in interest cost, the city has financed interest payments in the capital budget through the use of short-term debts of 5 years or less. Discussions with Jeffrey Weiss have been most helpful on this point. Now, however, the city has gone too heavily into short-term debt and is under great pressure to substitute long-term for short-term debt. But if the interest costs are to be funded by long-term debt the problem of pyramiding will be made far worse. The way to deal with the problem is to get the interest out of the capital budget and back into the expense budget. In future this problem can be avoided if the Health and Hospitals Corporation routinely receives payments for interest in its reimbursement from third-party payers rather than by way of the city.

Policy Recommendations

Despite frequent concerns expressed over more than half a century there is as yet no effective system for controlling costs or for rationalizing utilization. But within the framework established by the reimbursement and regulatory systems there are, nevertheless, important opportunities for action by policy makers in New York City. There has been far too much acceptance of the view that costs of health care, or costs of programs such as Medicaid, are uncontrollable by action at the local level. In fact these costs depend upon services and facilities decisions that are determined as much by local action as they are by actions taken elsewhere. The point can be easily illustrated.

We know, for example, from the national experience with health maintenance organizations that under an HMO system sound medical care can be provided with many fewer hospital beds. Yet the city has not offered as an option to its own employees an HMO plan which ties in insurance for both inpatient and ambulatory care. We know that preadmission surgical screening can greatly reduce the frequency of unnecessary surgery. Yet the city has moved far too slowly in its efforts to establish a surgical screening program to cover all municipal employees. The introduction of national health insurance will raise further issues of this sort.

One of the most important problems facing the city is the already great excess of hospital beds and the danger of still further over expansion of facilities. In order to deal with the problem, the following actions should be taken by the city: The city should plan immediately for a one-tenth reduction in demand for municipal inpatient services (the result of the shift of medically indigent patients to voluntary hospitals that would come about with the introduction of a comprehensive national health insurance program). This adjustment would be in addition to those already required by declines in utilization and those which will be required to offset new municipal facilities as they open up.

The city should press the state to disallow many of the more than 4,000 hospital beds which have been approved for expansion but are not yet under construction, and to refuse any new approvals except in the most extreme circumstances. At the same time, permission to replace existing facilities should be suspended and reviewed.

146

The city should ask the state to examine whether a less costly alternative can be found to the 10,000 nursing home and health-related facility beds which have been approved but are not yet under construction.

Since 1960 the number of voluntary beds has increased by the same amount as municipal hospital beds have decreased. The city should seek a reversal of this pattern and (a) hold the line on voluntary beds when municipal beds decrease; and (b) deliberately use the leverage of decreasing the number of municipal beds to bring about a reduction in the number of general care hospital beds in the system.

The city and the voluntary hospitals should explore the possibility of setting up health service consortia which link groups of municipal and voluntary hospitals in such a way that staff is allowed to treat patients in any hospital in the consortium.

The city should examine the ways in which the $370 million currently spent for subsides to HHC and for affiliation contracts can be used to promote the development of health services consortia. In addition to these measures, a number of additional actions are necessary.

The city should press the state for reimbursement of hospital-based ambulatory care on the basis of specific service provided rather than on a flat per visit rate. The city should examine the issues raised by collective bargaining, over-staffing and work roles in order to avert adverse effects on productivity and innovation. The city should cease the practice of pyramiding loans and instead fund interest payments on the bonds floated through independent authorities in the capital rather than the expense budget. It should allow interest payments which are part of hospital reimbursement rates to be received directly by the Health and Hospitals Corporation. The city should seek revision of the legislation establishing the Health and Hospitals Corporation in order to (a) make more explicit the provision for reducing the size of the city's funding commitment to the Health and Hospitals Corporation as funds are replaced by national health insurance; (b) permit city payments to HHC under a wider range of legal and organizational arrangements; and (c) allow city payments to HHC to be conditional upon the fulfillment of performance standards.

The introduction of national health insurance will bring to the fore many new problems, including many that cannot be anticipated at this time. It is essential that high priority be given to developing and implementing responses in advance wherever early action is possible. In addition to seeking other views and following up on recommendations made here, there is a need for a parallel analysis of efforts to shape the delivery system through actions at the state level, and of the city's stake in its development.

References

[1] For some national estimates see Joseph Newhouse, Charles Phelps and William Schwartz, "Policy Options and the Impact of National Health Insurance," *New England Journal of Medicine* 290:24 (June 13, 1974), pp. 1345–1359.

[2] Irving Leveson, et al., "Trends in General Care Hospital Use in New York City, 1950–1970," New York City Health Services Administration, June 1972, in Irving Leveson and Jeffrey Weiss (editors), *Analysis of Urban Health Problems*, New York: Spectrum Press/John Wiley and Sons, 1976. (The study covered all beds in general care hospitals.)

[3] This is part of a national pattern which can be expected to continue. (See Irving Leveson, *Poverty and Public Policy*, New York: Hudson Institute, July, 1975.)

[4] Public hospitals do not find that most empty beds fill up and they have been experiencing large declines in occupancy rates across the country. (See Irving Leveson and Regina Reibstein, "The Economics of Hospital Utilization Under Insurance," New York City Health Services Administration, May, 1974. Preliminary findings were reported in the May 1974 *Proceedings of the Social Statistics Section of the American Statistical Association.*)

[5] For further discussion on this point see Herbert Klarman, "Approaches to Moderating the Increases in Medical Care Costs," *Medical Care*, 7:3 (May–June 1969), pp. 175–190.

[6] U.S. Bureau of Labor Statistics, *Industry Wage Survey, Hospitals, 1966 and 1969.*

[7] Irving Leveson and Gelvin Stevenson, "Trends in Physicians in New York City, 1959 to 1970," *New York State Journal of Medicine* (September, 1974), pp. 1844–1852.

[8] Irving Leveson et al., "The Recent Growth in Hospital Based Ambulatory Care," New York City Health Services Administration, November 1972, in Irving Leveson and Jeffrey Weiss, *Analysis of Urban Health Problems.*

[9] Ronald Rudolf, "Out of Pocket Costs for Medical Care in New York City, 1969–1970," New York City Health Services Administration, May 1974.

[10] Associated Hospital Service of New York, One Day Census, March 1971, computed from data reported in Health and Hospital Planning Council of Southern New York, *General Hospitals and Related Health Services in Brooklyn, June 1974*, Table 16.

[11] Ronald Rudolf, "Out of Pocket Medical Expenditures," New York City Department of Health, 1975, Table 11, based on data from the New York City Population Health Survey.

[12] American Public Health Association, *Minority Health Chart Book*, October 1974. (The data cited were derived from studies of Karen Davis at the Brookings Institution).

[13] "Performing Major Surgery on Hospital Costs," *Business Week*, May 19, 1975.

[14] Section 1a, paragraph 7386, Chapter 5, Title 18, Public Health Law of New York.

The National Health Planning and Resources Development Act of 1974 and National Health Insurance

FRANK VAN DYKE

In this paper, emphasis is placed upon (1) the organizational framework established by the National Health Planning and Resources Development Act; (2) what the various levels of government will do to carry out the act; and (3) some questions about how the legislation may work in local areas. Unless we understand the new planning law and some of the opportunities and problems, real or imagined, it may create, we cannot discuss how health insurance could or should relate to it. In particular, since P.L. 93-641, signed on 4 January 1975, places additional responsibilities on local administrations, as well as added planning functions at state and federal levels, we should examine this new system to determine whether it is a useful vehicle to tie to national health insurance.

As one reads the House and Senate testimony leading up to passage of the bill one is impressed by the lukewarm or hostile attitude of those who testified. Except for the planners, mainly the Comprehensive Health Planning (CHP) Agencies, there was relatively little support. Why did it pass? In this case, Congress was thinking of money. The rapid increase in health expenditures without any end in sight brought normally cautious committee members to recommend, and Congress to enact, a drastic measure which they hope will place limits on the costs of medical care.

In examining the findings and purpose of the new law, note the relative stress placed upon economics and changes in the delivery system. Section 2 (a) (1) states: "the achievement of equal access to quality health care *at a reasonable cost* (underlining added) is a priority of the Federal government." Section 2(a) (2) adds: "The massive infusion of Federal funds into the existing health care system has contributed to inflationary increases in the cost of health care and failed to produce an adequate supply or distribution of health resources, and consequently has not made possible equal access for everyone to such resources," Section 2(a) (4) goes on to say: "Increases in the cost of health care, particularly of hospital stays have been uncontrollable and inflationary, and there are presently inadequate incentives for the use of appropriate alternative levels of health care, and for the substitution of ambulatory and intermediate care for inpatient hospital care."

Certificate-of-need legislation, which began in New York State, attempted to place limits upon the growth of health facilities. Prior to certificate-of-need, Hill-Burton required area planning for facilities development. Later, both Comprehensive Health Planning Agencies and Regional Medical Programs (RMP) were created to plan for some parts of the health system. Any successes of these various attempts to plan were obscured by rising costs and the inability of the health system to provide care to some parts of the population. All of them provided an administrative framework in which state and local public officials, providers and consumers gained experience in the health planning process. Thus the new law builds upon this reservoir of state and local personnel engaged in planning.

Overview of Public Law 93-641

The law combines three existing agencies at federal, state and local levels. Hill-Burton, Comprehensive Health Planning and Regional Medical Programs will operate as a single program. In the broadest sense the law establishes review mechanisms for federal expenditures for personal health. It will develop a system of federal resource allocation which is intended either to control or influence how federal health dollars are spent and also to influence expenditures made by the private sector. Section 1502 of the law lists ten national health priorities for planning and resources development. These priorities taken together would require changes in financing of medical care, manpower development, facilities construction and organization of services. In the language of the law "it is the purpose of this Act to facilitate the development of recommendations for a national health planning policy, to augment areawide and State planning for health services, manpower and facilities and to authorize financial assistance for the development of resources to further that policy." More specifically the law does several things: (1) It will create a national system of health resource indices, and methods and systems of monitoring costs. This primarily federal function would develop baselines to be employed by states and localities in day to day determination of allocation and would also serve as yardsticks for use by the secretary in approval or disapproval of specific recommendations from states and local areas. (2) A major function will be approval or disapproval by health systems agencies (HSAs) of federal funds for the area. Action taken under this resource allocation function would ultimately be reviewed by the secretary. (3) Another area covered is certificate-of-need for facility construction. The law requires that this be done by state agencies. (4) Still another major provision of the act requires evaluation of continuing appropriateness of services and facilities. If the purpose of the law could be summed up in a sentence it would be that the expenditure of federal funds for health services will be planned, monitored and controlled through a new planning process.

The machinery to carry out this lengthy act is as intricate as the requirements of what is to be done. Unlike some previous pieces of health legislation the law intends to establish federal control. Consequently, final authority for decision making rests with HEW. The Secretary will be assisted by an advisory council. On certificate-of-need and grants for construction, HEW will be advised by state councils, and on federal health grants or contracts to localities, HEW will be advised by area-wide councils.

National Administration of the Law: Planning Responsibilities

Probably the most sweeping effect the law can have upon the health system is the direction to the secretary to establish by regulation within eighteen months "a statement of national health planning goals developed after consideration of priorities—which goals to the maximum extent practicable should be expressed in quantitative terms." Taken together with other sections of the law, this statement of goals can be considered as a national plan for development and use of health resources. More specifically, the secretary is required to establish "standards respecting the appropriate supply, distribution and organization of health resources." The requirement that planning shall be expressed in quantitative terms is especially interesting because it would enable the secretary to avoid the vagueness of many planning documents. These goals, if they are stated in regulations of some reasonable precision, would be the national framework for the expenditure of federal funds for health. To use an example, one of the priorities in the law calls for multi-institutional arrangements for the sharing of support services necessary to all health service institutions. The secretary could require that the annual implementation plan of the Health Systems Agencies (which will be discussed later) include development of multi-institutional arrangements; he could also require that grants and contracts to a health service area must conform with a health service area plan in this respect. Perhaps a more cogent example follows from the very heavy emphasis in the law on ambulatory care. If a state was not in substantial compliance with the national planning goals for provision of outpatient facilities, the secretary could withhold Title 16 funds for hospital construction for the entire state or for individual projects.

What obstacles can we foresee to the development of a national plan for health services? In recent years, federal health officials have complained that they have not been able to find the technical personnel required to develop sophisticated systems of review and monitoring of health systems. Undoubtedly there is a scarcity of such people. But one wonders if this is the root of the problem. Technicians are useless without leadership, and leaders, however committed they may be, cannot operate effectively in an environment in which the rules change every few months. Master planning has gone out of fashion, yet in order to be effective, leaders as well as technicians must operate in a framework which has reasonably explicit goals and which permits both continuity and orderly change. A successful example of this type of federal planning has been the Hill-Burton program. The intent of the program was to expand hospital facilities in the country based upon priorities established by law. Over the years, despite mistakes and problems, this intent has been carried out. In contrast, neither CHP nor RMP, viewed from a national perspective, have been particularly successful. One can speculate that this was caused by rather vague goals, quickly shifting priorities and by uncertainties of intent and purpose, rather than by any lack of leadership or technical competence. Obviously, a comprehensive national plan for health services is more difficult to develop and administer than the three programs it will replace. But it would have a reasonable chance for success if priorities have some continuity, and if the priorities are tied to the expenditure of federal funds for health.

Data Gathering

At a somewhat more technical level we should examine carefully the requirement that national goals, to the extent possible, be expressed quantitatively. As an example of the problems, let us look at the overriding priority in the law of emphasizing ambulatory care (and presumably placing less emphasis on inpatient care). Two recent studies reach diametrically opposite conclusions on the demand for ambulatory care in a free-market setting. The Newhouse finding estimates a huge increase in demand under national health insurance.[1] In contrast, a household survey made in Quebec before and after the introduction of universal compulsory health insurance found that differences in volume of physician services between the two periods were minimal.[2] Although these studies do not in an exact way compare like with like, the short-range Quebec experience and the Newhouse estimates for a somewhat longer period vary so wildly that we are left wondering about the state of the art. This lack of precision is not, of course, limited to health planning. How then, can the secretary develop the quantitative data required by the Act? The answer, I think, is to take successful instances in the field of health and emulate them. The National Center for Disease Control, with

152

a clear purpose in view, has established, over a period of time, data gathering systems. These data are used in developing trends and projections which are employed by federal, state and local health officials. Such systems cannot be set up overnight and they are expensive. But without a carefully established data-base, national health planning will be fragmentary at best. If it is to succeed, the secretary must have the authority and the funds to collect and maintain the quantitative information required to establish national health planning goals.

Technical Assistance

Several pages of the law describe the types of data and technical assistance the secretary must supply to the state and area-wide agencies and must obtain for his own use. For example, the secretary will specify "the minimum data needed to determine the health status of the residents of a health service area and the determinants of such status." He must also establish a national health planning information center for "use in the analysis of issues and problems." Possibly the most difficult technical tasks the secretary must accomplish within one year of enactment of the law is to establish a uniform system for calculating costs of services and volume of services in health service institutions and to establish a uniform system of calculating rates to be charged by health insurers. In addition, the secretary must classify health service institutions according to (among other things) the complexity of services provided. Finally, the secretary must establish a uniform system for reporting by institutions of costs, volume of services and rates. The law does not, however, require institutions to participate in any system which is developed. A fair presumption is that this intense activity required of the secretary is preparation for national health insurance.

State Administration

The governor of each state will establish a state health planning and development agency under agreement with HEW. The state agency will be advised by a Statewide Health Coordinating Council, appointed by the governor, and composed of representatives of the local area-wide agencies and others, including public officials. At least 60 percent of the council will be representatives of the local agencies, and a majority of the entire council will be consumers. The law describes in considerable detail the process by which the governor is to establish the administrative machinery by agreement with the secretary, although it does not absolutely require the state to take any action at all. If, however, after four years, an agreement with the secretary is not in effect, the secretary may not make any grants, loans, or contracts in a state under the Public Health Service Act or any of the other laws which provide federal health funds to a state.

The state agency will develop a state administrative program which, among other things, must provide for "the collection, retrieval analysis, reporting and publication of statistical and other information related to health and health care" and requires providers of health care to make statistical and other reports to the state agency.

Medical Facilities

One of the important functions of the state agency is to develop a state medical facilities plan. This facilities plan must be consistent with the state health plan (described later). Each state, as under Hill-Burton, will receive an annual allotment in accord with the national health priorities listed in the act. Not less than 25 percent of the allotment must be spent for outpatient facilities in medically underserved areas, and at least half of this money for outpatient facility construction must be allocated to rural areas. The lack of emphasis upon inpatient care is underscored by the requirement that not more than 25 percent of the funds may be obligated for new inpatient facilities, and that those facilities be constructed only in areas which have experienced recent rapid population growth. For the first year, $150 million is appropriated for these purposes with the restriction that each state receive at least $1 million. It is unlikely with this limited amount of money that this section of the law will have much effect on redirecting priorities, especially in New York City and New York State. If we should have a national health insurance law, large sums of federal funds for construction will be needed. This section of the law also provides funds for loans and loan guarantees for construction and for special project grants to eliminate safety hazards and to meet hospital code standards. The law also strengthens the authority of the secretary to compel hospitals to provide "freecare" under Hill-Burton grants or under new grants from federal funds.

Certificate-of-Need Program

A second major function of the state agency is to develop and administer a certificate-of-need program. Determination must be made "prior to the time such services, facilities, and organizations are offered or developed or substantial expenditures are undertaken . . ." (Sec 1523 (a)). Certificate-of-need decisions will be based upon the state plan. The states will have at least two years to develop a program under regulations which have not yet been issued. Eugene Rubel, former Director of the Bureau of Health Planning and Resources Development has said, "I think every single certificate of need program now in existence will have to be changed as a result of this law." New York State, which has the oldest certificate-of-need legislation in the nation, has had problems in implementing the law, especially recently. The New York State Metcalf-McCloskey Act antedates the Comprehensive Health Planning Law, and the administrative mechanisms in the state for carrying out both pieces of legislation have never been fully integrated. We have parallel health planning bodies at the state level and in some of the localities. We also do not know what effect Metcalf-McCloskey has had. No comprehensive study has ever been made. We do know from simple observation that construction of inpatient facilities continues in areas which are officially described as over-bedded. This may be caused by the lack of hard definitions of need for facilities or by an unwillingness to stick to the definitions in particular instances. In any event this problem may be solved for us if the secretary employs his authority by regulation and describes what each certificate-of-need program shall do. The state agency will also serve as the designated planning agency for the purposes of Section 1122 of the Social Security Act. This function is somewhat limited for planning purposes because it takes effect (by withholding Medicare and Medicaid funds) only after an unapproved facility is constructed.

Rate Regulation

As various versions of the health planning bill were discussed in the House and Senate, one of the most controversial provisions was dropped. This would have required the states to establish a program of rate regulation for health care. In its place the secretary is authorized to enter into agreements with not more than six states which have authority under state law to carry out rate-regulation functions. The intent of the law is to go further than either federal or state governments have thus far gone in rate regulation, e.g., "create incentives at each point in the delivery of health services for utilization of the most economical modes of services feasible . . ." (Sec 1526(a)). The Bureau of Health Planning and Resources Development has agreed that the Social Security Administration will implement this part of the planning law. SSA has had responsibility for incentive reimbursement under Medicare. This example of interaction between the federal planning agency and Medicare may be a precedent for joint action between planning and reimbursement agencies under national health insurance.

Appropriateness

Another controversial section of the law is a requirement that each Health Systems Agency shall review and make recommendations to the state agency at least once every five years as to the "appropriateness" of all institutional health services in the area (Sec 1513 (g)). This section, although it emerged without teeth to enforce it, nevertheless requires the state and area agencies to take note of inappropriate services and could conceivably lead to revisions of the state and local plans; this, in turn, would create difficulties for providers of "inappropriate" services. Unless this vague language is strengthened by regulation, however, it is difficult to see how, in practice, a state or local planning body could make a conclusive determination. The findings of appropriate or inappropriate services are to be made public.

The State Health Plan

The primary responsibility of the state agency and the statewide Health Coordinating Council is to prepare and approve a state health plan. Each of the health systems agency plans and their implementation plans, as well as the state facilities construction plan, must conform to the state plan. The state plan, in its totality, must be made up of the plans developed by the health service areas and will be reviewed and revised annually. Should the state make a decision which is not consistent with local goals or priorities, it must explain its decision in a detailed statement to the Health Systems Agency.

The effect of the law on the state is to "federalize" such health planning as exists and to require states which have not carried out such functions as certificate-of-need for facilities to institute them. The penalty for not doing so is withdrawal of federal health funds. It can also be said that even if such a drastic step is not taken, the secretary, through his powers to approve or disapprove specific requests for funds, could, in effect, act as the health planning agency for a state.

Local Area Planning: Health Systems Agencies

The first step in establishing Health Systems Agencies has been completed. The law defines the criteria for determining the boundaries of health service areas. The governor of each state and the secretary decide where the boundaries are to be.

A health systems agency can be a non-profit corporation, a public regional planning body, or a unit of local government. The governing body, or boards of the agency, will have a majority of members who are consumers, but not greater than 60 percent. The consumers must be broadly representative of "social, economic, linguistic and racial population, geographic areas and major purchasers of health care" (Sec. 1512C). The remaining places are to be filled by providers who must represent health professionals, institutions (hospitals, long-term care facilities and

HMOs), health insurers, professional schools and the allied health professions. As either consumers or providers, public elected officials, other government officials and representatives of public and private health agencies will be members of the governing body. The governing body may not be larger than thirty, unless it has established an executive committee of not more than 25 members. If a health systems agency chooses to have an executive committee, it must delegate to it authority to take action on all matters except the establishment and revision of the health systems plan and the annual implementation plan. A health systems agency may establish sub-area advisory councils to advise the governing body. The secretary will amplify by regulation, standards and criteria, although the law is reasonably specific about the formation of a health systems agency and the composition of its board. These regulations have not yet been issued.

The local agency, like the federal and state levels of administration, will combine the functions of CHP, RMP and Hill-Burton. Thus there is no successor agency. A new agency will be formed.

Area Health Services Development Fund

Another section of the law, as has been noted, establishes an area health service development fund. The secretary will make a lump sum grant to each HSA, and the HSA will use the fund for grants or contracts to public and private non-profit entities for projects and programs which the agency determines are necessary to carry out the health service plan. The amount of money for any HSA for this purpose will not be more than one dollar multiplied by the population of the area. This provision of the law replaces the present arrangements for local grants or contracts by RMP.

HSA Board Composition

Taking the law at face value, many CHP agencies would meet the new standards for the composition of HSA boards. One difference would seem to be in the way CHP boards have been required to function. As it is, executive committees of the CHP have not been entitled to exercise the authority of the agencies. A change in the law has made that possible. One of the decisions which will need to be made in each health service area is whether to have a board with a membership greater than thirty and an executive committee, or a lesser board membership without one. When the CHP agency in New York City was being organized, an effort was made to make the board relatively small. It was felt that, by creating sub-area councils, the many interests that P.L. 89-749 required to be represented would be satisfied with sub-area representation. They were not;

providers in particular each with a different interest insisted upon central board representation. Voluntary hospitals could not have one representative—each of the major systems needed representation; similarly, proprietary and municipal hospitals, each for very good reasons, wanted a place on the board. As one proceeded through the list of providers each of them sought a place in the decision-making body. Although less populous areas with less diversity than New York City have been able to create relatively small CHP boards, it was not possible and probably not desirable to do so here. If important segments of the provider or consumer communities are left out of the planning process they will use their exclusion as basis for opposition to the agency.

Locating the new agency outside the framework of city government would have the advantage of freeing it from local budgetary controls and the restrictive requirements of municipal civil service. A possible disadvantage of forming a free-standing health systems agency is that under certain circumstances it might not be accountable to the public in the area. Public accountability is a perplexing issue. In this instance the law requires that HSAs shall conduct their meetings in public, give adequate notice of meetings, issue public reports and hold public hearings. It goes so far as to define a quorum. But, aside from general statements on the composition of the planning body, the law does not touch on the most important issues—how the first board is to be selected and how a structure is to be created which would permit the changes in composition and membership which, for want of a better phrase, would represent and continue to represent the public interest.

There is another way of looking at this matter. Organizationally, the HSAs are local arms of the secretary. He establishes them, supervises them, pays them. He must approve their health systems plan (HSP) and their annual implementation plan (AIP). They recommend directly to him (not through the state) the approval or disapproval of federal health funds for the local area. As noted, HSAs, unlike "B" agencies, will be federally funded in full. Although they may receive and spend non-federal funds, and may be entitled to federal matching for such funds, federal matching will "not include any funds contributed to the Agency by any individual or private entity which has a financial, fiduciary, or other direct interest in the development, expansion, or support of health resources."

In this organizational model we would hold the secretary accountable for the actions of the bodies which he has established. If he permits narrow interests to dominate the local planning bodies, our recourse would not be to local public officials or state public officials but to the federal government. In summary, it should be said that our experience in public administration with "free floating" authorities has not been happy. Removed from public accountability and from day-to-day responsibility toward any elected or appointed public official, they have sometimes become a vehicle for spending public funds or making public decisions for essentially narrow purposes. Local decision-makers must be alert to this broad issue as HSAs are formed.

Data Collection

"A health systems agency shall have a staff which provides the agency with expertise in at least the following: (1) Administration, (2) the gathering and analysis of data, (3) health planning and (4) the development and use of health resources . . ." (Sec 1512(b) (2). As noted previously, the law lays stress on use of quantitative data and technology in developing plans. The above section relating to local planning reinforces this intent. As all of us know from experience that in New York City hard health-planning data is difficult to come by, especially on a sub-area basis. The law lists six specific types of data which the agency will collect and analyze, including: health status of residents; status and use of the delivery system; the effect of the delivery system on health status; an inventory of health resources, including personnel; utilization patterns; and environmental and occupational health factors affecting health. New York City has some of this information scattered in dozens of public and private agencies. Some of it has never been collected and some of it, e.g., the effect of the delivery system on health status, except in a gross sense, would be especially difficult to obtain. Nevertheless, this is what is expected of us.

At a first glance at these requirements, as well as some others in the law, it would seem as though the HSAs, like CHP and RMP, are being programmed for failure. These expectations are beyond accomplishment unless we make a basic assumption: If the federal government wants the states and localities to have an extensive data base for health planning, it must establish a national system of data collection. This national system could be decentralized to the states and health services areas, or data collected by the federal government could be provided to the planning areas. Necessarily, although the law does not say so, provider-based data on costs of services would need to be part of such a system if the overriding purpose of the new planning law—the prudent use of limited resources—is to be carried out. The alternative to a federal health data system is not mere fragmentation. We simply do not have the manpower available—with the required high degree of skills—to be shifted to 200 or more state and local health planning agencies in order to develop and maintain sophisticated data systems. It is also unlikely that the federal government would furnish the large sums necessary to establish many separate data-collection systems.

159

The immediate federal intent, however, is to use existing data and to employ the resources of the Cooperative Health Statistics System of the National Center for Health Statistics. The cooperative system, elaborate in concept and voluntary in nature, was established to provide a national uniform data base with the ability to disaggregate data by area; it will not, however, be fully operational for a number of years. The Social Security Administration, it is hoped, will be able to provide Medicare data to state and local planning bodies. In addition, if funds could be made available, the New York State Department of Health should be able to supply HSAs with data, particularly as it relates to institutional planning. If we think of the data collection responsibilities of the HSAs as an evolving process, it is possible to foresee that, over a period of time, they will have a data base supplied from federal and state sources and supplemented by local special studies. With the advent of national health insurance, provider and patient-related data could be fed into the federal, state and local planning endeavors. However, for the next several years at least, we have a law which requires planning but which is without the data systems to support it.

Planning Function

The primary responsibility of the health system agencies is to develop two plans: The first, a health systems plan (HSP) will be a statement of goals which is "consistent with the national guidelines for health planning policy issued by the secretary—respecting supply, distribution and organization of health resources and services . . ." [(Sec. 1513 (b) (2)]. The second plan will be an annual implementation plan (AIP) which will describe the objectives and priorities which are necessary to achieve the goals in the HSP. These plans will be supplemented by specific plans and projects.

Another example of the law's intent to provide a unified approach to health planning is found in the requirement that HSAs coordinate their activities with other federally-supported health agencies such as PSROs. In particular, HSAs are expected to arrange that activities of other planning and review agencies fit into the health service plans and annual implementation plans. The HSAs will assist the state planning agencies in their responsibilities for facilities construction by recommending the need for any new institutional health services and by recommending priorities each year for modernization, construction and conversion of facilities.

Disposition of Federal Funds

The "proposed use" clause of the law is probably the strongest weapon possessed by the HSAs to enforce their HSPs and AIPs. The

HSAs will "approve or "disapprove" each proposed use of federal health funds for the area, including federal health funds under control of the states. This does not apply to Social Security Act funds. The agency will have 60 days to make a review of each proposed grant, contract, loan, or loan guarantee and, if it disapproves, will notify the secretary. The secretary may overrule the decision of the HSA, but only after asking the opinion of the state health agency. He must also make a detailed explanation of his decision to the HSA. This authority of the HSA over the use of federal funds in an area could have the beneficial effect of coordinating and directing the priorities of federal health resources. As a practical matter, it may be asking too much of a locality to expect it to refuse to accept federal project funds. One wonders whether, instead, the notoriously uncoordinated flow of federal health funds to thousands of projects each year could not, somehow, through the planning process, be better integrated at the federal level before these funds reach the health service areas. Some previous experiences with federal revenue have not been reassuring. It may be that the system of federal grants for specific purposes—carefully coordinated at the federal level—is the wiser way to achieve national goals. In our own locality attempts to control or curtail the use of health resources have been disappointing. Gouverneur Hospital was not needed as an inpatient facility, yet pressure was such that the city built a redundant hospital. In Manhattan, over-bedded by standards of the Health and Hospital Planning Council, no facility of any consequence has been closed. In fact, some institutions which are able to find the necessary money have continued to expand. The question, then, is whether a locally created council of consumers and providers could withstand the pressures for expansion. What would their interest be in curtailing the expenditure of federal dollars coming to the area via Medicare or national health insurance? Would they not, in fact, become the advocates of bringing more, rather than less, to the locality through open-ended financing?

In the continuing drama about health care costs the providers wear the black hats and the consumers the white hats. This arrangement appears to suit most of us. The providers are motivated by greed and a desire to retain power; the consumers look to the public welfare. Like many soap operas, this scenario contains elements of truth and, in fact, sometimes approaches reality. The flaw in this simplified attitudinal value system becomes apparent when neither consumers nor providers have incentives to develop and maintain cost-effective health delivery systems. In fact when consumers are without the skilled staff leadership or data to support a point of view, they often share with providers a desire to add to existing health resources in their communities—whether or not such additions could meet criteria for expansion. It is especially difficult for consumers to accurately evaluate existing community resources, even though they may be well aware of existing deficiencies. The gap in expertise between developing goals and achieving them is particularly wide for the consumer part of the health planning partnership.

If the decision that consumers and providers must make is whether to spend or not to spend federal funds in their communities, they will, more often than not, decide to spend the money. If the planning process were to be conducted in a somewhat different framework, however, a different result might be obtained. If, as a result of the health planning law and national health insurance, each health service area had to work with a "budget" ceiling—one based upon nationally developed criteria—and had, as well, some discretionary funds to allocate as part of the planning process, one can see a situation in which both consumers and providers alike would be prompted to review wasteful or low-priority health activities in order that funds might be freed up for more urgent needs. If this new system of health planning were to be viewed as one of local allocation of national resources based on nationally determined priorities, and with a "budget" for each area, then the local boards could probably fulfill successfully their roles as local arms of a national system.

As an illustration of the ability or lack of it of local bodies to plan for a health system, let us examine controls on hospital construction under Medicare. The Medicare reimbursement formula—like Blue Cross formulas—includes allowance for hospital depreciation. This allowance is a part of the daily rate received from Medicare by the hospitals. Setting aside funds for depreciation of buildings is an accepted corporate practice. But Medicare, by returning depreciation allowance to each hospital, acts on the theory that each hospital will continue in perpetuity. It is true that hard-pressed hospitals often use money received for depreciation for operating expenses. But a HSA Board will find it difficult to plan for reduction of beds, to close redundant facilities, or to move facilities from areas where they are no longer needed if Medicare or national health insurance reimbursement formulas are based on the assumption that every institution should exist forever.

Let us suppose that, instead of returning a depreciation allowance for construction to each hospital, national health insurance established a facilities depreciation fund. Under such an arrangement state and local planning bodies would be able to allocate construction funds for priority projects. As a negative control, institutions would not have health insurance dollars at their own disposal for construction. Certificate-of-need would then become a positive rather than a negative control. This old idea would appeal to few institutional managers. But we are faced with the dilemma of changing, however slowly and painfully, from open-ended financing of all parts of the health system to more selective financing of nationally determined priorities. This is the direction P.L. 93-

641 is taking us. The beginning of this paper mentioned that the congressional motivation for the new law was control of money for health. This new vehicle for allocation of resources is untested. It cannot work unless it actively participates in allocation of resources, especially those enormous sums which will flow from national health insurance.

Some General Implications and Observations

Is it likely that national health insurance will relate to the health planning law? A careful reading of two quite different current approaches to national health insurance may give us a clue. H.R.1, introduced by Mr. Ullman in January 1975, carefully builds upon the current methods of financing and administering of health insurance with one significant departure. Like the Nixon bill in the last session, it actively promotes HMOs. Why does this somewhat conservative or middle-of-the-road measure establish Health Care Corporations and then give them a generous financial edge in competition for subscribers? The answer lies, not in any desire to change the delivery system but in the current belief that HMOs—operating under capitation—will save money. Like the Professional Standards Review Organization (PSRO) law (a special interest of a conservative senator) which requires utilization review of care rendered to Medicare and Medicaid patients, H.R.1 would introduce delivery-system changes as a means of controlling health expenditures. If the assumption is correct that an overriding concern of Congress is to control health costs, one can foresee that only a slight redrafting of the Ullman bill would make the Health Care Corporation areas coterminous with, or subdivisions of, the health service areas.

S.3, the Kennedy-Javits-Corman bill introduced in the current session, had language added at the last moment which refers directly to the new planning law. In various sections of the bill, and in various contexts, the administration of health insurance is tied to the Health Planning and Resources Development Act. For example, the local administrative areas for health insurance would have the same boundaries as the health service areas. The Kennedy-Javits-Corman bill, of course, is much more ambitious than the Ullman bill. If it is enacted, the authority of the secretary, combined with his existing authority under P.L. 93-641 to make changes in the delivery system, would be greatly enhanced. But under either "conservative" or "liberal" health insurance formulations, however ill-defined these terms may be, we can reasonably expect that the administration of national health insurance will be coordinated, or perhaps integrated, with health planning.

The allocation of resources for health is now largely a function of the free market—to the extent that it exists in health economics. Superimposing planning controls on a free market economy is extraordinarily difficult to manage, as we have found in areas such as agriculture. Neither P.L. 93-641, nor any of the other principal health insurance bills before Congress, contemplates a completely directed health delivery system such as the National Health Service of Great Britain. Rather the new planning law charges the various authorities at federal, state and local levels with maintaining an intricate system of checks and balances that directs resources to priorities in health delivery, and restrains or cuts off resources to unneeded or unwanted parts of the system—within the context of American free enterprise. This may be looked upon as a step toward making free enterprise work in health.

The complicated and cumbersome administrative machinery designed to carry out the purposes of P.L. 93-641 is not an accident; it is deliberate. Public planning has not been popular in the United States. It has overtones of socialism. The new law follows our basic legal system which diffuses power among several branches and levels of government. To make the planning pill more palatable, the administration and Congress decided to distribute the exercise of the powers conferred under the act among not only federal, state and local bodies, but to so constitute those state and local bodies that power would be shared by large groups with varied viewpoints. The checks and balances in this administrative system are such that, at best, the planning process will be slow—as perhaps it should be. At worst, we run the risk which is one of the faults of CHP, of so emphasizing process to the subordination of content that little else takes place; the form but not the substance of planning. If this should happen what will the consequences be? One possible consequence, without some other intervening factor such as change in the law, is fairly clear. If organizations at the state and local levels should fail to meet the criteria established by the secretary, they can be replaced by him.

It has been said that national health insurance will increase the demand for health services (although the short-range Quebec experience does not seem to bear this out). In our economy, if demand increases, prices increase, except where planning is effective in channelling demand to lower-cost modes of delivery or in preventing unnecessary care. The chief weapon at hand, considering our present knowledge, is to restrict access to inpatient beds and direct patients to ambulatory services. The law, as has been noted, begins this process by the negative control of restricting funds for building new inpatient facilities and by encouraging construction for ambulatory care. Control in the form of certification-of-need is designed to limit all construction to that considered necessary in the annual implementation plan.

Limiting facilities, however, even if successful, treats only one part of the problem. In the medical care economy "demand" is controlled by

164

physicians and the planning law does little about restricting access to physicians or limiting their practice. One can surmise that, unless a national health insurance law directs payment to "desirable" medical care practices and discourages payment for "undesirable" diagnosis or treatment, the total costs of care will continue to rise. Kennedy-Javits-Corman attempts to treat this aspect of economic and social planning by a number of devices one of which is to place some restrictions on payments for the practice of surgery. It also, like the Ullman bill, encourages prepaid group practice as a means of limiting demand. The function of restricting demand is, of course, merely one side of health planning. In a more positive sense, the planning law would encourage the addition of resources to some areas and to some groups in the population. This is a more congenial aspect of planning in this country, although a planned expansion based on priorities is less familiar to us than an expansion in all directions at once.

If planned expansion is to proceed in some orderly fashion there must be linkages—between the planning law, manpower legislation and national health insurance. At this writing, manpower bills are just beginning to be considered by Congress. It is interesting to note that each of the ten priorities of P.L. 93-641 is directly connected to manpower. Presumably these priorities or others will be the focus of a manpower law. Although manpower legislation may not be devoted exclusively to the needs of a national health insurance system, it should direct attention and funds to personnel which are crucial for national health insurance. For example, if dental services are to be part of a health insurance measure, it is important to consider dental manpower needs with specific reference to the scope and volume of those services which dentists and ancillary dental personnel will be expected to deliver, as well as the time at which such services will become covered under the law. The phasing in of dental benefits could be accompanied by a manpower bill timetable for the production of dental and ancillary manpower if shortages should result from increased demand. This example can be applied to many other professions as well, either in the form of priorities for producing new workers or redirecting the labor of existing personnel.

One of the lessons of Medicare is that provision of benefits by law does not deliver services. Regional and socioeconomic differences in the use of services by the Medicare population relate, in part, at least, to the availability of services. Thus, if the first listed priority of P.L. 93-641 ("The provision of primary care services for medically underserved populations, especially those which are located in rural or economically depressed areas") is to be carried out, then either a manpower law, or a health insurance law, or both, must address itself to those incentives or penalties which will lead to the pressure of sufficient manpower in these

165

underserved areas or populations. We must face the possibility that the attempt by the law to control the supply and demand of services and manpower will not succeed. The purposes of the law are ambitious and the administrative devices to carry it out, as has been noted, are elaborate. If it should happen that it does not work, we can only conclude, based on what we know now, that something stronger will replace it.

During the last fifteen years or so we have been on a path or, perhaps more accurately, on an unpaved rough track, which leads in the direction of a managed health economy. What has been little appreciated or understood as a part of this effort are the attempts to establish controls, however halting, that have been made by the private sector, particularly by Blue Cross. Some of the Blue Cross plans have, openly or covertly, encouraged state regulation of hospital construction, and many of them have adopted reimbursement formulas which tend to restrict hospital costs and hospital expansion. But voluntary health insurers are not in a position to direct the hospital economy. Not only do they have ties to providers, but few of them cover a large enough segment of the prepaid hospital-care market to give them a dominant role in hospital planning.

Medicare has had less influence on directing the health delivery system than some observers had expected in 1966. The language of Title 18 was written to enable providers to render services in their accustomed ways and to pay them in the traditional manner. The only departure from this principle was to encourage hospital-based radiologists, pathologists and anesthesiologists to render separate bills to patients. Although Medicare now pays a significant share of health-care dollars to providers, it has had little success in attempting to direct those dollars, at least in a positive planning sense. In fact, as the Medicare law intended, the Social Security Administration simply paid its money into the system as it existed. Congress has now gone in another direction with P.L. 93-641, and yet one curious omission from P.L. 93-641 deserves some comment. Title 18, with its pattern of payments into a creaky delivery system, is reputed to have caused, in part at least, the rapid inflation of the costs of medical care to everyone. Yet the drafters of the new planning law did not specify that both the Social Security Administration and the Secretary must take positive steps to see that federal Medicare funds be spent in accordance with federal planning priorities. Thus the most effective way of enforcing planning decisions was avoided by both Congress and the administration.

This discussion of the National Health Planning and Resources Development Act of 1974 has been largely in terms of a short-range time frame, without the benefit of knowing what kind of national health insurance we will have. The obvious point has been made that neither planning nor health insurance will be especially effective without linkages.

It has also been said that the financial and technological resources available to the secretary to carry out the planning law are limited, and that the organizational framework is cumbersome. It would seem clear then, that if we expect far-reaching changes quickly we will be disappointed.

In a more optimistic vein we may say that as a data base for national health planning is developed, and as state and local planning bodies gain experience, we can look forward to a rationalized system financed by national health insurance. But more than anything else, real progress will depend upon a national will to bring about the result.

The various local units of CHP and RMP were faced with an age-old problem:

> "Mother, Mother I want to swim."
> "Yes my darling daughter.
> Hang your clothes on a hickory limb
> but don't go near the water."

So our suspicion lingers that we will be asked to plan just a little, but not too much.

References

[1] Joseph P. Newhouse et al., "Policy Options and the Impact of National Health Insurance," *New England Journal of Medicine* 33:24, June 1974.

[2] Louis Munan et al., "Population Health Care Practices: An Epidemiologic Study of the Immediate Effects of a Universal Health Insurance Plan," *International Journal of Health Services* 4:2, 1974.

Measurement of the Impact of National Health Insurance—A Conceptual Framework

PAUL M. DENSEN

This paper will address the basic considerations which must enter into the development of an information system to assess the impact of national health insurance (NHI) on the health delivery system of New York City. The quality of the information system is bound to have a direct bearing on how effectively professional and fiscal resources will be allocated in the implementation of NHI.

Whatever the details of the particular national health insurance legislation which may be passed by Congress, there are three broad areas in which its impact may be assessed. These relate to: (1) the *cost* of health care; (2) the *equity* of the arrangements for the distribution of services among different groups of the population; and (3) the health *status* of the population. Each of these three areas may be divided into a number of sub-areas, but the relative importance of the three will depend upon the way in which the legislation is written. At this writing we shall address all three areas and will assume for purposes of discussion that NHI will have the following four features. (These assumptions seem to be those most likely to be incorporated in NHI legislation. They are not necessarily those which the writer would like to see embodied in legislation.)

(1) The entire population will be eligible for benefits which are broad in scope but not all-inclusive; (2) deductibles and co-insurance features will be included in the legislation; (3) payment for services will be on a fee-for-service basis (in the case of health maintenance organizations [HMOs] an agreed-upon premium per person enrolled will be paid to the HMO for those services either mandated under the legislation or allowed for in the implementing regulations); and (4) some system of fiscal intermediaries will operate to make the payments for services.

In the first section we shall consider the *kinds* of measurements needed to assess the impact of NHI in each of the three areas mentioned above. The second section will outline the elements of the *information system* required to obtain such measurements.

The Kinds of Measurements Needed to Assess Impact: Cost

Current debate in Congress about NHI is the result in large part of the rising costs of medical care. In assessing the impact of any program of

NHI which Congress may adopt, the fiscal aspects of the program may be viewed either from the perspective of the individual consumer of health services who is concerned about how his pocketbook is affected, or from that of the government which is concerned with establishing priorities and allocating scarce resources among a number of competing public programs, as well as with providing a measure of accountability to the public.

Expenditures from the Standpoint of the Consumer

The consumer will want to know how effective NHI will be in helping him meet his medical bills. The general kind of information needed may be illustrated by some data available on the Medicare program. In fiscal 1974, the average expenditure for an aged person was $1,218 as contrasted with $528 in fiscal 1967, the first year of the program.[1] In 1974 Medicare and Medicaid picked up about 60 percent of this bill whereas only a little more than one-half was paid for by public funds in 1967. During the same period, however, average out-of-pocket expenditures for an aged person increased from $195 to $415.[2] On a gross level the same kind of information is needed about all consumer expenditures for health care but for purposes of optimal resource allocation—i.e., seeing that the benefits of NHI effectively reach all groups of the population—data for various sub-groups of the population are far more important. What proportion of the health expenditures of the poor, the elderly, the minority groups are met by NHI? What proportion of total income is accounted for by the health expenditures of each of these groups? Do the poor spend proportionately more of their income for hospitals or drugs than other groups of the population? What proportion of the income of the elderly is spent for nursing home care, and of this how much is covered by NHI?

To answer such questions information will be required on per capita expenditures classified by such demographic variables as age, sex, socio-economic status and minority group status. In addition, for each of these groups of the population it will be essential to have a picture of what the money is spent for: hospital care, both inpatient and outpatient; physician's services; dentist's services, etc.; drugs and drug sundries; eyeglasses and appliances; nursing home care, etc. (It will be noted that these variables fall into three general classes—population variables; provider variables; service variables. The next section will discuss methods of obtaining these classes of information.)

Expenditures of the System

The total expenditures of the system should be classified in the same manner as the per capita expenditures. The adoption of NHI will result in

169

a transfer of funds from the private to the public sector and, at the same time presumably, within the public sector itself, from state and local to federal funds. The extent to which these transfers take place, and whether there are differential transfers among age groups (children vs. aged for example) or for different kinds of expenditures (hospital services vs. ambulatory care) is of great importance for program planning and fiscal policy at the state and local level. If, for example, NHI covers most of the costs of health care for children but not for the elderly, state and local funds for children released by the introduction of NHI might be reallocated for programs for the aged. It is essential, therefore, to be able to classify the expenditures of funds for personal health services by source— federal, state or local; by type of expenditure; and by age and for special groups such as crippled children, the blind, etc.

One of the factors influencing the amount of money available to pay for services is the proportion of total income which is spent for administration of the system. Although the costs of monitoring a system are becoming a matter of general concern, relatively little is known about them. For example, P. Morton Ganeles, Director of Finance, Hospital Association of New York State, in an interview with Katharine Bauer, a member of the staff of the Harvard Center for Community Health and Medical Care, stated: "The cost of the New York State Utilization Review System, to be operated by the State Department of Health *if* agreements and funding are worked out, is estimated to add $2.00 per patient day on an average for the state; in New York City, the per diem cost would be $2.50 for a 300-bed hospital. The cost per admission is estimated to be $13.50."

In any system which contains a deductible or a co-payment feature, administrative expenses associated with the monitoring function may be very large, both in absolute dollars and on a proportionate basis. In view of the fact that there is some question about whether the effect of deductibles is to discourage use by the poor[3]—the very group that needs help the most—such information could be very important. It is, of course, difficult at this writing to know whether the implementation of the fiscal aspects of a NHI program will be carried through fiscal intermediaries or not. But assuming, as indicated previously, that this proves to be the case, the administrative expenses of the intermediaries should also be known. These administrative expenses should be presented on a per enrollee or per claim basis, as suggested by Weiss[4] and as since adopted by the Social Security Administration for Medicare.[5] A tabular summary of the above information is set forth on page 171.

The Issue of Equity

The question of equity in the provision of health services is complex and may, as Fein[6] points out, be viewed from a number of perspectives.

Tabular Summary A
Information Desired on Expenditures for Personal Health Services

	Individual (Per Capita) Expenditures	System Expenditures
Total Covered Expenditures	X	X
Age, sex, SES	X	X
Type of expense (Hospital, medical, nursing, etc.)	X	X
Source of Funds	X	X
Federal, state, local		
Administrative		X
Related to deductible and/or co-insurance		X
Other		X
Out-of-pocket expenditures	X	
Age, sex, SES	X	
Type of expense	X	

One definition of equity centers on access to health care among all classes of the population. (Many economists distinguish between horizontal and vertical equity. The former refers to the provision of essentially the same set of health services for persons in approximately the same economic circumstances; the latter concerns "fairness" in the provision of services for persons in different economic circumstances.)

Access means not only being able to obtain care when it is needed, but the availability of the right kind of care at the right time. As Donabedian puts it, "the proof of access is use of service, not simply the presence of a facility."[7] Access is concerned with the *kind* of care received (process) as well as the amount of care. It thus contains an element of *quality* as well as quantity. Indeed, since the kind of care received may ultimately affect the patient's outcome, the relation between access and health status must, at some point, also be examined. (See the discussion below of measurement of health status, and for a more detailed considera-tion of the concept of access see Aday and Anderson.[8])

Fundamentally, the measurement of accessability of various kinds of health services offered requires a knowledge of the patterns of utilization of those health services among the various socioeconomic and demo-graphic groups of the population. (Though various "indices of access" have been proposed [see Aday and Anderson] they all begin with this basic information.) Thus it will be desirable to know the following for each group of the population classified as to age, sex and socioeconomic status: the frequency of encounters per unit of population (1) by type and place of service—hospital inpatient services, surgery or non-surgery, physician and related services, extended care facility services, hospital outpatient services, emergency services, home health services; (2) by purpose of encounter—acute care, case management, health mainte-nance, preventive care; (3) by type of provider—primary care physician,

171

specialist (by type), physician's assistant, nurse practitioner or other non-M.D. provider; (4) by utilization—of laboratory, X-ray and other support services, such as the pharmacy for prescribed drugs, dialysis units, etc., and (5) by diagnosis. (It is important that the rubrics used to describe the utilization patterns of the population be the same as those used for classifying expenditure patterns.)

Such information will reveal differentials in the patterns of utilization among the different groups of the population both in the amount and kinds of services utilized. If, for instance, it is found that the rate of utilization of physician's services by pre-school children is very much higher among the more well-to-do groups of the population than among the poor and, at the same time, that there are parallel differentials in the rate of immunization on entry to school, then the need to develop more effective pre-school immunization programs among the poor is clear. On the other hand, if the rate of immunization is found to be low in *all* socio-economic groups of the population, then the system as a whole is functioning inadequately, and system-wide changes need to be made.

If NHI results in a more equitable access to facilities and services, it may be hypothesized that, over time, there will be a lessening in certain differentials which now exist among various age and socioeconomic groups of the population; for example in the extent and timing of the utilization of various *kinds* of services, and in certain health status measures. In the testing of this hypothesis we begin to address the issue of quality. For example, if good prenatal care is readily available to all, and if resources are specifically allocated for high risk pregnancies and high risk neonates, then one might expect early identification of these high risk groups to lead to an improvement in continuity of care for both mothers and infants. Were this to occur, then the differences in the rate of complications of pregnancy and of perinatal mortality in whites and non-whites should gradually lessen. Similarly, one may postulate that an equitable distribution of resources would increase the proportion among children entering school of those who have completed the recommended course of immunizations and decrease the variation in this proportion among the several SES groups. Additional measures of the extent to which the allocation of resources under NHI (fiscal, manpower and facilities) results in an equitable distribution of the amount and kinds of services among different groups of the population may need to be derived from special studies.

In adults, measures of the frequency of Papanicolaou tests among women in the different SES groups, of the stage at which certain forms of cancer are diagnosed, and of the frequency of microscopic confirmation may provide insights—at least in a statistical sense—into whether the "right" kind of care is obtained at the "right" point in time. (For a

172

Tabular Summary B-1
Information of Potential Use in Assessing Equity

	DERIVED FROM ROUTINELY AVAILABLE RECORDS								SPECIAL STUDIES		
	Inpatient Utilization			Ambulatory Utilization		Pren. Care					
	Admission										
	Surg.	Non-Surg.	Days Care	Encounters per person per Year	Dist. of Persons by No. Enc/Yr.	Trimester First Seen	Immunization Rates	EPSDT Findings	Referral Patterns for Specific Conds.	Pap Smears	PSRO Data on Adherence to Standards
Age, Sex, SES	X	X	X	X	X	X	X	X	X	X	X
Dg. Problem	X	X	X	X				X			X
Reason for encounter											
Acute care				X							
Mgmnt. of chronic problem											
Health maintenance or prevention											
Place of service											
Office, OPD				X		X					
Emergency Room											
Home											

173

discussion of the interpretation of the results of screening tests for cervical cancer see Knox.[9]) It will be noted that measures such as these are, in general, available from existing reporting mechanisms such as vital statistics or other normally available information systems. Alternatively, they could be obtained through the operation of the NHI information system itself, as discussed later.

Availability of Resources

The preceding information will permit an examination of who uses what at what cost. Insofar as it reveals differential patterns of utilization among the various socioeconomic groups of the population, and insofar as one judges it desirable to beneficially alter these patterns by reallocating resources of money, manpower or facilities, it then becomes necessary to know something about the geographic distribution of manpower and facilities in the city. For example, if NHI covers dental care, and if it is found on school health examinations or in the EPSDT program that oral health is not as good among the children of poor families as it is among those of more well-to-do parents, then the reason may be either an inadequate supply of dentists, a maldistribution of dental services, improper nutrition, or some combination of these factors. (A more widespread acceptance by communities of the efficacy of fluorides as a preventive of dental decay would help to deal with the problem.) In any case, it would be important to know about the number of dentists per unit of population and their geographic location. In general it is desirable to have a picture of the kinds and distribution of manpower and facilities available to provide the services needed by the various socioeconomic and demographic groups of the population. The range of information required to assess the availability of resources is set forth in Tabular Summary B-2.

Impact of National Health Insurance on Health Status

Of the three broad areas in which one may wish to examine the impact of national health insurance, that which concerns itself with the health of the population at large is likely to prove most difficult and frustrating to assess. As the chronic diseases have assumed proportionately greater importance in the total health picture of the population, it has become more difficult to show any relationship between input of resources into the health system and changes in specific health measures of the population. As Victor R. Fuchs[10] points out, the marginal return for a marginal investment in the health system is small at the present time. Implicit in the concept of equity described above is the assumption that

174

Tabular Summary B-2
Information on Availability of Resources Numbers and Ratio to Population

| | MANPOWER | | | FACILITIES | | | |
| | | | | | Chronic | | |
	No.	Rate		Acute	Hosp.	Long-Term Care	Special Care: Mental, Rehab., Blind, Deaf, etc.
Type of provider and specialty	X	X	Ownership (Public, Private)	X	X	X	X
Type of practice (Solo, partnership, group, HMO, etc.)	X	X	Number of Beds	X	X	X	X
			By Type	X	X		
Geographic location by census tract	X	X	By Level of Care		X		

175

equal access to the right kinds of services and facilities at the right time will decrease the differentials in various measures of health status among the several socioeconomic groups of the population. Moreover, even were it to be shown that this assumption holds, it must be recognized that the amount, kind and quality of health services received are not the only determinants of the health status of the population. There is a considerable body of evidence that this is far from the case.[11]

In spite of the difficulty of showing any relationship between availability of health services and health, the population will continue to seek medical care, because much of the population's needs are related to what Fuchs calls the physician's "caring function" as well as to his curing function. This being so, the effort should be made, whenever possible, to determine whether and to what extent the health of the various groups of the population would be improved under NHI. One of the reasons for making such attempts is that the more we know about the impact of national health insurance—how it affects the population in regard to cost, equity of distribution of services and health status—the more likely it will be that we can allocate resources efficiently, either through administrative arrangements, or through legislation, or both. We shall attempt, therefore, to suggest some approaches to measuring the health status of the population.

Measurements of Health: Mortality, Morbidity, Functional Status

The likelihood that national health insurance will significantly reduce the general mortality of the population, i.e., the crude death rate, is not very great. However, the fact that there are at present major socioeconomic differentials in mortality from certain causes among different subgroups of the population suggests ways in which the impact of NHI on health status might be assessed. For example, in relation to the issue of equity, we have previously discussed access to prenatal care and the desirability of looking at the continuity of prenatal care among pregnant women in the various groups of the population. Assuming that this prenatal care is good prenatal care, and that such other matters as nutritional advice and education about good health habits are generally available, one can hypothesize that the availability of such care will have an impact on the outcome of pregnancy, specifically on the perinatal mortality rate. The extent to which the workings of NHI will be reflected in this specific case, as in other instances, will depend in part upon the specific benefits provided by the legislation. It is clear, therefore, that efforts to measure the impact of national health insurance will need to be related as much as possible to the provisions of the legislation, and to whether or not specific programmatic activities are developed in relation to those provisions.

In the same way, following the suggestion of Rutstein,[12] one may examine the occurrence of preventable deaths such as tuberculous meningitis, before and after the initiation of NHI. In this way indices of "preventability" could be developed for particular geographic regions and for specific socioeconomic groups. Special studies might be required to separate the influence of NHI from other factors influencing the trend of such indices.

It is conceivable that the operation of national health insurance programs would be reflected in the five-year survivorship rates for specific chronic diseases. The general line of reasoning is as follows: early diagnosis and treatment of certain chronic diseases have been shown to be reflected in the five-year survivorship rate of individuals contracting these diseases. (It is important to compare expected survival beyond any given age with actual survival since, in general, the earlier the age at which diagnosis is made, the greater the probability of five-year (or any other period) survival.[13]) If national health insurance increases access to good quality care, one might hypothesize that there will be an increase in the early diagnosis and treatment of such conditions as cancer of the cervix, cancer of the breast, certain forms of heart disease, hypertension, cerebrovascular accidents and possibly others. In this connection the literature should be systematically reviewed with these possibilities in mind, and efforts made to discover at what stage persons with these conditions have been identified, proper treatment instituted and what the survivorship rates have been.

Morbidity may be discussed under two headings: incidence and prognosis. Incidence refers to the number of *new* cases of a disease developing during a given period of time per unit of population. The class of services which falls under the heading of primary prevention is likely to be important here. The classic example is frequency of immunization, since immunization has already been shown to decrease the incidence of communicable diseases. There are, however, relatively few procedures that bear such a one-to-one relationship with incidence of disease as does immunization. In most cases, one has to attempt to measure the incidence of the disease itself. In New York City, for example, there are still groups of the population, particularly immigrant groups, that have a relatively high incidence of tuberculosis. Again, if national health insurance brings about greater equity (accessibility) among the several groups of the population, it may be postulated that the frequency of chest X-rays and skin tests among selected groups of the population will be increased. Initially this might result in an increase in the number of newly discovered cases of tuberculosis in these population groups. As these sources of infection are brought under control, however, the number of new cases discovered may then be expected to decline.

In the incidence of cardiovascular and cerebrovascular diseases, and of cancer of various forms, a considerable body of evidence is building that the health habits of the population are one of the major determinants. For NHI to have any impact on the incidence of these diseases, we will first have to learn how to effectively influence the health habits of the population[14] and, second, to provide in the legislation for payment for services shown to be effective. At the moment, it is unlikely that incidence of these conditions will be affected by the passage of national health insurance.

The general principle underlying the attempt to measure the impact of national health insurance on the prognosis, or the course, of illness from various conditions follows the same rationale as that given for the five-year survivorship studies for specific conditions; namely, that if national health insurance improves access to care from the standpoint of both quality and quantity, then one might expect to find earlier diagnosis and treatment and this, in turn, should have an impact on prognosis.

The discussion to this point of the impact of NHI on the health of the population has been largely related to a specific disease or condition. Little has been suggested in the way of measuring the general health status of the population. In this connection it would be desirable to have some measure of the ability of the population to function in its normal environment, i.e., a measure of functional status. One such measure is days lost from work or, more generally, days of disability or days lost from usual activities. There is some evidence in the literature that days of disability tend to increase when coverage under an insurance program is increased. This may reflect unnecessary utilization of the health care system, or satisfaction of an unmet need, or both. These measures of health status are set forth in Tabular Summary C-1.

Before and After National Health Insurance

The discussion so far has focused on identifying the impact of NHI on differentials in costs, equity and health status among different socio-economic groups of the population on the assumption that the differentials should decrease if national health insurance becomes effective. One may also attempt to assess the impact of NHI from a before and after standpoint. Has the passage of national health insurance made it possible for various groups of the population to pay for health services more readily than before? Has the economic burden of illness been reduced as a result of the passage of the legislation? Rather than attempt to answer

Tabular Summary C-1
Potential Measures of Health Status

Mortality
  Perinatal mortality
  Mortality for specific causes, proportion of total deaths classed as preventable
  Five-year survivorship rates

Morbidity
  Incidence
    Immunizations (a surrogate for the incidence of certain communicable diseases)
    Specific diseases
      Tuberculosis among certain specific groups of the population
      Venereal disease
      Proportion of cases of certain diseases which may be classed as preventable
  Prognosis
    Course of illness landmarks for specific conditions

Functional Status
  Days of Disability
  Bed Days

All measures should be obtained specific for age and socioeconomic status.

these questions for all groups of the population, it might be best, at least in the beginning, to approach them by examining the data for certain specific groups of the population in which the information is presently accessible in existing record systems.

One such group is the aged, for which data are accumulated in the Medicare program. Articles which have appeared in the *Social Security Bulletin* over the last few years have indicated that Medicare has been able to meet some of the problems of the aged.[15] These records continue to be available, and as NHI is introduced, one will be interested to know what changes take place in the ability of the elderly to meet their medical costs and to proceed from this to an examination, not merely of the expenditures of the elderly, but to some picture of the kinds of changes that take place in their patterns of utilization.

We shall not pursue this topic further except to make the point that currently available information about certain other population sub-groups may be pertinent to the measurement of the impact of NHI and may be used with less expense, probably, than is entailed in the development of special studies requiring specially designed records.

Elements of the Information System

We turn now to a consideration of the principles which must govern the design of the information system so as to yield measures of the kind discussed in the first section. The reader is urged to bear in mind the assumptions concerning the characteristics of NHI set forth in the introduction.

179

The perspective from which the first section has been developed is that any attempt to appraise the effectiveness of NHI in dealing with the issues of cost, equity and health status must approach the problem from a population standpoint. Thus the various measures discussed were expressed per unit of population as well as, at times, per unit of service or per utilizer. It follows that the fundamental requirement of a meaningful information system is a count of people classified, minimally by age, sex, ethnic group and socioeconomic status. These counts will form the denominator for the rates. The numerator information on expenditures, utilization and health status will also need to be classified in the same manner. We will first consider the sources of information for the population data which form the denominator.

Population Information

The primary source of population information is, of course, the decennial census which contains data on the age, sex, ethnic group (white, non-white, other) and socioeconomic characteristics of the population for the city as a whole, as well as for each census tract.

As we have indicated, the information on socioeconomic status is particularly important in addressing problems of equity and related problems of allocation of available resources. Several indicators of SES are available through the census: among them the distribution of families and unrelated individuals by income: the proportion of families below the poverty level of income; the years of schooling completed for individuals 25 years old and over; the occupation of employed individuals 16 years old and over and households by mean value of owner-occupied units, or by mean gross rent. All of these measures have their uses, and various attempts have been made to combine two or more, but if only a single measure is desired, it is suggested that years of schooling completed be used. (For a brief discussion of the measurement of socioeconomic status see reference 11). It appears to correlate highly with health although the correlation may lessen in the future if increasing proportions of the population finish high school.

In the context of this paper, a basic difficulty which will be encountered in using census data is that it very quickly becomes outdated, especially in a highly mobile population. In intercensal years, information on the distribution of the population by socioeconomic status is often not available except from special surveys of one kind of another. Any serious attempt to assess the extent to which NHI is successful in achieving its goals will, in all probability, require some systematic kind of population survey at reasonably frequent intervals; this will serve not only to develop reliable denominator data but also to make possible the comparable classification of numerator data.

Cost and Utilization Data: The Claims Document

The assumption that payment for services will, in general, be made within a fee-for-service structure means that a claims document will have to be submitted to the fiscal intermediary. This claims document will serve two kinds of purposes—one with respect to the individual in determining whether or not the deductible or co-insurance requirements have been satisfied in the particular case, and the other a statistical purpose; in that it is the basic source of the utilization and cost information required for the numerator of the measures dealing with these areas. It is essential that careful thought be given to the content and design of the claims document.

Deductible and Co-Insurance Features

Insofar as satisfaction of the deductible or co-insurance features are concerned, the procedure presently in use in the Medicare program places the burden of proof on either the consumer or provider to show through receipted bills that the requirements have been met. This has led at times to awkward and even painful situations for individual consumers and providers—especially those not accustomed to keeping records. An alternative approach, which appears to offer some advantages over the Medicare procedure, would be to have the provider submit his bill to the fiscal intermediary, who would reimburse the provider for covered services and simultaneously check the computer files to ascertain whether the deductible (or co-insurance) had been satisfied. If so, the transaction will have been completed. If not, the fiscal intermediary would bill the consumer for the amount of the deductible. Assuming that the NHI legislation is so written that the provider must accept assignment, the suggested procedure would obviate the need for any discussion of bills between provider and consumer and would minimize the paper work required to complete the transaction. Further, the consumer would not have to keep records to prove he had met the deductible.

There will, in general, be two broad classes of claims documents— one for ambulatory care services and one for inpatient services. In both cases the identifying information is essentially the same and is set forth in the Uniform Hospital Abstract Minimum Basic Data Set[16] or the Ambulatory Medical Care Records Uniform Minimum Basic Data Set.[17] It consists of the patient's name, a unique identification number, residence, date of birth and sex.

Consumer Information

It will be noted that none of this demographic information pertains directly to socioeconomic status. Nevertheless, some mechanism for obtaining SES data on consumers is essential. It is unlikely that SES information, such as years of schooling completed, or income, could be added to the claims document itself, as it is not needed for day-to-day administration of the program. Its usefulness will not be readily apparent to either the consumer or the provider and hence the information is not likely to be reliably entered. The ultimate effect would be to complicate the system unnecessarily. It might be possible through the use of the address information to classify the claims according to the socioeconomic characteristics of the census tract in which the consumer resides. Again, however, the usefulness of this approach would be hampered by the lack of reliable intercensal data on the SES of the population. If the legislation is so written as to make the deductible a function of income, then information on income status of those who make claims will be required. This would permit classifying the numerator by income status. Similar information for the denominator could be derived from the population survey.

Since, as we have already seen, a population survey would be desirable to provide intercensal denominator data, the same survey could also provide numerator data or at least sufficient data to permit, together with the NHI identification number, linkage with the information on utilization and costs in the claims file. The adoption of this combined survey and claims document approach should yield the kind of data required to examine the equity issue in the manner described in the first section.

Provider Information

In addition to including information identifying and characterizing the patient, the inpatient and ambulatory care claims document should contain information characterizing both the institutional provider (the hospital, long-term care facility or other institution) and the professional provider (doctor, dentist, nurse, etc.). The specific information desired is set forth in the reports on data sets previously referred to. This information, together with the information described below on kinds of services, will permit analysis of *who* provides *what* services to the population.

Services Information

The third class of information desired on the claims document concerns the services provided to the patient and the reason for these services. Since these differ in the inpatient and ambulatory settings we shall discuss them separately.

The inpatient claims form should contain information on diagnoses, length of stay, procedures performed and disposition of the patient.

182

Similar information should be obtained for inpatient care in long-term care facilities. The method of recording these items is discussed in detail in reference 16. In general, the ambulatory care claims forms should contain the same classes of items, but would differ in detail for such items as services and procedures. It would be desirable, if possible, to include, along with the diagnosis, the patient's principal problem, complaint, or symptom which led to the episode of care. This item should be useful for purposes of health services research and for studies of the natural history of the illness. It should aid in studying the degree to which preventive services are provided to the population.

The ambulatory care claims document presents a problem in processing not present in the inpatient document. A natural point at which to present the latter for payment is at the time of the patient's discharge from the inpatient facility. There is no similar "natural" point for the ambulatory care form. If a separate encounter form is submitted after each patient-provider contact, a mountain of paper would result. If the form is presented at the conclusion of each episode, it would result in an irregular schedule of payments to the provider. It is possible that claims for patients seen should be submitted at a given interval of time such as a month. Although considerable thought needs to be given to this problem of system design, it is beyond the scope of this paper. To some extent the answer will depend on the way the legislation is written.

Billing Information

The information required for billing purposes is the last class of information needed on both the inpatient and ambulatory care claims form. This should consist of itemized charges for the various services or procedures indicated as having been provided. Both total charges and non-covered charges should be identified. If a uniform classification of cost-centers were adopted by the hospitals, then the inpatient claims form could be designed to permit identification and allocation of charges to these cost centers. This would permit analysis of the contribution of the different hospital departments to the cost structure and would aid in rate-setting procedures.

The information on charges, and the related information on payments kept by the fiscal intermediary will determine the satisfaction of the deductible or co-insurance requirements, as well as the analysis of costs of the program as described in the first section. By correlating the charge information from the claims forms with annual cost budget reports from the hospital, some assessment can be made of the impact of NHI on hospital finances. Whether or not the claims forms should contain information on the expected source of payment, as is recommended in the present reports of the National Committee on Health and Vital Statistics (see references 16 and 17), will depend once again on the specifics of the legislation.

Manpower and Facilities Information

Information on manpower and facilities of the type given in Tabular Summary B-2 will be derived largely from data submitted to state licensing agencies, and from the annual reports of the American Hospital Association, the American Medical Association, the American Dental Association and the Registry of Nurses. This information should be brought up to date annually, and the general characteristics of both manpower and facilities set forth along the lines indicated. Up-to-date information on the distribution and characteristics of health manpower is relatively lacking. Yet a little thought given to the organization of the files of the licensing agencies should make possible not only the distributions mentioned above, but also the construction of life table functions for each of the various types of manpower. (For example, there is the "survivorship function" so that one may obtain the probability that a person entering a given professional field in New York City in a given year will continue in that field t time units later. A good illustration of the use of this function is provided in reference 18.) These would indicate the expected length of service of any given class of professional under a given set of conditions. Such information would then permit analysis of the effect of changing these conditions on the supply of manpower.

Information on Health Status

Like the information on manpower and facilities, the information on health status will derive from records other than the claims documents. Among these are the vital statistics records which will provide data on perinatal mortality and which, because of the inclusion of years of schooling completed on the birth certificate, can be classified by socioeconomic status. The death certificates, of course, also provide information about mortality from specific causes.

Other routine sources of information concerning various aspects of the health status of the population are school health records, which show immunization status at the time of entry to school and, depending on the content of the school health examination and the reliability of recording, the prevalence of such conditions as hearing defects, eye defects, orthopedic defects and dental defects. This information, together with additional data derived from the EPSDT program for Medicaid children, should permit comparison of the health status of children among the several SES groups, as well as an analysis of trends over time within the groups. The PSRO program, while largely concerned with the process of care, may have the potential for providing information on health status, or for making possible special studies about health status. This should be explored.

Because of the possible significance of five-year survivorship rates in an examination of the effects of national health insurance on the equity issue (as described in the first section) special studies should be conducted to elicit such rates. Since the information on diagnosis will be contained on the claims forms, it should be possible to establish a cohort of individuals who receive a given diagnosis for the first time in a given year; then to follow up these individuals in successive years to determine their survivorship rates. Care will have to be exercised to be sure that the cohort is complete and that the total number of individuals in the cohort is accounted for in each successive year. Nevertheless, the necessary methodology is available to carry out such studies, and efforts should be made to incorporate them in the evaluation of the NHI program.

There is at present no routine reporting system which provides information for the entire population with respect to measures of functional status, such as days of disability or days spent in bed because of illness. The National Health Survey collects this kind of information for the United States as a whole and for the SMSAs, but the sample is too small to permit estimates for subgroups of the population within the SMSAs. It would appear that this kind of information is best obtained through systematic population surveys directed at the needs of the local areas.

It was pointed out in the first section that attempts to measure the impact of national health insurance on health status should be related to the benefit provisions of the legislation. A fruitful approach to this analysis would focus on specific programmatic activities which are part of the benefits package of the legislation, and whose aim is to improve health in some specific way. Gordis' study on rheumatic fever in the inner city of Baltimore[19] is an example of this approach.

The Population Survey

We have stressed the need for a systematic population survey to provide numerator and denominator information not otherwise available from routine records; information such as out-of-pocket costs and socioeconomic characteristics of the population and of utilizers. (The usefulness of a population survey in assessing the effects of a health insurance program is well illustrated by the reports of the Current Medicare Survey,[20] and the work of Enterline and his colleagues[21] on the Quebec experience before and after the introduction of the province-wide health program.)

Much of the information which has so far been derived from survey data has been cross-sectional in nature. But the existence of a population survey creates the opportunity to carry out longitudinal studies on samples of the population. Such studies could, for instance, contribute to an understanding of the impact of national health insurance on the continuity of care. Longitudinal studies would permit the observation of the patterns of utilization and referral of the various SES groups of the population, particularly if the data gathered were to be linked with information from claims documents for members of the sample. There is a vast potential here which has scarcely been tapped.

Some of the potentials of the population survey might be realized in a very limited way for the New York City SMSA as a whole because the National Health Survey does publish information on selected health characteristics for the SMAs and identifies the New York City SMSA as an entity. However, there are no breakdowns of this material for smaller geographic areas or by socioeconomic status; information which would be essential to the effective allocation of resources within the SMSA. To get this information would require much larger samples than are currently being used in the National Health Survey program. The possibility that the NHS Sample might be enlarged to make it possible to examine the impact of national health insurance more effectively should be explored.

Some Caveats and Organizational Considerations

It seems best to approach the idealized conceptual framework presented here incrementally, setting some priorities for the development of the information system, while keeping the ideal framework in mind when addressing the issues of system design. In the nature of the case, the heart of the information system must be the procedure for submitting and paying claims, including the satisfaction of the deductible or co-insurance features of the legislation. Top priority should be given to the design of this aspect of the system. Once this is in place and functioning, assessing NHI can begin. Because of the importance of socioeconomic status in examining the impact of NHI on different groups of the population, it may well be that the next priority should be accorded to methods of determining the socioeconomic status of both the general population and of the utilizers, so that the distributional effects of NHI can be examined. The discussion on the need for a household survey is germane here. At an appropriate point efforts should be directed toward the integration of the various sources of information bearing on expenditures, utilization and health status, and to the launching of various special studies along the lines suggested in the body of this paper.

186

The linkage of information from one set of records with that from another brings up the issue of confidentiality. This is a knotty problem, particularly when efforts are made to use a widely applicable identifier, such as a social security number. Nevertheless, if any serious effort is to be undertaken to evaluate the impact of NHI on the population, some means of overcoming this problem, while still protecting the public, must be found.

Finally we come to the issue of where responsibility and authority to develop and manage the information system, and to analyze the data flowing from it, should rest. Since the Social Security Administration has had a long and, by and large, successful experience in administering a claims reporting system with Medicare, it would seem appropriate to assign to it the responsibility and authority for developing and administering the claims program under NHI. At the same time, as Frank Van Dyke has pointed out,[22] the Health Systems Agencies created under the National Health Planning and Resources Development Act of 1974 are to have access to expertise in the gathering and analysis of data through the Cooperative Health Statistics System of the National Center for Health Statistics. The kinds of activities which the CHSS Centers must undertake under the planning act will involve pulling together from a variety of sources information regarding the workings of the health system at the level at which health services are delivered. This is exactly the kind of activity which local areas must develop a capacity for in order to make the most of NHI—an ability to analyze their own problems and to adjust their resources to cope with them.

Whether or not CHSS units at the local level will be in a position to assume such responsibilities will depend upon adequate financing and the delegation of authority to accomplish their tasks. Neither of these conditions presently exists. Yet under NHI the need for a strong analytical unit at the local level will be essential if resources are to be allocated so that the system may operate at a high degree of effectiveness from the standpoint of both costs and benefits. Given, then, the need for such a unit, what can be done now to plan for it?

As a first step, a review should be undertaken of the provisions, if any, for an information base in the national health insurance legislation presently being considered by Congress. This review should probably take place at the national level, with the views of local areas being sought. Both the Social Security Administration and HEW should be involved in such a review, with coordination through the secretary's office, and with specific participation of the National Center for Health Statistics and the Office of Research and Statistics of the Social Security Administration.

The review should take place within a framework such as that suggested in this paper and should determine whether the following points are provided for in the bills:

1. Recognition of the need for a well-organized information system at both the national and local levels for effective functioning of national health insurance.

2. Adequate funding for all levels of the information system. There should be ample precedent and experience to draw on in the workings of both the National Health and Resources Development Planning Act of 1974, which provides funds to develop a data base for planning purposes, and the old Hill-Burton Act. (The latter's approach called for local areas to submit a plan for the local program of hospital development. If the plan fitted in with the overall guidelines established, federal funding was approved. In this way local needs were recognized but at the same time a national program developed.) The same approach might be adopted for the funding of strong, well-defined, analytical units at the local level.

3. Responsibility for the implementation of the information provisions of the bill to be clearly fixed and not left vague or ill-defined.

Second, HEW and the Social Security Administration, through the review group mentioned above, should begin, as soon as possible, planning the elements of an information system for national health insurance. Since the exact form the legislation will take is unknown, such planning must be done within a framework which will permit an incremental approach. At the same time, it should be sufficiently flexible to require changes in detail only in order to accommodate itself to the particular legislation, rather than requiring a massive restructuring. This discussion paper presents a suggested framework.

Given agreement on the basic elements of the information system, the next step should be development of the detailed system specifications required to gather the data, including budgetary estimates. This is a complex task, and it is not too early to begin now.

While this detailed planning is going on at the national level, selected local areas, such as New York City, should be funded through the 1974 planning act so as to begin pulling together from various sources the pieces of information called for by the federal guidelines. Particular attention should be paid to the kind of authority required to collect the information and to fiscal requirements at the local level. The expenditure of funds under the planning act for such long-range planning is not only legitimate but should prove a worthwhile investment. As Van Dyke has pointed out, "For the next several years, at least, we have a law which requires planning without data systems to support it."

To sum up, it is to be hoped that we have learned from the past that the time to plan is now, before legislation is passed, for the information system required for an effective functioning of a national health insurance bill. There is still time to think and to invite constructive criticism. To lose this opportunity would be an egregious oversight; to plan now would represent a demonstration of responsible leadership.

References

[1] Barbara S. Cooper and Nancy L. Worthington, "Medical Care Spending for Three Age Groups, 1966–1971," *Soc. Sec. Bull.* 35: 5 (May 1972).

[2] M.S. Mueller and Robert M. Gibson, "Age Differences in Health Care Spending, Fiscal Year, 1974," *Research and Statistics Note*, Soc. Sec. Adm., Office of Research and Statistics, Note No. 6, May 13, 1975.

[3] A.A. Scitovsky and N.M. Snyder, "Effect of Co-insurance on Use of Physicians' Services," *Soc. Sec. Bull.* 35: 6 (June, 1972); C.E. Phelps and J. P. Newhouse, "Effect of Co-insurance: A Multivariate Analysis," *Ibid.*

[4] Robert J. Weiss, W.H. Wiese and J.C. Kleinman, "Trends in Health Insurance Operating Expenses," *NEJM* 287: 13 (Sept. 28, 1972).

[5] M.S. Mueller, "Private Health Insurance in 1973: A Review of Coverage, Enrollment and Financial Experience," *Soc. Sec. Bull.* 36: 2 (Feb. 1973).

[6] Rashi Fein, "On Achieving Access and Equity in Health Care," *Milbank Memorial Fund Quarterly* Vol. L, No. 4, Part 2 (Oct. 1972).

[7] Avedis Donabedian, "Models for Organizing the Delivery of Personal Health Services and Criteria for Evaluating Them," *Milbank Memorial Fund Quarterly* Vol. L., No. 4 (Oct. 1972).

[8] L.A. Aday and R. Anderson, *Development of Indices of Access to Medical Care*, Ann Arbor, Michigan: Health Administration Press, 1975.

[9] E.G. Knox, "Cervical Cancer" in *Screening in Medical Care*, Nuffield Provincial Hospitals Trust, Oxford University Press, 1968.

[10] Victor R. Fuchs, *Who Shall Live?* New York: Basic Books, Inc., 1974.

[11] E. Kitigawa and Philip M. Hauser, *Differential Mortality in the U.S.: A Study in Socio-Economic Epidemiology*, Cambridge, Mass.: Harvard University Press, 1973.

[12] David D. Rutstein, *Blueprint for Medical Care*, Cambridge, Mass.: MIT Press, 1974.

[13] David L. Sackett, "Screening for Early Detection of Disease: To What Purpose?" in "Preventions and Health Maintenance Revisited," 1974 Annual Health Conference of the New York Academy of Medicine, *Bull. N.Y. Acad. of Med.* Vol. 51, Jan. 1975.

[14] Marc LaLonde, "A New Perspective on the Health of Canadians," Government of Canada, Ottawa, April 1974.

[15] Paul M. Densen, "Public Accountability and Reporting Systems in Medicare and Other Health Programs," *NEJM* 289 (Aug. 23, 1973). See references 1 and 2.

[16] "Uniform Hospital Abstract: Minimum Bases Data Set," U.S. National Committee on Health and Vital Statistics, Vital and Health Statistics Reports, Series 4, No. 14, National Center for Health Statistics, Dec. 1972.

[17] "Ambulatory Medical Care Records: Uniform Minimum Basic Data Set." U.S. National Committee on Health and Vital Statistics, Vital and Health Statistics Reports, Series 4, No. 16, National Center for Health Statistics, Aug. 1974.

[18] Margaret D. West, "Estimating the Future Supply of Nurses," *Am. J. of Nursing* Vol. 50, No. 10, Oct. 1950.

[19] L. Gordis, "Effectiveness of Comprehensive Care Programs on Preventive Rheumatic Fever," *NEJM* 289, Aug. 16, 1973.

[20] Jack Scharff, "The Current Medicare Survey: The Medical Insurance Sample," *Soc. Sec. Bull.* (April 1, 1967); Howard West, "Five Years of Medicare—A Statistical Review," *Soc. Sec. Bull.* (December 1971); Social Security Administration, Office of Research and Statistics, "Current Medicare Survey Notes."

[21] P. Enterline et al., "The Distribution of Medical Services Before and After 'Free' Medical Care—the Quebec Experience," *NEJM* 287 (Nov. 29, 1973).

[22] Frank Van Dyke, "National Health Planning and Resources Development Act of 1974 and National Health Insurance," A Discussion Paper prepared for the Task Force on the Impact of National Health Insurance, N.Y. Regional Medical Program, May 22, 1975.

Organized Ambulatory Services and the Enforcement of Health Care Quality Standards in New York State

STEVEN JONAS

Two of the many problem areas in health care are quality control and the provision of ambulatory care in organized settings. Among other things, New York State's response has been through inspection and regulation carried out under Article 28 and related provisions of the Public Health Law of the State of New York, through subsidy of local health departments under the "Ghetto Medicine" law, and in New York City, under the same law, the New York City Health Department provides funds to help voluntary hospitals operate their in-hospital ambulatory services.

This study was carried out during a three-month period, March–May, 1975. It relied primarily on personal interviews with persons in hospitals, health departments and influential positions in affected communities. Published papers, public documents and some relevant unpublished materials were reviewed as well.[1,2]

Article 28 of the Public Health Laws of the State of New York is a product primarily of the Folsom Report,[3] and is often referred to as The Folsom Act, although it is not just a single law but a collection of many, having been amended on a number of occasions.[4] The Folsom Report was the product of the Governor's Committee on Hospital Cost, established by Nelson Rockefeller in May 1964 to study the costs of general hospital care, the apportionment of responsibility among state agencies concerned with hospital care, and to make recommendations for improving the situation.[5] The committee recommended a nine-point program.[6]

Detailed proposals to implement the nine major recommendations were made, amounting to over 50 sub-recommendations.[7] Naturally, not all of them have been put into law, regulation, or policy. The three principal aims of the legislation which has been developed over the years on the basis of the Folsom Report, and on subsequent relevant experience are: (1) a program to regulate the number and type of hospital beds in the State of New York, usually referred to as the "certificate-of-need" program (actually a further development and strengthening of the program which had been started by Chapter 730, Laws of 1964 [the Metcalf-McCloskey Act]); (2) a program for rate-setting in hospital insurance programs; and (3) a uniform, statewide hospital licensing (operating-certificate) law controlled by the New York State Department of Health.[8]

The Implementation and Effects of Article 28

What Was Supposed to Happen

According to the "Declaration of policy and statement of purpose" of Article 28, "Hospital and related services including health-related service of the highest quality, efficiently provided and properly utilized at a reasonable cost, are of vital concern to the public health." Unfortunately, no specific goals were set and no baselines defined.

What Has Happened under Article 28

No comprehensive reviews or evaluations of Article 28 activities, carried out either by the department itself, or by outside observers, are available. Annual reports of the New York State Department of Health are not particularly revealing,[9] referring only briefly in spots to Article 28.[10] According to Andrew Fleck,[11] the department has always interpreted its powers in relation to the quality of medical care very narrowly. ("Narrow" would sometimes seem to mean "virtual inaction".) As long ago as 1963, in Article 2, the commissioner was empowered to "cause to be made such scientific studies and research which have for their purpose . . . the improvement of the quality of medical audits within the state."[12] There is little evidence that anything has been done with this power. As far as the Section 2803 powers are concerned, Fleck said that the department has interpreted "the power to inquire into the operation of hospitals and to conduct periodic inspections of facilities with respect to . . . standards of medical care . . ." (Section 2803 [1]) as one limited to a Joint Commission on the Accreditation of Hospitals (JCAH) type of inspection of hospital medical staff organization. As to the powers given to the Public Health Council to inspect and review hospital operations under Sec. 2803 (2), Fleck said that council has never implemented them and that, in effect, this was "their problem."

What Has Happened to Quality Control of Ambulatory Care under Article 28

The provisions of Article 28 which concern quality control in ambulatory services are implemented through the Hospital Code portion of the Health Code, Part 703 and sections 720.17 and 720.18. The ambulatory care provisions of the code apply only to care given in organized settings, not in private doctors' offices. In New York State it is probable that a higher proportion of ambulatory care is given in organized settings than in most other states because of the large number of hospital clinics in New York City. Nevertheless, it may be assumed that the proportion provided in private doctors' offices still approaches the national average of 80 percent,[13] particularly because of the high doctor/patient ratio experienced by this state. Thus, even if the ambulatory care provisions of the code were to be fully applied, the bulk of ambulatory care in the state would remain unregulated.

In a series of interviews,[14] a wide variety of persons concerned with the implementation and effects of Article 28 stated that, in relation to the enforcement of the ambulatory care standards, nothing had in fact happened, at least to mid-1975. The contrast with what has happened under the Ambulatory Care Program of the New York City Health Department is quite striking.

Findings: "Ghetto Medicine"

The Development of the Original Legal Basis of the Programs: Legislative History

In April 1920, Herman Biggs, then Commissioner of Health for the State of New York, noted the severe problems which many rural communities were having in obtaining medical services.[15] To deal with the problem, Biggs proposed legislation which would have encouraged the establishment throughout the state of local health centers that would house medical school, public health nursing and public health education services; that would coordinate all existing rural public health activities for tuberculosis, venereal disease, maternal and child health and the like; and that would provide laboratory and X-ray services and general medical services, both outpatient and inpatient—all on a sliding fee scale, or free, if necessary. A modified version of this proposal to provide state aid to counties wishing to undertake such programs was, indeed, passed by the state legislature in 1923, but by that time Biggs was dead, as was the "Progressive Era," and nothing ever came of it.

In 1967, the New York State Department of Health decided to have another try at implementing Herman Biggs' idea of directly involving health departments in the delivery of general medical services.[16] The department was concerned about health care shortages in the rural areas of the state, as Biggs had been. But it was also concerned about the increasing health care deficits in the so-called "ghetto" areas. The general idea was to pass legislation enabling local health departments to establish general medical clinics (which they could not do previously), to charge for services provided in them (contravening the tradition of free-to-all-at-the-time-of-use health department services), and to waive the fees if they chose to do so. The programs envisioned would, in fact, have been

193

financed for the most part by the state's then broad-coverage Medicaid program since it was estimated that about 90 percent of the persons using such centers in the neighborhoods in which they would presumably be established would be Medicaid-eligible.

In 1968 the program was created, not by a bill which had the label "Ghetto Medicine" on it, but by two *separate* bills, each of which contained very brief amendments to the Public Health Law. The label "Ghetto Medicine" was invented by Andrew Fleck as part of his program to deal with potential opposition; the "two-bill" approach was a part of the same strategy. On June 5, 1968, Chapter 572 of the New York State Laws of that year passed the state legislature without debate. It allowed health commissioners in the several local jurisdictions to waive or compromise the collection of fees. (At that time commissioners could charge only for nursing and paramedical services in the home.) In fact, these amendments had nothing to do with a change in departmental policy on home nursing services; they were preparing the way for another amendment to come.

On June 17, 1968, Governor Rockefeller announced a three-part program for improving the delivery of health care in low-income urban and rural areas. The program would include mobile detection units, "neighborhood health facilities" and a neighborhood health worker program. The proposal for neighborhood health facilities was buried in verbiage about the other components of the program, and a great deal of emphasis was given to the aspects of maternal and child-health care in these facilities.

On June 22, 1968, Chapter 967 of the Laws of 1968 passed the legislature without debate. It amended the Public Health Laws to allow the health commissioners in the various local government jurisdictions to establish general medical services and to charge for such services. Since the Medicaid law provides that institutions cannot bill for services to Medicaid-eligible persons which are given free to non-Medicaid-eligible persons, the latter feature was necessary if the centers were to be able to collect Medicaid reimbursement. A modification of Chapter 35, Laws of 1969, allowed the health commissioners of the various jurisdictions to institute sliding-fee scales. Chapter 967 was accompanied by a brief statement from the Governor outlining its true purposes. Thus was "Ghetto Medicine" established.

Early Attempts to Implement the Program

Regulations were written to implement the program, originally Health Code Sections 40.10 (a) (2) and 40.10 (c) (2). With Part 703 of the code, these constitute the state regulations concerning "Ghetto Medicine"

194

program content. The most relevant portions of Section 40, describing criteria for receiving state aid, are:

> (2) State formula aid can be provided for the cost of maintaining and operating clinics and program as follows: (i) Approved preventive, diagnostic, consultation and detection clinics and programs. (ii) Approved general medical clinics, subject to the following conditions: (a) A letter of intent as specified in Section 710.2 of the New York State Hospital Code must be transmitted . . . (c) A fee schedule must be established . . . (d) A county or part-county health commissioner may, in his discretion in proper cases . . . waive the collection of such fees . . . (e) The administration of the clinic shall be under the general supervision of the county health commissioner . . . (f) clinic services may be provided by the contract . . . (g) An advisory committee of not less than seven persons, representative of the community served, shall be appointed by the county health commissioner. A majority of the committee shall be made up of persons not directly engaged in the health profession.

Regulations for state financial aid are in Section 39.3 (d):

> (1) . . . State aid will be based on prior approval of specific local programs, after application by the locality, and review and approval by the State Commissioner of Health . . . no claimant shall receive more than 50 percent of its total expense.

The 50 percent state-aid formula for the "Ghetto Medicine" program is traditional for local government categorical public health programs. It was assumed that since most patients using services would be Medicaid-eligible, the unreimbursed part of the cost would be low, and that a 50/50 sharing approach would put no undue burden on the state or on the local government jurisdictions. This is the origin of the "deficit-funding" character of "Ghetto Medicine" which was later carried into its transformation as a hospital-subsidy program in New York City.

The early approaches undertaken in New York City to implement "Ghetto Medicine" involved contracts with voluntary hospitals to operate general medical services in district health centers.[17] Outside of New York City, "Ghetto Medicine" programs were developed in six counties: Albany, Erie, Westchester, Monroe, Nassau and Suffolk, yet we were unable to find any state health department summary reports on "Ghetto Medicine," either excluding or including New York City. Nor does any mention of "Ghetto Medicine" appear in the department's Annual Reports for 1969 or for 1971–73.[18] Total state expenditures, however, for "Ghetto Medicine" outside of New York City for 1972–75 were: 1972—$834,732; 1973—$998,396; 1974—$1,622,221; 1975 (est.)—$2,172,530. The major expenditure has occurred in New York City.

"Ghetto Medicine" in New York City; The Origins of the New York City Ambulatory Care Program

In the 1968 legislative session, the same one which passed "Ghetto Medicine" without debate, major cutbacks were made in the state's Medicaid program. The legislature took the heart out of the "Ghetto Medicine" program (which was to have been funded largely by Medicaid) before it could be started. Oddly enough, no one seemed to realize at the time what the implications of the Medicaid cuts really were for the "Ghetto Medicine" program. Nevertheless, in New York City, the health department stubbornly pushed ahead with its contract idea, determined to try to implement the "Ghetto Medicine" concept even with reduced support from Medicaid.

In 1969, the voluntary hospitals of New York City, which provide about 50 percent of all hospital clinic visits in the city, were thrown into a tizzy by further Medicaid cutbacks and by a state freeze on Medicaid reimbursement rates to hospitals. As a result, they brought increasing pressure to bear on Governor Rockefeller. (Although the state administration wanted to help, it did not want to call a special legislative session.) Casting about for an existing piece of legislation which might do the trick, "Ghetto Medicine" was discovered. Since the Health Code Section 40.10 (c) (2) (ii) (f) did allow for the provision of services by contract, the way was left open—using a great deal of imagination—for the New York City health department to contract with voluntary hospitals for the provision of ambulatory services, even if they did happen to be existing services in existing clinics. Governor Rockefeller found $6 million and made his move. Thus a whole new chapter in the development of the health care delivery system in the United States was begun without the addition of even one new chapter to the laws of the state in which the beginning was made.

Original Characteristics of the New York City Ambulatory Care Program [19]

The New York City health department moved rapidly to implement, in its new form, the "Ghetto Medicine" program. Officially, it came to be called the "New York City Ambulatory Care Program," or ACP, the term which we shall use, but many persons still refer to it as "Ghetto Medicine." Since the approach in the original "Ghetto Medicine" program had been for the state to provide direct support for program deficits incurred after all third-party payments had been collected, this approach was continued in the subsidy program for voluntary hospitals. To meet hospital deficits for ambulatory services covered by the contracts, state

196

dollars would match city dollars on a one-to-one basis to the limit of the state appropriation for the purpose for any given year.

The first contracts covered the period December 1969 through June 1970. Twenty-nine hospitals applied for funds. Twenty-two contracts were negotiated and signed for a total of $9.5 million. Many policies and precedents were set during the incredibly hectic first seven months of the program's existence. Although by law three parties were involved in each contract negotiation—the state department of health, the city department of health and the hospital—it was the latter two which were the major participants, with the state playing an approval role only.

The major provisions of the first prototype contract were: (1) services provided by the hospital's clinics were to be "comprehensive" and "family-oriented": (2) the Commissioner of Health of New York City was to have general supervision over the program; (3) the hospital was to provide all resources necessary to provide a broadly comprehensive set of specified services; (4) there was to be a Director of the Ambulatory Care Unit whose appointment must be approved by the city health commissioner; (5) there was to be an Ambulatory Care Advisory Committee; (6) preference in future employment was to be given to persons residing in "economically deprived areas served by the Unit;" (7) an appointment system was required; (8) the unrestricted right of inspection was given to the city health commissioner or his/her designee, and operation reports had to be made available at the request of the commissioner; (9) patients referred for admission from the ambulatory service to the hospital itself had to be admitted and treated under the same rules as were applied to any other admittees; (10) the hospital was specifically constrained from reducing total volume of service; there had to be a maintenance of effort at the same time that services were being improved—in fact, the hospitals were specifically prohibited from using the money for new services, except as specified in the contract, but had to use the funds to maintain and improve existing services; (11) all Medicaid eligibility and collection responsibilities lay with the hospital; (12) termination was allowed upon 30 days notice; (13) a fee schedule was required.

In the context of the manner in which most government funds were, and are, given to voluntary hospitals, these provisions were truly revolutionary. For the first time, and by contract, funds were given to hospitals to pay for services *in the hospital*, according to standards of care established for hospital ambulatory care services. Fees and charges were standardized. Community participation, particularly in relation to contract enforcement, regulation and inspection, was accepted by the hospitals at the same time that they committed themselves to program improvements and while maintaining their previous level of effort. Detailed regulations (at first called "guidelines") pursuant to that proto-

197

type contract have been written over the years and have evolved into the contract "schedules." A consideration of the experience of the first 15 months of the program in some further detail is reported in the papers by McLaughlin, et al.[20] and Betty Bernstein.[21]

Status of the New York City Ambulatory Care Program in 1975

By 1975, the major contractual elements of the first contract, as outlined above, had all been retained, but the language had been refined and more detail added. The major substantive addition was a partial default provision, which we shall discuss below. The "schedules" which supplanted the original "guidelines" came to constitute a formal attachment to, and integral part of, the contract. Schedule A contains the provisions for, and the rights and duties of, the community advisory groups, now called "Community Boards for Ambulatory Care." Schedule B, not completed by 1975, contains prototypical community board by-laws. Schedule C contains specific contract requirements for individual hospitals, in addition to the general program requirements spelled out in the contract and accompanying schedules. Schedule D contains the Outpatient Department Guidelines. Schedule E contains the Emergency Room Guidelines. Schedules F and G are concerned with the fee schedule and administrative rules. (Samples of the contract and schedules are available from the New York City Department of Health, the contracting hospitals and the community boards.)

Several points and observations are worth making at this juncture. Meaningful community participation is an extremely important aspect of the ACP. The master contract is now negotiated on a city-wide basis between representatives of the voluntary hospitals and the city health department. Representatives of the community boards, and other representatives of community interests selected by the city department of health, take part in the negotiations. The present payments to hospitals are related to the deficits which they incur in their ambulatory care programs as reported in city health department audited figures. In no year since the existence of "Ghetto Medicine" has the city treasury matched the funds made available for the program by state appropriation. Since 1973, the state has provided certain funds which voluntary hoapitals in the ACP may match with their own money raised through voluntary contributions.

The ACP as an entity is nowhere mentioned in the New York State Public Health Laws. It was maintained on a year-to-year basis by appropriation only. Likewise, the city never enacted a local law embodying the ACP and further, the very detailed city ACP regulations have never been incorporated into its own health code. The program is, in fact, probably of questionable legality, particularly when its origins are taken into account. The state health department has, in general, maintained a hands-off posture in relation to the ACP, and contracts apparently receive the legally required approval of the state health commissioner rather automatically. No city health department inspection team has ever been accompanied by a state health department representative. All of this means that the collective power which the two departments have has never been put together.

Community Role [22]

According to several informants, including David Pomrinse,[23] the strong political pressure which had been brought to bear on Governor Rockefeller by interests in the city who were opposed to aiding the voluntary hospitals without also helping the municipal hospitals was, in part, responsible for creating a strong community presence in the program. According to Lowell Bellin,[24] the voluntary hospitals were so desperate for money that they were ready to accept almost any conditions.

Some of the history of the development of the community role in the ACP has been described.[25] As of 1975, there was a community board for each hospital, originally called "The Ambulatory Committee." Membership ranged from 11 to 17, with an average membership of 15. These boards had a consumer majority of no more than 60 percent. It was intended that about one-half of the consumer representatives be patients who use the services themselves, with the balance representing community organizations. At least eleven meetings per year, including at least three public meetings, were required. Each board had its own annual budget of $2,000 supplied by the city health department.

From 1971 there was a city-wide steering committee of representatives of the ambulatory care community boards. This evolved into the Consumer Council to the New York City Health Department, also referred to as the Ambulatory Care Consumer Advisory Committee. It met with city health department officials on a monthly basis to discuss problems and prospects of the ACP as a whole. It had 30–40 members representing all of the community boards, plus several city-wide health consumer organizations. Like each community board, the consumer council had an annual budget of $2,000 supplied by the city health department.

The rights and scope of work of the community boards are spelled out in Schedule A of the Contracts. Briefly, they are: (1) the right to full discussion of issues deemed important by the board; (2) the right to consult with responsible officials and outside authorities; (3) the right to make specific recommendations to responsible officials; (4) the right to health education programs for the community; (5) the right to inspect the ambulatory services based on a plan presented to and approved by the commissioner of health; (6) that the community board shall be involved in the early stages of planning and have the right to be consulted within adequate time about policies affecting ambulatory care.

The community boards are to "advise and consult" with the hospital and the city health department on the following items: quality of care; physical plant standards; maintenance of facilities; patient registration; patient eligibility; fee schedules; billing for self-pay patients; staffing patterns; establishment of Health Priorities; hours of service; review and follow-up of patient grievances; methods of handling patient admissions from outpatient department; complying with the terms of the contract; all reports to be made available to the community board; development of a patients' rights' document consistent with the general aims of the agreement. The community board had the use of the site-visit report, as well as information available from patients, to provide the community and the department of health with a rating report of the hospital for its compliance with major items in the body of the contract.

As might be expected, the quality of performance of the community boards varies. No objective evaluation of community board functioning has ever been published. Most evaluations are anecdotal and subjective, although most observers from the provider, consumer and health department perspectives consider that the boards do a good and valuable job.[26] The community role in the ACP is one of contract enforcer. With some degree of variation, the boards appear to be active and productive.

Evaluating Hospital Performance Under the ACP

Standards and Procedures for Evaluation

Schedule D of the ACP contract, covering clinics, required that the hospitals deliver or provide for: comprehensive health care; continuity of care; basic services in medicine, pediatrics, surgery, obstetrics and gynecology, prenatal care, family planning, psychiatry and vision and dental care—at convenient hours and frequencies on an appointment basis, with a plan for caring for non-appointment patients; a maximum two-week wait for a new-visit appointment; thirty minutes to be allowed for a complete history and physical examination for a new patient; no more than five patients per hour per physician for re-visits; patient privacy; patient knowledge of who his/her physician is; the nature and seriousness of his medical condition, and the treatment being provided; the establishment of formal patient grievance procedures in consultation with the committee; the availability of social workers; a unit record system; a fully responsible director of ambulatory care. Schedule E for emergency services included the following standards: the emergency unit to be integrated into general hospital operations; minimum staffing standards; a triage system; readily available record review; holding areas. These standards are comprehensive and inclusive. One is continually impressed with the stress given in them to the quality of patient care.

City Health Department Evaluation Procedures

Participating hospitals are inspected by the department's Bureau of Ambulatory Care with a frequency of slightly more than one time per year. The community board is an integral part of the evaluation procedure. Structure, process and, occasionally outcome measures of quality are used. Inspections are done not just on a "one-shot" basis—but include written comments, and, on occasion, follow-up visits. In addition, they are related to payments. Prior to 1974, inspections were an all-or-nothing proposition in that if a hospital failed all or part of an inspection the only possible penalty was dismissal from the program. Partial default, a much more sensitive tool, was implemented in 1975. After review has taken place, part payment can be withheld from a hospital with particular deficiencies until the deficiencies are corrected, without eliminating the hospital from the program entirely. This kind of approach means that hospitals can be assisted in improving while at the same time having a real incentive to improve.

Outcomes of Evaluations

Hospital evaluation reports under the ACP are public documents. A comprehensive set of reports has been put together by the United Hospital Fund of New York.[27] In 1975, reports on Misericordia and Mount Sinai were published by the Consumer Commission on the Accreditation of Health Services.[28] The major feature of these evaluation is that they have breadth, depth and real concern for the welfare of patients. It is no surprise that there is a wide range of opinion regarding the evaluation/inspection program and the city health department's approach to it. Health department officials, present and former, regard them positively.[29] Gary Gambuti of St. Luke's Hospital[30] feels that the site-visits have been "terrible"; that the inspectors are "untrained and do not know what they are looking for." Hammerling[31] feels that site-visits and reports "are positive, but too rigid," but that the hospital and the New York City program "share the same concerns." He sees the city as "a partner striving for common goals" and resents what he calls their tendency to play "an adversary role" and their "lack of patience." Another source felt that the health department had to be careful to avoid getting

201

into a "check-list rut" in its approach to inspection/evaluation. An additional source, known to be a strong supporter of consumer interests in health, characterized some health department recommendations as "absurd." He referred to the lack of continuity of inspectors, remarked that it is very difficult to make assessments in one day and that some major problems are missed. Schwarz noted a tendency to defensiveness on the part of professionals being inspected.[32] If nothing else, inspections under the ACP shake people up about themselves, as well as about their building and their program.

No comprehensive evaluation of the ACP has ever been carried out, and there is no ongoing evaluation system for the ACPs. Thus, as with the Article 28 program, no one really knows if the ACP makes a difference insofar as the quality of care is concerned. There has been one small-scale attempt at objective evaluation of the ACP at a particular time, and there are, of course, many subjective evaluations which we encountered in the course of our interviews. In 1973, Schwarz et al. examined the experience of twenty ACP hospitals in relation to 17 program criteria for the period January 1, 1970–January 1, 1973 (Table 1). Most of the criteria are structural, but a few, like physician continuity, are process. For whatever it is worth, the experience shows progress on all but two measures (9 and 15) and compliance with criterion 15 was at a high level at the start of the program. Significant improvement in numbers of hospitals complying were found for physician continuity, institution of a sliding-fee scale, professional review of diagnostic test results, the institution of chart audits and the establishment of a consumer board. The study has not been repeated nor does it consider parameters of utilization, quality of medical care, or costs. It does, however, show that, on these criteria, the ACP had positive effects on the ambulatory services in the contracting hospitals.

The subjective evaluations of the ACP by persons from the health department side,[34] the consumer side[35] and the provider side[36] all tended to be positive, although some providers, particularly those who did not speak for attribution, were highly critical. The major achievements of the ACP are considered to be: the maintenance of service; the creation of a single standard of care; standardization of fees and charges; acceptance by hospitals of the contract method of payment; the creation of community boards with a meaningful role; the introduction of process standards into the evaluation process; probable improvement of medical care quality; up-grading of ambulatory care staffing; improvements in dignity and comfort for patients; the creation of a patient grievance mechanism; the creation of appointment systems; the reduction in the number of specialty clinics; better social and nursing service. The most serious continuing problems are the most intractable for OPDs everywhere—incomplete or missing medical records; delays in getting appointments for new visits; long waiting times; weakness in the position of Director of Ambulatory Care.

In summary, there is no broad-based objective assessment of the ACP, but there is a remarkable agreement, for the most part, between hospital directors, directors of ambulatory care, city health department officials, and consumer representatives that the ACP has been a good thing and has achieved noticeable improvements in voluntary hospital ambulatory services in New York City.

The Voluntary/Municipal Hospital Struggle

A major struggle which has enlivened the history of the ACP since its inception has been the attempt by a coalition of city officials and certain city-wide consumer-representative groups, such as the Citizens' Committee for Children, to persuade the state government to allow "Ghetto Medicine" funds to be used to subsidize ambulatory services in municipal as well as voluntary hospitals. An early view of this struggle was cited above.[34] Nothing has changed since that time.[35] It should be noted that, despite the change in administration in Albany, as of the Spring of 1975, the position of the state government on the question remained the same.

"Ghetto Medicine" in Suffolk County[36]

A few of the counties in the State of New York have attempted to develop programs along the lines of the original "Ghetto Medicine" concepts: Albany, Erie, Monroe, Westchester, Nassau and Suffolk. According to Andrew Fleck,[37] the fact that the program did not generally catch on is due to three factors: (1) The 1968–69 Medicaid cutbacks sharply reduced the available third-party reimbursement for general medical services in local health departments, thereby increasing the amounts which local governments would have had to supply from their general revenues, even though these would be matched by the state; (2) local health departments do not comprise "accounting entities" within their jurisdictions, so that incoming funds disappear into general revenues, thus making it difficult to establish an identifiable program; (3) local health officers were not very interested.

In our original report there was a fairly lengthy description of the program in Suffolk County which was based on a study carried out in the spring of 1975 and written by Ms. Virginia Neary, a student in the School of Social Welfare, Health Sciences Center, State University of New York at Stony Brook. We only have space here to present briefly the conclusions of that piece. As of mid-1975, the Suffolk County Health Department operated three health centers which were supported in part by "Ghetto Medicine" funds.

The major problems have been with the county health department and the county government; enormous delays, lack of understanding, conflicts with the civil service system, and county insistence on running pieces of the program itself even while contracting with local hospitals to run the bulk of the programs. We do not know what the experience has been in the other five counties in the state which have "Ghetto Medicine" programs but in Suffolk, at least, red tape and bureaucracy abound and make program implementation slow and frustrating.

The community role in Suffolk is very different from that in New York City. A major reason for this is related to the major differences in the roles of the two health departments. In the city the department has two clear roles: money provider and inspector. On the one hand, it is money-giver; on the other, it has insisted on being, in part, program operator as well. It is directly involved in nursing service, building ownership and maintenance, equipment purchase, family planning and dental services, transport services and outreach programs. Thus the community, in dealing with the county, must relate to it as a part of the program administration as well as the money-giver. Since as program operator the county appears to border on the inept, the community groups often find themselves in an adversary position with it. This is in sharp contrast to the New York City situation in which the health department's role is clear, and the department and the community boards most often find themselves as allied in attempting to improve the various services programs.

Objectively and rationally, quality control and organized ambulatory care are two areas which should receive a great deal of stress in a health care system. For a variety of reasons, neither receives such attention other than that of the rhetorical variety. In this work, we studied these two "orphans," and have tried to see, in a particular context, how they have made out when thrown together. Some of the observed experience, from the point of view which deplores the third-class status of quality control and organized ambulatory care, has been good, some of it bad. However it is possible to learn positive lessons from both experiences.

Discussion: The New York State Health Department General Powers and Article 28; Broad Powers Granted to the Commissioner and the Public Health Council

We were able to find no evidence that the broad powers concerning the quality of medical care granted to the New York State Commissioner of Health and to the Public Health Council under the Public Health Laws have ever been implemented to more than a very minor degree. The

204

question is why. Part of this has to do with narrow interpretations placed upon the statutes by the department itself which may relate to the historical reluctance of health departments to tangle with organized medicine. In this regard, notice the care and circumspection with which the "Ghetto Medicine" legislation was introduced and passed. It was aimed toward districts in which there were few private practitioners; public hearings were purposely avoided, as Fleck pointed out; the bills came up at the end of the legislative session; and the doctors happened to be distracted by Governor Rockefeller's interest in a state health insurance program. In any case, non-implementation of the general quality powers in the Public Health Laws of the State of New York certainly avoided potential struggle over the issue. Finally, it appears as if the health department simply had too much to do with a limited staff, and that it may well have been lawsuit conscious and subject to political pressure, as in the nursing home situation.[38]

The articles of the hospital code relating to hospital ambulatory care simply have not been implemented. The state health department, until very recently, has not seen ambulatory care as a priority. Frank Cicero, who is responsible for the operating certificate program, refused to say, despite repeated prodding, that the department needs more staff. He did say that for the past several years most of his inspectors were tied up with the nursing home situation. As if to emphasize the importance of shortage of staff in a year of massive budget cuts and personnel firings, Governor Carey added 36 auditors to the staff of the state health department.[39]

In discussing the limitations of the Article 28 program, one must consider the role of the state legislature. There is no record of legislative hearings ever being held about the performance of the department of health in any of these areas, neither in implementing specific Article 28 programs nor in carrying out its general responsibilities for quality control under Articles 2 and 28.[40]

In summary, the record in relation to Articles 2 and 28 is spotty. Virtually nothing has been done in hospital ambulatory care. There has been activity in short-term hospital inpatient services and in long-term care, but that activity remains essentially unevaluated in any objective sense, except for one study of certification-of-need. The powers of the department are plentiful and the legal sanctions are strong. Implementation has been, at best, inconsistent.

The "Ghetto Medicine" Program; The State Government and "Ghetto Medicine"

The New York State Health Department created the "Ghetto Medicine" program. It did not come off as planned, however, and the department seemed to lose interest. As with Article 28, the legislature, too, has had little interest, and "Ghetto Medicine" (or ACP) has thus become, primarily, a program of the New York City health department. It is a fascinating program. It is creative, it is apparently productive and it has achieved certain changes in the operations of voluntary hospital clinics in New York City for relatively small outlays of funds. One of the most amazing things about it, in fact, is the extent to which hospitals will go on changing, or attempting to change, or at least appearing to change, in order to get (in proportion to their total budgets) a relatively small amount of money. It makes one wonder what they would do if they had to make changes to get large amounts of money.

In terms of objective evaluation, New York City has been somewhat better, but not too much better, than the state has been. Clear goals for the program were stated in the first prototype contract, and there are periodic, although episodic, attempts by the Bureau of Ambulatory Care to measure achievement of these goals. There is still, however, no on-going program of objective evaluation. Although the academic literature concerning the ACP is not voluminous, at least there *is* such a literature, descriptive and evaluative, produced by persons both inside and outside the city department of health. (The department's concern is to establish the fact that there are connections between the ACP and improvements in the health care of the people of New York City.) Despite the lack, however, of a clear, objective evaluation mechanism, which is certainly needed, the subjective view of almost everyone interviewed is that the program is working and producing positive results.

The ACP has challenged the basis of the whole structure of the participating voluntary hospitals in New York City in two vitally important areas: quality control and ambulatory care. For quite some time, in dealing with the JCAH and operating certification, hospitals have accepted audits by outside agencies of quality of care on the basis of structural standards. However, they, or more specifically their medical staffs, have traditionally maintained that quality auditing which examines discrete instances of delivery of care was the private province of the medical staff alone, and that anything else would be "interference with the practice of medicine." The ACP, which uses process as well as structural standards in its auditing procedures, and thus looks at discrete instances of care delivery on a routine basis, has cracked this barrier, and has probably cracked it once and for all. Furthermore, hospitals are being forced to reorient their basic thinking on ambulatory services; on their organization, structure and place in the hospital hierarchy.

The ACP has kept voluntary hospital clinics open, some of which probably would have closed. It has introduced the principle of the contract mechanism to control the transfer of government money to

206

private institutions for the support of their own services. Private institutions have, of course, contracted with government before, but it has always been for money to run a program *someplace else*—an affiliated municipal hospital, a neighborhood health center, a drug program, or the like. (Under the Medicare and Medicaid programs the major amounts of government monies coming into hospitals come in on a cost-reimbursement basis, and the contrast is striking.)

The ACP has introduced meaningful community participation into hospital operations. Many of us who struggled through the "community control" issue in reference to neighborhood health centers and municipal hospitals came away with a rather jaundiced view of the whole affair.[41] In the ACP, the contracting hospital is clearly in charge of the operating program; the city health department is in charge of the money and the inspections; the community board is in charge of contract enforcement, relating to both contractor and contractee. This is different, creative, productive of positive change and has potential for wide application.

The ACP has also required maintenance of effort, a lowering of financial barriers to care for the "near-poor," publication of ACP inspection reports (in contrast, it is only recently that Article 28 inspection reports have come into the public domain), program audits and fiscal accounting—with these reports being made public as well—and the introduction of the concept of partial default. This will probably be followed by the extremely interesting system of linking reimbursement to performance, an approach which has important ramifications.

Most observers have felt that specific improvements have been made in hospital ambulatory services. Among them, not necessarily in order of importance, are: the requirement for a Director of Ambulatory Care; the institution of an appointment system; the removal of interns from emergency rooms; the requirement for primary care physicians and the implementation of the concept of comprehensive care; reduction in the number of specialty clinics; increased social services; the introduction of patient drug profiles; and the institution of nurse conferencing.

Problems do remain in areas which have been the toughest nuts to crack in hospital ambulatory services: the limited authority of the directors of ambulatory care; the medical records system, with lost charts and unposted test results; lengthy, although reduced, patient waiting times; and long delays in first appointments for new patients. There are also problems in the inspection process itself, relating to frequency, staff shortage and the limitations of the one-day visit.

Why was the ACP implemented as it was? The explanation is not completely understood by us, but it has the following elements: the hospitals needed money desperately; consumer participation happened to exist already in the state regulations for the original "Ghetto Medicine" program; these regulations, the only possible legal basis for the ACP, contained the contract option which was the only way that money could be funnelled into the voluntary hospitals. Thus, what we consider to be the two basic elements of the ACP—the contract mechanism and the community role in contract enforcement—were in the program, perforce, if it were to have any legal basis at all.

Conclusions

"It doesn't matter how many teeth you have if you can't close your mouth."

In dealing with the problems of enforcement agencies, some people want to say that "the only thing we [they] need is more teeth." But it is quite obvious that the state health department does not, or cannot, use the powers which it already has. It has the teeth, but for a variety of reasons, only some of which are entirely understood, it cannot close its mouth. In contrast, the New York City Health Department has, in law, only a few teeth, the gum structure is very weak and, objectively, the teeth are very wobbly. In fact, one well-aimed blow could probably knock them out. But the city health department closes its mouth hard (again for a variety of reasons, not all of which are well understood) and the few wobbly teeth appear to leave their mark.

The Key Ingredients of the ACP

Three of the ACP's many features stand out: money attached to standards; the contract mechanism; the community role in contract enforcement. To understand that the ACP needs all three to make it work one need only compare it with two other programs under which the city government gives money to voluntary hospitals for providing services. Under the Medicaid program, the city's voluntary hospitals receive amounts of money far greater than the amounts received under the ACP. There are Medicaid performance standards, and so there is money attached to standards. But there is no contract—Medicaid monies are paid out on a cost-reimbursement basis. There is no input from the community for enforcement of standards, and, for whatever the reasons, in New York City there is little or no enforcement of standards for institutions under Medicaid. The New York City Health and Hospitals Corporation contracts with voluntary hospitals and medical schools to supply medical staff and certain other services for most of the city's hospitals. There is money attached to standards, and there is a contract, but there is little or no input from the community to contract enforcement

208

and contract enforcement under the so-called affiliation agreements is reputed to be weak.

Here, then, are two instances in which there are money and standards and, in one of them, a contract, and little or no enforcement. One should not think, however, that the magic answer is in input from the community. There have been many instances in New York City, particularly in the neighborhood health center movement, in which there were very high levels of input and in which program output left much to be desired in terms both of quality and quantity. The secret of the success of the ACP is in its melding of the elements.

The Approach to Community Participation Is Innovative and Productive

As we pointed out, we did little evaluation of the process of community input to the ACP. However, as far as we could tell, the "who is in charge here" questions which bedeviled the neighborhood health center movement (particularly that of the Office of Economic Opportunity) have been left behind by the ACP. The community representatives' principal role is clear: contract enforcer, to both the contractor and the contractee. This, to use an overused word, is *meaningful* community participation. In other words, it is *productive*.

The Original Concept of "Ghetto Medicine" Has Its Problems

We looked at the program of only one of the six counties outside New York City which have tried to implement "Ghetto Medicine." We do not know if Suffolk County's experience is typical, but the reviews of its program are, at best, mixed. The experience shows very clearly the tremendous limitations which county governments have in trying to implement an innovative program. If the Suffolk County experience is any indication, county government is not the ideal instrument for something new, regardless of the reasons for its limitations. One of the major reasons for the almost complete failure of the original "Ghetto Medicine" program to alter the profile of health care in New York State was that county government was chosen as the linch-pin.

Article 28 Is Selectively Enforced

It is obvious that Article 28 has had no effect, positive or negative, on hospital ambulatory care in New York State. The overall effects of Article 28 remain virtually unevaluated with the exception of one retrospective statistical study of certification-of-need. A factor in this selectivity may be the virtual lack of public involvement in its work. In one area of its Article

28 activities, the nursing home industry, the state health department has recently shown itself responsive to public pressure and has shown that it can benefit from public support in carrying out its responsibilities.

The Future Potential of the Voluntary Hospital System Is Great

It is popular in some quarters to seek the solution to the problems faced by the American health care system in a "government takeover" of that system. Yet the voluntary hospitals which participated in the ACP program have shown themselves capable of positive change. It is true that in many cases change is made with great reluctance and may be, at this early stage, more apparent than real. Furthermore, changes in terms of program, approach to community participation and approach to quality control are being made for the stepchild only—ambulatory care—while the hospital continues to play the role of overprotective mother to its pride and joy—the inpatient services. But history moves only one step at a time, except in revolutionary situations. Change has begun, and the voluntaries are participating or, as some might put it, being forced to participate. It would appear that the results of our study lend some credence to the view that, to the extent that positive change is possible within the limits of our present socioeconomic system, the voluntary hospital system, when forced to become accountable to the public and responsive to the broad mass of the people which it serves, is reasonably well equipped to undertake the necessary changes in our health care system.[42] It is just not known what the effects of Article 28 and programs like it really are. Yet the country plunges ahead, legislating like mad. This is probably our most important finding and should be borne in mind as our recommendations are considered.

References

[1] Steven Jonas, "Issues in National Health Insurance in the United States of America," *The Lancet* July 20, 1974, 143; House of Representatives, Committee on Ways and Means, *National Health Insurance Resource Book*, Washington, D.C.: USGPO, 1974; R.D. Eilers, "National Health Insurance: What Kind and How Much?" *New England Journal of Medicine* 284:881, 945, 1971; E.R. Weinerman, "Organization and Quality of Service in a National Health Program," *Yale Journal of Biology and Medicine* 44:133, 1971; and K. Davis, *National Health Insurance* (Washington, D.C., The Brookings Institution, 1975).

[2] Committee on the Costs of Medical Care, *Medical Care for the American People* (Chicago, 1932, Reprinted U.S. Dept. of Health, Education, and Welfare, Washington, D.C., 1970); National Commission on Community Health Service, *Health is a Community Affair* (Cambridge, Mass., 1966); National Advisory Commission on Health Manpower, *Report* (Washington, D.C., Government Printing Office, 1967; R. Battistella et al., "Crisis in American Medicine," *The Lancet* 1:581, 1968; Health Task Force of the Urban Coalition, *Rx for Action* (Washington, D.C. 1969; Daniel Schorr, *Don't Get Sick in America,*

(Nashville: Aurora Publishing Inc., 1970); and Citizens' Board of Inquiry into Health Services for Americans, *Heal Yourself* (Washington, D.C., 1971).

3 "Report of the Governor's Committee on Hospital Costs," M.B. Folsom, Chairman (New York, 1965).

4 New York State Department of Health, "Decade of Legislation," mimeographed (Albany, October 13, 1971).

5 "Report of the Governor's Committee," p. 2.

6 *Ibid.*, p. 3.

7 *Ibid.*, pp. 3–11.

8 Hollis S. Ingraham, "Hospital Affairs. New Mission for the State Health Department," *New York State Journal of Medicine* March 15, 1966, 771; D. Solomon, Director, Hospital Construction Finance, New York State Department of Health, interview, Albany, May 13, 1975; Frank Cicero, Deputy Commissioner, New York State Department of Health and Jane Garry, Director, Bureau of Ambulatory Care, New York State Department of Health, joint interview, Albany, May 13, 1975; Andrew Fleck, Assistant Commissioner, formerly First Deputy Commissioner, New York State Department of Health, interview, March 7, 1975; and G. Bernstein, formerly Assistant Commissioner, New York City Department of Health, presently Director of Development, Church Charity Foundation, Brooklyn, interview, March 10, 1975.

9 New York State Department of Health, *Our Mission: Your Health, Annual Report, 1969* (Albany, May 1970); New York State Department of Health, *New York State's Health, Annual Report, 1971* (Albany, May 1972); New York State Department of Health, *New York State's Health. Annual Report, 1972* (Albany, April 1973).

10 New York State Department of Health, *Annual Report, 1973* (Albany, April 1974). *Annual Report, 1969*, pp. 2–4; *Annual Report, 1971*, p. 3; *Annual Report, 1972*, pp. 9, 17; and *Annual Report, 1973*, p. 10.

11 Fleck interview.

12 Chapter 326, Laws of 1963, New York State Public Health Laws, Section 206 (1) (j).

13 J.B. Tenny et al., "National Ambulatory Medical Care Survey: Background and Methodology," *Vital and Health Statistics*, Ser. 2, No. 61, 1974, p. 2.

14 Benjamin Wainfeld, Director of Community Medicine, Brookdale Hospital, Brooklyn, interview, March 26, 1975; Stanley Reichman, Director of Community Medicine, Hospital for Joint Diseases, New York, interview, April 4, 1975; Alden Hammerling, Assistant Vice-President for Ambulatory Care Services, Roosevelt Hospital, New York, interview, April 2, 1975; S.D. Pomrinse, formerly Director, Mount Sinai Hospital and Medical Center, New York, interview, April 4, 1975; Bernstein interview; and Cicero and Garry joint interview.

15 C.-E.A. Winslow, *The Life of Herman M. Biggs* (Philadelphia: Lea and Febiger, 1929), Chap. XVII.

16 Most of the legislative history of "Ghetto Medicine" came from the interview with Andrew Fleck, March 7, 1975, and unpublished documents supplied by him. Other material was also used, as noted.

17 M.C. McLaughlin et al., "Ghetto Medicine: Program in New York City," *New York State Journal of Medicine* October 1, 1971, 2321.

211

[18] New York State Department of Health, *Annual Reports 1969, 1971-73.*

[19] This section is based on the interviews with Dr. Fleck, Mr. Bernstein, Dr. Wainfeld, Dr. Reichman and Dr. Pomrinse; McLaughlin et al. cited above; and A. Schwarz, presently Assistant Commissioner for Evaluation and Institutional Review, New York City Health Department, interviews, March 12, and April 16, 1975, and subsequent telephone conversations.

[20] McLaughlin et al., "Ghetto Medicine."

[21] Betty Bernstein, "What Happened to 'Ghetto Medicine' in New York State," *American Journal of Public Health* 61:1287, 1971. See also relevant letters, *AJPH* 62:3, 1972.

[22] Material for this section comes from cited publications, interviews cited above with Dr. Wainfeld, Mr. Hammerling, Dr. Pomrinse and Mr. Schwarz; other interviews cited below with Ms. Z. Fearon and Mr. G. Gambuti, and from interviews with other persons who did not wish to be quoted directly.

[23] Pomrinse interview.

[24] Lowell E. Bellin et al., "Phase One of Consumer Participation in Policies of 22 Voluntary Hospitals in New York City," *American Journal of Public Health* 62:1370, 1972.

[25] McLaughlin et al., "Ghetto Medicine," Betty Bernstein, "What Happened to Ghetto Medicine," and Bellin interview.

[26] The Consumer Commission on the Accreditation of Health Services. "Ambulatory Care Program—A Role for the Consumer," *Health Perspectives* 2, January-February, 1975; Z. Fearon, Chairperson, Consumer Council to the New York City Health Department, interview, April 4, 1975; M.F. McCann, *The Ambulatory Care Program: A Manual for Consumers* (New York Community Health Institute, 1974); and Wainfeld, Hammerling and Schwarz interviews.

[27] United Hospital Fund of New York, "Workbook for the Study of Ambulatory Care in New York City" (New York, no date, but presumably 1975).

[28] The Consumer Commission, "Ambulatory Care Program."

[29] Lowell E. Bellin, Commissioner of Health, New York City Department of Health, interview, March 12, 1975, and Bernstein and Schwarz interviews.

[30] Gary Gambuti, Executive Vice-President, St. Luke's Hospital, interview, March 25, 1975.

[31] Hammerling interview.

[32] A. Schwarz et al., "A Ghetto Medicine Program," *Social Work* November 1973, 90.

[33] A. Schwarz et al., "Evaluating Ambulatory Care in New York City," New York City Department of Health, process, *op. cit.*, 36ff.

[34] Bernstein, Schwarz and Bellin interviews.

[35] The Consumer Commission, "Ambulatory Care Program," and Fearon interview.

[36] Wainfeld, Pomrinse and Gambuti interviews; Rosenberg paper.

[37] Betty Bernstein, "What Happened to Ghetto Medicine."

[38] Report of the New York State Moreland Act Commission, "Regulating Nursing Home Care: The Paper Tigers" (Albany, October 1975), and A. Stein, "Report on Nursing Homes

and Health Related Facilities in New York State," The Temporary State Commission on Living Costs and the Economy (Albany, April 1975).

[39] New York State Department of Health, "News Release" (Albany, December 31, 1975).

[40] Joint Legislative Committee on the Problems of Public Health, Medicare, Medicaid and Compulsory Health and Hospital Insurance, Annual Report, Legislative Document #40 (Albany, 1967); *ibid.*, Legislative Document #14, 1968; *ibid.*, Legislative Document #19, 1969; *ibid.*, Legislative Document #8, 1970; and Herbert Miller, Chairman, New York State Assembly Health Committee, interview, April 10, 1975.

[40] Joint Legislative Committee, Annual Report, Legislative Documents #40, 1967; #14, 1968; #19, 1969; #8, 1970, and Miller interview.

[41] Steven Jonas, "A Theoretical Approach to the Question of Community Control of Health Services Facilities," *American Journal of Public Health* 61:916, 1971.

[42] J.G. Freymann, The American Health Care System: Its Genesis and Trajectory (New York: Medcom Press, 1974), Chaps, 18–23.

NOTE: This paper is an abridged version of the original report of the study "Organized Ambulatory Services and the Enforcement of Health Care Quality Standards in New York State," which was carried out for the task force in the Spring of 1975. The bulk of the original report will appear as part of a book, *Aspects of Ambulatory Care Quality Control in New York State: Implications for National Health Insurance*, published by the Springer Publishing Company, New York, N.Y.

Impact of National Health Insurance on Labor-Management Health and Welfare Plans in New York City

BETTY G. LALL and FRANK GOLDSMITH

Unions as Major Purchasers of Health Care

This paper explores ways in which labor-management health plans might be affected by national health insurance legislation. It is followed by excerpts from a study of the views of trade union leaders at the local level on this subject.[1]

There are about 10,000 labor-management health plans around the country, at least 300 in New York City alone. Considering that about one-fourth of the work force of 86 million is organized, and that for every unionized worker there are an average of three members of his family who are also beneficiaries, labor-management health plans represent a considerable portion of the population.

New York City is considered a union town. The New York City Central Labor Council, AFL-CIO, claims a membership of one million workers in more than 80 different industries who belong to almost 500 local unions affiliated with the American Federation of Labor-Congress of Industrial Organizations. (This number of workers plus their families would suggest that almost half the population of the city is covered to some extent by union-negotiated health plans.) There are, in addition, many unions in New York City that are independent, without AFL-CIO affiliation; they include, among others, the International Brotherhood of Teamsters and the United Automobile Workers. Some industries are more heavily represented and unionized than others. The men's and women's clothing industry, for example, is heavily unionized, while office workers and workers in retail establishments are for the most part not highly unionized.

There are some very large unions in the city, such as Local 23-25 of the International Ladies Garment Workers Union with more than 20,000 members, and at least one, Local 2 of the United Federation of Teachers, with more than 50,000. There are many small local unions in the city as well, with memberships of 500 or less, and they naturally lack the resources for major activities; they have small treasuries, few staff members, and limited office and headquarters space. Some of them, however, belong to district or regional councils and hence are able to

214

utilize the resources of the district. For example, District Council 37 of the American Federation of State, County, and Municipal Employees services 43 locals and represents over 100,000 workers.[2] Another introductory point to make about workers and their unions is that New York City, with one of the highest costs of living of any city in the country, consists of many industries which are characterized as low-wage. Workers in these industries tend to work for employers with relatively few employees; that is, fewer than 500 at a single work location.[3]

Evolution of the Bargaining for Health Benefits

World War II conditions caused many unions to bargain for health benefits as part of their collective bargaining agreements. Wages and prices were controlled at the time and as unions found themselves unable to bargain for wage increases, they were able, instead, to obtain the equivalent of monetary gains in the form of health benefits. Thus, the early 1940s saw large amounts of funds being poured into the health delivery system. Early benefits stressed hospitalization, since this was one of the most costly aspects of health care. This was followed by surgical coverage, in-hospital medical costs, ambulatory care and later, by the development of a comprehensive package. A subsequent development was the addition of dental care and provision for drugs. As health costs have mounted along with the interest of union members in new items to add to their health benefit package, the amount negotiated for health has risen. For those unions which negotiate a percentage of payroll for health and welfare, the amount going for health at the present time ranges from 5 to 8 percent of the total payroll of workers covered. The usual practice is for unions to take the money available and to work with actuarial consultants or with an insurance company (or similar third-party carrier in health) to decide what benefits will be purchased and at what cost. Another group of unions negotiates for health care with management not in monetary terms, but in terms of actual benefits to be provided, e.g., number of days for hospitalization, dollars for surgery, doctors' visits, laboratory services, etc.

Growth of Union Health Centers

Many unions in New York City found that negotiating health benefits did not automatically provide their members with good medical care. Members were often given second class treatment by providers; many workers did not have a family doctor at all, and when the need arose went to the emergency room in the hospital closest to their homes. To meet some of the health needs of their members, 22 New York City

215

unions negotiated with management to construct and operate health facilities. One of the 22, the Hotel and Motel Trades Council, maintains health facilities at six locations. Seventeen of the health centers are in Manhattan, six in Brooklyn, and two each are located in the Bronx and Queens. They represent a variety of industries: five in the maritime trades; three in the garment industry; three from the retail and wholesale industry; others from the construction trades, electrical manufacturing, the teamsters, hotel trades, etc. Among the centers the range of persons eligible is vast, from 4,000 to 350,000. All centers but three include the spouse as eligible, and all but five include some family coverage. Most centers were erected near the members' place of work and several were placed in the vicinity of the union headquarters, or in the headquarters itself. As a result, the utilization rate of the centers has changed over time, particularly as members moved to different parts of the city or the suburbs, and as their work took them farther and farther afield. Utilization rates vary in most unions, in several cases by as much as 50 percent. The highest utilization rate for the family was 40 percent in the case of Local 1205 of the International Brotherhood of Teamsters.

Services vary considerably, with most centers providing several diagnostic or screening tests. The vast majority provide electrocardiograms, chest X-rays and blood and urine analysis. Only a few, however, offer screening for hypertension, and less than a majority take Pap smears and pulmonary tests. Sixteen centers provide primary care, a development that grew out of earlier experiences with providers for diagnostic care only. Center administrators discovered that many members did not have a doctor to whom the results of the screening could be sent, and so the union decided to offer physician services at the center itself. Although most doctors are not full time but work on a subcontract basis, a few centers offer medical specialties such as pediatrics, obstetrics, dermatology, orthopedics and urology.[4]

Membership satisfaction with union health centers appears to be high, although there are no recent concrete surveys that can be cited in this regard. Utilization, too, has remained high, and where decreases have been noted the main causes appear to be change in a member's place of residence or work, or reduction in the number of persons employed.

For unions which negotiated a health and welfare fund—as opposed to specific services—the inflation in health costs threatened the survival of the fund. If unions negotiated for more money to go into the fund so as to keep even with rising costs, as well as to add services, they were taking money away from wages or other benefits desired by the membership. To avoid this, there were at least fifteen local unions in New York City that divested themselves of their third-party carriers (insurance company, Group Health Incorporated, HIP, Blue Cross, etc.) and became self-insured. Thus the union took on the function of paying provider bills directly. To do this the administrators of the health plan became sophisticated in the handling of claims, especially in knowing when charges were unreasonable. Over the years union leaders have reaped substantial organizational gains as a result of collective bargaining for health benefits, primarily because unions could point to health and other benefits as something the worker would not have, or not have as fully, were there no union bargaining on his behalf.

Issues Concerning Unions and National Health Insurance

Unions prefer to use the term health security rather than health insurance. They do not think that insurance companies and other third-party carriers have done much to improve the quality of health care and to monitor costs. In short, according to the labor movement, insurance companies have contributed nothing to the health system except to act as a costly intermediary. Because health costs have risen substantially, and because unions have not been able to curtail the fragmentation which has resulted from numerous locals purchasing health care separately from powerful health care providers, the labor movement has put a high priority on achieving federal legislation to establish a comprehensive health security system in which there is a single payment source; namely, the Social Security Administration of the federal government. This is a fundamental goal of labor and one on which it is least likely to compromise.

Although there are many different bills before Congress concerning the establishment of a system of national health insurance, or parts thereof, the legislation referred to in this paper is primarily the Kennedy-Corman Bill—not necessarily because it embodies concepts supported by the labor movement, but because it is the most comprehensive bill with respect to benefits and financing mechanisms. Thus it would have the greatest impact on the health plans of the labor movement.

In considering the impact on union health plans of health security legislation it seems essential to include at least two other health bills already enacted into law which form aspects of the new health security system that the Congress is in the process of developing. One is the recent law creating Health Systems Agencies; the second is the legislation covering Health Maintenance Organizations, which constitutes a means for changing the delivery system through prepaid group practice centers. The fact that the legislation requires every employer to offer HMO as an option in employee health plans means that unions must contend with this important aspect of public policy.

Recent Collective Bargaining Negotiations and Health Benefits

Of ten unions responding to questions about time spent on health and related benefits in the recent negotiations with management, six said it has increased; one reported a decrease in time spent and three said no change. For those who said bargaining on health matters took more time, only one union said benefits increased. For the rest, they believed they had to bargain longer just to stay even. In many cases this meant that employers agreed to pay more money into health funds to keep benefits from being reduced.

Only five unions stated that health benefits increased during recent contract talks. These included maternity and dental benefits; an increase in the number of home visits paid for; and the lowering of the deductibles for major medical insurance. For the most part, unions complained that the increases in health costs combined with a recession that was forcing large scale unemployment, made it difficult to maintain benefits at past levels. Both industrial practices and the extent of recent unemployment affect the solvency of union health funds. Since employers do not pay into health funds for employees who have been laid off, as the economy enters a recession, health funds are gradually depleted. Therefore unions have been using a variety of devices to maintain health funds at an appropriate level to continue to pay benefits. For example reserve funds which had been fairly ample were dipped into in order to pay increased costs.

Views of the Current Health Care System

Health care in the United States is not viewed favorably by union leaders. These leaders, many of whom have had extensive experience with the health system on behalf of their members, believe almost unanimously that health care is far too costly, that it provides too much profit for practitioners, duplicates efforts, is uneven in the quality of health rendered, is full of bureaucracy, is impersonal and operates on a double standard: one for the rich and one for everyone else. Union leaders interviewed were asked what specific grievances members have about the health system. Membership complaints centered around the money problems presented by the cut-offs, co-payments and deductibles which accompany medical coverage through Group Health Insurance, HIP, Blue Cross and through the commercial carriers (Travellers; Aetna, etc.). Blue Cross computer delays also meant that members received late reimbursement. This often resulted in a financial burden to union members. This finding conformed to the stated desire by union leaders to eliminate these costs under the current, negotiated health fund coverage and to insure that these costs are covered by a national health insurance bill. The union leadership seemed to judge proposed health legislation by a single criterion—how much of the cost will be covered. They were not impressed by the number of benefits to be covered but by the extent of coverage for each benefit. Some union leaders also expressed views about how health matters are organized at the government level. The fact that various responsibilities for health care are given to federal, state and local governments confuses union members as well as the administrators of union funds. These leaders called for the formation of a single system. Few of them thought that a health insurance system organized by both the private and public sectors would eliminate the problem.

Anticipated Impact of National Health Insurance on the Union Health Fund Package

About half of the union leaders have not thought about the impact national health insurance would have on their health plans. Moreover, many reported that none of their employers expressed any interest in national health insurance either during contract negotiations or in trustees' meetings. Of the many leaders who have considered how a national health security or insurance program might affect the union, almost all expressed general support for the concept. Some recognized, as discussed below, that the Kennedy Bill would not make any substantive changes in health care delivery or resolve other health care issues outside of strictly financial considerations. A few union leaders noted that they already had a comprehensive health package and they wondered whether NHI would bring the members anything new. One leader said he definitely would not want to give up the existing health plan while another thought that a role for the union in the health field would remain no matter what kind of legislation was passed. Generally, they indicated clearly that they saw no possibility of the union health fund apparatus being legislated out of existence either by fiat or by becomming superfluous. One union leader stated that he assumed that the union welfare fund would be "grandfathered in" under any national health insurance program.

At least two unions had taken the step of incorporating new language into their collective bargaining contracts which anticipates federal legislation. The language reads: "In the event that equivalent Group Insurance shall be provided by virtue of any Federal, State of Municipal law, mandatory in nature, the benefits hereunder shall cease on the date benefits under said law shall become effective."

The likelihood is that this kind of clause will eventually be included in all of these agreements upon enactment of such legislation as described above. Evidently, however, this language was considered fairly routine because the unions said that no serious discussion of NHI took place with management during recent negotiations. One union leader stood out in expressing the view that NHI should enable the union to get out of the health business and instead devote its full energies to "real" trade union matters. This leader thought that too much time had to be spent on health. One very skeptical union leader refused to be interviewed by saying that, "When they pass national health insurance, then I'll tell you the impact it will have on our health program."

Use of Health Funds Released

Many students of health care legislation assume that a federal program of national health insurance would be sufficiently comprehensive so as to release funds that are now spent for health in union health plans. If this occurs, it would be important for health planners to know what decisions union leaders might make with respect to the future use of such "released" funds. The range of choices has been thought to be broad, e.g., additional health benefits or other non-health benefits such as prepaid legal services or educational scholarships; provision for greater pensions or putting the monies into increased wages.

When asked how they would use released funds, union leaders exhibited some bewilderment. They agreed generally that any national health insurance program, including National Health Security, would not cover all the benefits and the fullest extension of those benefits which their members now enjoy. The overwhelming majority of the leaders, therefore, would spend these monies in the health area. They envisioned using any "freed" monies to buy additional coverage for the membership specifically in the area of preventive medicine. They would fill the gaps in health coverage not covered by a federal program. Of new programs to be considered, special mention was made of programs in preventive care; mental health; dental, optical and prescriptive drug benefits and combining with other unions to form health maintenance organizations. Also, in the health field, some leaders would try to eliminate deductibles and co-payments so as to release the burden of health costs from the member.

A few unions would explore prepaid legal services, the extending of existing scholarship programs, the establishment of vacation programs for the membership and the extending of existing summer camp programs for the families of members. Only one union expressed interest in converting such monies into wages. Those locals of national unions with national agreements which therefore are without control over their health and welfare funds will not have any option, if they desire additional benefits, than to purchase them from union dues.

Role of Health Fund Staff Under NHI

Under some forms of national health insurance the union would no longer be required to administer a health fund's finances completely. Leaders were asked what consequences this development might have for the fund's administrative staff. Another reason for raising the question was to learn whether some union leaders would prefer to maintain a health fund and staff as important union political assets or whether, on balance, they would reduce or eliminate such staff positions so as to curtail the union's involvement in health care.

Union leaders were agreed that the use of health funds to purchase health benefits for the membership was no substitute for national health insurance. They see the union health programs as a stopgap until a national health insurance bill is enacted that will relieve them of the responsibility of buying health care benefits, and in some cases delivering health care directly, through union medical centers. The leaders did not state this outright in every case, but certainly alluded to the logic behind it. One union leader who has had extensive experience in union health care matters said specifically that he could not wait for the day when the union would be rid of this function and the federal government would provide the benefits.

If Congress passed an NHI bill which relieved unions of some of their health fund duties, several leaders saw the necessity of keeping a non-clerical staff to help monitor federal NHI programs to make sure the member gets what is legally provided. The leadership in some cases also said that the health staff should act as ombudsman for the union membership to guarantee that the health care received is of high quality. Some union leaders were eager to have key health fund staff serve on local, regional and national boards of advisors. However, most said that these would need to be more than advisory boards in order to make sure that the "bureaucrats" do their job correctly. Other leaders said that these jobs should be given to trained rank-and-file activists. One important labor suggestion was that if the Social Security Administration were to become the administrator of a NHI program, many of the union health fund staff could be of great help in providing the personnel to make it an efficient, effective system. Most saw this as a very important step. However, many leaders thought that union health fund personnel would simply be switched to other activities in the union.

Form of Administration for NHI

Labor's views on what is desirable in the administrative machinery for a system of national health insurance is a key element in how such legislation will be drafted. In this study, only two of the union leaders would give commercial insurance companies, Blue Cross and other private carriers a preference over public control and operation of NHI. Union negativism toward private groups stems from a belief that business and profit-making should not be part of the health system. Unions also oppose commercial carriers because of their belief that they have done nothing to control costs or to monitor the ways in which hospitals and physicians administer care to patients. Three unions view Blue Cross as somewhat better than the other commercial carriers, while one leader had the reverse opinion. He felt that Blue Cross was more to blame than the others for the critical state of the health industry today. Most unions, however, make no distinction. If the law permitted, several unions would remain or become self-insured in the event that commercial carriers were selected over public agencies.

While a majority favored the Social Security Administration as the preferred administrative mechanism for NHI, many unions would not want it to be designated without first having the legislation define the nature of the controls to be adopted. In others words, there is a healthy suspicion on the part of a large number of knowledgeable labor leaders that the government must improve its way of handling the people's money and of serving them efficiently and humanely.

Several unions would opt for the SSA only if a separate structure was created to handle health. They fear that otherwise money for health might be siphoned off for other purposes. An important aspect of union skepticism towards SSA is the government's experience in handling Medicaid. Many labor leaders believe the government does not yet have an adequate system to monitor bills and control health costs. Some also think that even SSA is cluttered with too much red tape and bureaucracy. One leader cited the difficulties already encountered in the administration of the Pension Reform Act (which presently costs more money to administer than previously) as a reason for being somewhat wary of government administrative efficiency.

A number of unions want SSA to be required to establish citizen boards which would have some voice in the handling of NHI. They want labor to be prominently represented on these boards, and they believe that their long experience in administering health care plans for their members, as well as their demonstrated interest in protecting the consumers, entitles them to such a role. These leaders would not exclude health professionals from these boards, and some explicitly said it was essential that these persons should be included. Many leaders also affirmed that they would not relinquish control over their health plans until they were assured that a federally sponsored and run program was providing coverage which was at least as good as the coverage their members presently enjoyed.

Health Programs the Unions Would Want to Continue That Might Not Be Covered Fully by Legislation

Union leaders repeated that the union would not "give up" any health care prerogatives until guarantees were provided which assured the membership of at least the health care coverage it now receives. Specifically, union leaders singled out fifteen different kinds of health benefits which they felt were sufficiently important to their members to be continued with funds which were now supplied by management under collective bargaining agreements. The programs mentioned most frequently were dental (15 unions) and optical (14 unions). The next highest were mental health (7 unions), major medical coverage (5 unions) and drug prescription (5 unions). Other programs emphasized for retention by one to three unions were medical check-ups (3) social service referral service (3), second opinion for elective surgery (2), union medical center (2), on-site hypertension screening (1) and maternity (1). Three leaders stated that it was difficult to isolate one or more programs that should be retained. Six union leaders emphasized the need to keep deductibles low and to avoid cut-offs. (Figures given here may be low because there is naturally an uncertainty about what specific benefits will be covered in NHI legislation.)

Labor Representation on Health Boards

At the present time, labor input in existing boards has been uneven and generally not very strong, either in numbers or in the quality of the service rendered. Unanimously, the twenty-five labor leaders interviewed wanted the trade union movement to be represented on community, regional and national boards concerned with health policy and the spending of public funds for health services. Some comments of the leaders were: "Labor should be involved in all levels of health care decision making." "Who else has a greater experience in fighting for consumer interests through negotiating with powerful management groupings for health care benefits than the labor movement?" "We have expertise which would greatly benefit all health planning boards in the HSA and also SSA advisory boards." Thus, the union leaders interviewed saw a major role for labor in both community and federal health programs.

The major reason for there not being more involvement in health care issues outside of union health programs was primarily a matter of lack of time rather than opposition to these programs. In addition to the fact that these leaders are usually very busy tending to union business, it is also true that several of them have not been able to become as knowledgeable as they might about what is happening in the community on health issues. Moreover, there is the future question of who takes the initiative—should labor leaders ask to serve on boards or should the organizers of boards seek out labor. Some leaders of labor think they should be asked. Others are willing to take the initiative.

Some of the leaders who were questioned stated that labor sometimes did not nominate or send its most competent people to represent them. They felt that labor should not consider board appointments as a kind of patronage, but should recommend those with genuine knowledge and skills. There was considerable criticism expressed over the poor representation which labor has had in the past within the health care system and elsewhere. Many said that while labor was often critical of community groups which become involved in health care issues for their own purposes, there was a real self-criticism over labor's own record in this regard.

One of the major problems toward union involvement in community health planning boards is the "spread of membership" which unions have throughout New York City. How can a local union which represents over a thousand members request representation rights in one local community board when its membership is spread over five boroughs? This situation resulted in labor having only one member on the Comprehensive Health Planning Agency (CHPA) city-wide board of directors to represent the NYC Central Labor Council, AFL-CIO. Union leaders considered this to be unsatisfactory. The two large hospital workers' unions also had but one member each on the board.

Occupational Health and Safety and Union Health Plans

Occupational health and safety became a serious concern of many unions with the passage of the 1970 Occupational Safety and Health Act. In this study about one-half of the unions provided some services on occupational health and safety to the membership. Health and safety committees, the training of shop stewards in how to implement the Occupational Safety and Health Act and involvement in studies concerning potential health hazards at the workplace were the most common forms of union-sponsored activity. At least six unions had experienced occupational health problems including stress, noise, fumes, gases, fiber, mouth cancer, asbestosis and silicosis.

Over half of the union health plans could recover the medical records of their members if they decided to institute a system of surveillance to ferret out occupational disease before it took its toll in workers' lives and disability. Only one union, however, had actually started the process of reorganizing its medical record-keeping in order to establish an occupational surveillance system. Several unions, according to their leaders, did not have any apparent occupational health problems. Almost all the leaders, however, held the view that workmen's compensation should cover the cost of illness caused or contributed to by the workplace. Many unions have in their health plans provisions for annual medical examinations and one leader stated proudly that 75 to 80 percent of the members took advantage of this benefit. They felt that such practices were essential to a good program of preventive health, and they recognized that such programs, when tied to checks to occupationally-related disease, would constitute further improvement.

Union leaders were convinced that under national health insurance federal funds should be available for hospitals and that both the municipal and voluntary ones needed additional financial resources. Most of them did not think that a distinction should be made between the voluntaries and municipals with respect to the dispensation of federal funds. Related to this point was a reluctance on the part of union leadership to resist the cutbacks now being forced on the city hospitals. The cutbacks were regretted, but under the present system of different levels of care it was evidently considered not worth fighting to prevent such cuts. Several leaders stressed the importance of effective controls being placed on the manner in which federal funds were spent. They wanted a system of accountability regardless of the type of hospital, and one concerned not only with expenditures, but with quality of care rendered. One union leader held up as a model the Veterans Administration hospitals where, in his opinion, quality of care was delivered at no charge to the users.

Conclusions

1. The success of a program for national health insurance will depend in large part on its effectiveness at the local level—how it is organized to serve people where they live and work, and how it relates to Health Service Agencies, hospital boards, city and county health departments, private medical groups, health maintenance organizations and labor-management health funds and programs. It is clear from interviews with local union leaders that national leaders have not consulted them about how a national health system should be operated at the local level. There is, therefore, a probable serious gap in the planning for a system of national health insurance.

2. Benefits for health of union members have reached a plateau with little or no increases in coverage and almost no change in the effort to reduce health charges paid by individual workers. These results further document the negative effects of rising medical costs on labor-management health funds.

3. While the social security system is favored by union leaders overwhelmingly as the best available mechanism to be given responsibility for administration of a program for NHI, there is widespread skepticism that, as presently organized, it can be effective in controlling costs. If a public mechanism is selected by Congress, it must devise ways to command the support and confidence of the leaders of health care consumers, particularly including those in trade unions.

4. Union leaders see little in the proposed legislation for national health insurance which would change the delivery of health care. They believe that current proposals deal primarily with the financing of health, and that the financing will not, initially, be comprehensive. They do not have much expectation that improvements in the delivery of care will be forthcoming in the future. Therefore, union leaders who are active and involved in health care for their members want the union to continue to function in this field.

5. Health care specialists drafting legislation for national health programs have not considered that the trade union movement is a vast consumer resource in the field of health. The workplace can be used extensively in implementing programs of preventive medicine, and the unions are a natural force to see that such programs are instituted and carried out. Unions not only have the capability to organize such programs, but through them they can also induce a kind of peer pressure that increases the probability of their success.

6. Drafters of health legislation need to distinguish between unions acting as health consumers and those serving as health providers. The overwhelming majority of unions, whose members are not part of the health care system, clearly regard themselves as consumers of health care.

Recommendations

1. Legislators and their advisers should consult health consumers and providers at the local level before health legislation is put into final form. Union leaders, with their sophistication and knowledge about the local health system and how it serves consumers, should be among the first to be consulted. Legislation should include ways to control costs, monitor quality and assure consumer input at the local level.

2. A study of the present structure of the social security system, especially its handling of Medicaid, would be instructive and should produce ideas to improve its role under NHI.

3. There is a need for further inquiry into how the method of delivery of health care should be changed at the local level. HMOs are naturally a part of this. Another part is the role union health plans can

undertake, particularly as ombudsmen and monitors of the quality and cost of care rendered. The experience of unions with the review of medical claims and the use of doctors' panels should be included.

4. Another recommended study concerns the ways in which trade unions and other groups associated with the workplace can assist in developing and implementing programs of preventive medicine at the workplace. Such programs might include screening for various illnesses, e.g., hypertension and work-related diseases.

5. Since union leaders are unanimous in wanting labor represented on community boards that have responsibilities in the health field, some inquiry should be made as to how this can be achieved in light of the difficulties labor has previously experienced in attempting to be appointed to and to serve on these boards.

6. Further discussion should be instituted on the means to integrate occupational safety and health programs and preventive measures into schemes for national health insurance. An analytical study should be pursued to devise a standard procedure to upgrade union medical records in order that they may become a part of a medical surveillance program in diagnosing, controlling and preventing job-related health problems.

7. In view of high union interest in health maintenance organizations, efforts should be continued to simplify and facilitate union involvement in this means of delivering health care to members of the labor movement.

8. There is a need for analysis of existing union health benefit packages and for comparing them with the various health benefit packages being offered in the various NHI proposals. Moreover, a study of the extent of use of health plans by members of unions would be instructive.

9. The extent to which unions should be encouraged to be self-insured groups for delivering medical care should be explored.

10. Most union leaders accept the probability that, at the outset, national health insurance will neither be comprehensive in number or benefits covered nor in covering all costs for each benefit. Consultation with union leaders and others about what should be included in each stage would appear to be a fruitful exercise.

References

[1] The study by Frank Goldsmith of the faculty of Cornell University's New York State School of Industrial and Labor Relations covered extensive interviews with presidents of 25 local unions in New York City.

[2] 1972 Trade Union Handbook (New York City Central Labor Council, AFL-CIO, New York, and the Education Committee of the Council).

[3] Alice H. Cook and Lois S. Gray, "Labor Relations in New York City," *Industrial Relations* 5: 3, May 1966. (There are in the city over 200,000 business establishments which have an average workforce of only 13.)

[4] For more information about union health centers, consult the publication, *Union Health Centers of New York City*, Trade Union Health Education Project of the Union-University Urban Affairs Program, Metropolitan Office of the New York State School of Industrial and Labor Relations, Cornell University, 7 East 43rd Street, New York, N.Y. 10017, June 1975. Copies of the questionnaire used in this study and the names of the trade union leaders interviewed are also available from the above address.

Appendix

Irving J. Lewis, of Albert Einstein College of Medicine, served as staff director of the project until August 1, 1975. He was assisted by Audrey G. Harris, staff associate, and by Marvin Lieberman, Ph.D., New York Academy of Medicine, and Herbert Lukashok, Albert Einstein College of Medicine, who served as consultants. On August 1, 1975, Dr. Lieberman succeeded Professor Lewis as staff director and continued in that capacity until September 1976.

The work of the Task Force on the Impact of National Health Insurance began on July 1, 1974, with the writing of a study prospectus in which the bsic issues which would be the focus of the task force's deliberations were decided upon. These are outlined in the prospectus.

The work of the task force included the following elements: task force meetings, prepared commissioned papers, and seminars.

Task Force Meetings

October 1974	Initial Meeting
December 1974	Ambulatory Care in Voluntary Hospitals Cost Constraints and Planning
January 1975	Medicaid—Experiences and Lessons: Implications for National Health Insurance
February 1975	The Canadian Experience and Lessons for the United States
March 1975	Possible Impact of National Health Insurance Upon the Health Budget of New York
	Local Controls for New York City: An Overview of Key Concepts, Interest Groups, and Policy Issues
April 1975	Implications of National Health Insurance for Ambulatory Care in New York City
May 1975	National Health Planning and Resources Development Act of 1974 and National Health Insurance
September 1975	Proposal for City Action in Dealing with Ambulatory Care Under National Health Insurance
October 1975	Organized Ambulatory Services and the Enforcement of Health Care Quality Standards in New York State
December 1975	Some Implications of National Health Insurance for New York City's Health System
January 1976	Restructuring Maternal and Child Health Services in New York City
February 1976	Final meeting

At the task force meetings various seminar papers were circulated in advance and discussed at the meetings and were usually focused around issues raised by the commissioned papers.

Papers Prepared for the Task Force

Ambulatory Care in Voluntary Hospitals, Herbert Lukashok and Eric Ploen

Cost Constraints and Planning, Joan Leiman

Possible Impact of National Health Insurance on the Health Budget of New York City, Jeffrey Weiss

Local Controls for New York City: An Overview of Key Concepts, Interest Groups and Policy Issues, James R. Posner

National Health Planning and Resources Development Act of 1974 and National Health Insurance, Frank van Dyke

Implications of National Health Insurance for Ambulatory Care Services in New York City, Charles Brecher, Karen Brudney and Miriam Ostow

National Health Insurance: An Assessment of its Impact on the Mid-Hudson Region, Anthony Berkowitz

The Impact of National Health Insurance on Maternal and Child Health Services in New York City, Betty J. Bernstein

Some Implications of National Health Insurance for New York City's Health System, Irving Leveson

Proposal for City Action in Dealing with Ambulatory Medical Care under National Health Insurance, George A. Silver

Impact of National Health Insurance on Labor-Management Health and Welfare Plans in New York City, Betty G. Lall

The Lessons of Medicaid, Howard N. Newman

Organized Ambulatory Services and the Enforcement of Health Quality Standards in New York State, Steven Jonas

Restructuring Dental Services in New York, Betty J. Bernstein

A Personal View of New York City's Medicaid, Henry J. Rosner

Impact of National Health Insurance on Union Health Plans, Frank Goldsmith and Betty G. Lall

Measurement of the Impact of National Health Insurance, Paul M. Densen

Seminars

To fulfill our obligation to broaden the participation and discussion of the issues, it was decided to hold a series of seminars for other decision makers in New York City. Approximately 50 persons attended each of the seminars:

January 1975   *Seminar on Primary Care*—Speakers: Nora Piore, Center for Community Health Systems, Columbia University; Norma Goodwin, M.D., New York City Health and Hospitals Corporation; Richard Berman, Cornell University Medical Center; Samuel Wolfe, M.D., Long Island Jewish-Hillside Medical Center

February 1975   *Seminar on Cost Containment*—Speakers: Mildred B. Shapiro, New York State Department of Health; Irwin

| April 1975 | Wolkstein, Bureau of Health Insurance, Social Security Administration; Irwin Birnbaum, Montefiore Hospital; Rashi Fein, Ph.D., Harvard University Medical School |

April 1975   *Seminar on Governance and Accountability*—Speakers: C. Arden Miller, M.D., University of North Carolina, School of Public Health; James G. Haughton, M.D., Health and Hospital Governing Commission of Cook County; Joseph V. Terenzio, United Hospital Fund; Ruth Atkins, Manhattan Office, Comprehensive Health Planning Agency for New York City

June 1975   *Seminar on Long Term Care*—Speakers: Robert Morris, Brandeis University; Marie Callender, United States Department of Health, Education, and Welfare; Beverlee Myers, New York State Department of Social Services; Mitchell Waife, Jewish Home and Hospital for the Aged

April 1976   *Seminar on the Impact of the Fiscal Crisis on Health Services in New York City*—Speakers: Ron Walter, Office of the Mayor; Joseph Terenzio, United Hospital Fund; Joseph Giglio, N.Y.C. Health and Hospitals Corporation; Betty J. Bernstein, Ph.D., Citizens' Committee for Children

May 1976   *Seminar on Data Needs for Health Planning and National Health Insurance*—Speakers: Paul M. Densen, Sc.D., Harvard University; Helen Thornberry, Bureau of Health Planning and Resources Development, Department of Health, Education, and Welfare; Roger C. Herdman, M.D., New York State Department of Health; Nora Piore, Columbia University; Muriel Ratner, Health Systems Agency of New York City, Inc.; Dorothy P. Rice, National Center for Health Statistics, Department of Health, Education, and Welfare; Marvin Roth, Department of City Planning; Leonard Schrager, Health and Hospital Planning Council of Southern New York; Melvin Schwartz, M.D., New York City Department of Health

Over 100 persons attended this all-day seminar on data needs which was planned with the assistance of the Data Advisory Committee.

Members of the Data Advisory Committee:

Marvin Roth, *Chairman*; George Allen; Blanche Bernstein, Ph.D.; Ann Cugliani; Jack Eller; Jack Ellinson, Ph.D.; Raymond Fink, Ph.D.; Peter Levin, Sc.D.; Purlaine Lieberman; Regina Lowenstein; Harry Meyer; Eric Ploen; David Robbins; Leonard Schrager; Melvin Schwartz, M.D.

Contributors

JESSE B. ARONSON, M.D., formerly Director, New York Metropolitan Regional Medical Program, New York, N.Y.

BETTY J. BERNSTEIN, Ph.D., Associate Director, Citizens' Committee for Children of New York, Inc., New York, N.Y.

CHARLES BRECHER, Ph.D., Senior Research Associate, Conservation of Human Resources, Columbia University, New York, N.Y.

KAREN BRUDNEY, formerly Research Assistant, Conservation of Human Resources, Columbia University, New York, N.Y.

PAUL M. DENSEN, Sc.D., Director, Center for Community Health and Medical Care, Harvard University School of Medicine, Boston, Mass.

FRANK GOLDSMITH, Project Coordinator, New York State School of Industrial and Labor Relations of Cornell University, New York, N.Y.

FREDERICK O'R. HAYES, formerly Budget Director, City of New York, New York, N.Y.

STEVEN JONAS, M.D., Associate Professor of Community Medicine, State University of New York at Stony Brook, Stony Brook, N.Y.

BETTY G. LALL, Ph.D., Director, Trade Union Health Education Project, New York State School of Industrial and Labor Relations of Cornell University, New York, N.Y.

IRVING LEVESON, Ph.D., Senior Research Analyst, Hudson Institute, Croton-on-Hudson, N.Y.

IRVING J. LEWIS, Professor, Department of Community Health, Albert Einstein College of Medicine, Bronx, N.Y.

MARVIN LIEBERMAN, Ph.D., Executive Secretary, Committee on Medicine in Society, the New York Academy of Medicine, New York, N.Y.

HERBERT LUKASHOK, Associate Professor and Acting Chairman, Department of Community Health, Albert Einstein College of Medicine, Bronx, N.Y.

MIRIAM OSTOW, Research Associate, Conservation of Human Resources, Columbia University, New York, N.Y.

ERIC PLOEN, formerly Assistant to the President and Director, Special Projects, United Hospital Fund of New York and Executive Director, Affiliated Risk Control Administrators, Inc., Great Neck, N.Y.

GEORGE A. SILVER, M.D., Professor of Public Health, Department of Epidemiology and Public Health, Yale University School of Medicine, New Haven, Conn.

FRANK VAN DYKE, Professor of Administrative Medicine, Columbia University School of Administrative Medicine, New York, N.Y.

JEFFREY H. WEISS, Director of Planning and Associate Professor, Downstate Medical Center, Brooklyn, N.Y.